Positive Ethics in Economics

Positive Ethics in Economics

Praxiology:
The International Annual of
Practical Philosophy and
Methodology

Volume 14

Edited by

Jérôme Ballet
Damien Bazin

Transaction Publishers
New Brunswick (U.S.A.) and London (U.K.)

This book is printed on acid-free paper that meets the American National Standard for Permanence of Paper for Printed Library Materials.

Library of Congress Catalog Number: 2005056881
ISBN: 0-7658-0325-9
Printed in the United States of America

Library of Congress Cataloging-in-Publication Data

Positive ethics in economics / edited by Jérôme Ballet and Damien Bazin.
p. cm.—(Praxiology : the international annual of practical philosophy and methodology ; v. 14)
Includes bibliographical references.
ISBN 0-7658-0325-9 (alk. paper)
1. Economics—Moral and ethical aspects. 2. Praxeology. I. Ballet, Jérôme. II. Bazin, Damien. III. Series: Praxiology (New Brunswick, N.J.); v. 14.

HB72.E87 2006
174—dc22 2005056881

Acknowledgements

This book is the result of several years of reflection carried out by the different authors. This publication would not have been possible without the support of and discussions with several colleagues. We wish to address special thanks to Pierre Antoine and Roland Guillon for the favourable climate they created, for their encouragement and valuable comments. We also thank Agathe Popelard for the translation of chapters 2, 4 and 7. Last but certainly not least, we wish to thank Professor Wojciech Gasparski who believed in the project and who encouraged us to pursue our goal right until the end.

Contents

Editorial: *Wojciech W. Gasparski* 1

Introduction: *Jérôme Ballet* and *Damien Bazin* 5

PART ONE: Altruism 21

On the Concept of Altruism: *Jérôme Ballet* and *Augendra Bhukuth* 23

Methodological Aspects of Altruism in Economics: *Jérôme Ballet* and *Sébastien Barillot* 41

Cooperation and Reciprocity: *Alejandro Caparros, Jean-Christophe Pereau* and *Tarik Tazdaït* 63

PART TWO: Commitment 93

Beyond Altruism: Commitment?: *Jérôme Ballet, Aurélie Carimentrand and Patrick Jolivet* 95

The Ideal Observer: A Figure of Economic Theory: *Jérôme Ballet* and *Damien Bazin* 119

Kantian Economics: Retrospect and Prospect: *Jérôme Ballet* and *Patrick Jolivet* 155

PART THREE: Responsibility 185

For a Positive Analysis of Responsibility and Duty: *Jérôme Ballet* and *François-Régis Mahieu* 187

The Economic Person and Responsibility: *Jérôme Ballet* and *Damien Bazin* 201

Some Reflections on Responsibility and Happiness in Economics: *Jérôme Ballet, Vinca Bigo, Jean-Luc Dubois* and *François-Régis Mahieu* 225

Notes about the Authors 239

Editorial

Wojciech W. Gasparski
Editor-in-Chief

Rationality, reason and responsibility are the three concepts this volume on praxiology and economics is based upon. The contributors to this volume named the approach the *positive economical ethics* as different from other approaches, mainly the normative economical ethics one. The question, therefore, is to what an extent it is a part of praxiological inquiry or how closely it is related to praxiology as a study of human action in general and/or with a special emphasis on actions characteristic for the domain of the economy.

To look for a proper answer to the above question one should recall Gunnar Skirbekk's praxiological anthology where he wrote the following in his introduction:

> Praxeology in our sense is a conceptual analysis and reflective discussion of the way human activities are interwoven with their agents and with the things at which they are directed within our everyday world. It is thus more clearly linked with the early Heidegger and the latter Wittgenstein than with Kotarbinski.

> In emphasizing the primacy of action in contradistinction to both passive perception and pure cogitation, praxeology thus understood fits in with a persisting modern trend, right from classical pragmatism to the praxis-philosophy of the Jugoslavs. From this praxeological perspective, the primacy of practice may be briefly elucidated as follows: (i) human insight is primarily located in actions; (ii) these are of various, overlapping kinds; (iii) the articulation of this insight calls for a careful elaboration of described instances of the activities in question (Skirbekk 1983, p.9).

This piece of Nordic praxiology (Skirbekk spells it 'praxeology') is a good example of a non-classic praxiological inquiry different in the method applied but not in the subject classic and variety of non-classic praxiologies are studying. The subject is human action. The method in the case of Nordic praxiology is "based on assistance on careful use of examples, invoking detailed descriptions and thought-experiments" (Skirbekk 1983, pp.9-10). Methods of classic praxiology are considered in various ways by various authors. As such, they are an apriorism characteristic for Ludwig von Mises, an analysis (philosophical) typical for Tadeusz Kotarbinski or a systemism employed by Mario Bunge (1989) and some other contemporary praxiologists (Gasparski 1987).

The approach presented in this book belongs to non-classic praxiologies, this time to a French chapter of a praxiological nonclassicizm. It is, however not the imitation of the Nordic approach although it is similar in a way to it because of its praxis orientation[1]. It is also related to the Misesian approach because of its involvement in economics in a positive, i.e., non-normative, way. The most peculiar thing is that although the presented approach is different than Kotarbinski's praxiology it is similar to the scheme of his practical philosophy named by him as ethics in a broader meaning[2]. Thus one may notice that for both Kotarbinski as well as for Jérôme Ballet and Damien Bazin praxiology is a part of ethics in its broader understanding.

The editors of the volume and the contributors to it, seeking positive characteristics of economical manifestation of human action, are in fact looking for elements of 'insider ethics', i.e., ethics characteristic for actors performing their activities within the scope of the economic milieu, and 'exchange ethics', i.e. ethics characteristic for interrelation between the 'insider' and 'outsider' of the milieu. Mario Bunge would rather call the two ethics in question the endo- and exo- moralities (Bunge 1989) respectively.

Praxiology may be considered in two different ways. One of them, let us call it static, considers it as a closed set of concepts and related analysis elaborated by the founding fathers once for all. The second way, let us call it dynamic, considers praxiology as an open area of purposeful human action taken voluntarily by its actor or actors. There is no doubt that only the dynamic way makes praxiology the live issue and the series is trying to promote this way. The approach presented in this book follows this path. Readers are invited to the debate, be it either supportive or critical. Both will add value to the development of praxiological inquiry, I am sure.

Notes

1. "The term *praxeology*, literally [implies] 'theory (logos) of action (praxis)' (...)" (Skirbekk 1983, p.9).
2. According to Kotarbinski it is composed of three studies: (i) felicitology or a study of happiness, (ii) praxiology or a study of action and its efficacy, (iii) ethics or a study of morality.

References

Bunge, M. 1989. *Treatise on Basic Philosophy: Ethics*, Vol. 8, D. Reidel, Dordrecht.

Gasparski, W. W. 1987. Praxiology, in: *Systems and Control Encyclopedia*, Pergamon Press, Oxford, pp.3860-3865.

Skirbekk, G. (ed.). 1983. *Praxeology: An Anthology*, Universitetsforlaget, Bergen.

Introduction

Jérôme Ballet
Damien Bazin
University of Versailles
France

Economics is often accused of being a-ethical, not to mention totally immoral. Pure and perfect competition is criticised and serves as a focal point in this denunciation. The criteria of efficiency are rejected in the name of rules of justice. It is thus common to assert that economics should be more ethical, more concerned with its social effects, for example, and that it should also be equitable. This is essential in fighting modern day poverty and foreseeing intergenerational equity. Redistributive measures, especially taxes, could be enforced for this purpose. Similarly, ethical taxes can be introduced in the event of financial corruption. Economics is thus assimilated to real consequences of a particular economic mode of functioning.

This, however, refers only to a specific part of economics. Economics has also developed a group of references associating itself to ethics. One could observe the presence of practical ethics in the economic analysis of behaviour that integrates certain modalities of ethical preference, altruism or, still more, a responsible calculation based on norms. In sum, this economic analysis integrates ethical considerations into preferences by differentiating them from economic considerations. Within this context, ethics appears either as a single substitutable characteristic amongst many others in the utility function or as an absolute priority in current economics that delimits all possible economic choices. Economics is henceforth associated with morality in man's daily life. A concept of *positive ethics* is thus created and aims at introducing a mode of reasoning which takes the adoption of ethical behaviour by individuals into account.

1. Positive Ethics in Economics: What does it Mean?

Positive ethics is highly different from normative ethics. The latter moralises economics in attempting to render it more just. The former, on the other hand, is first and foremost a model for the construction of theoretical economic reasoning. It is associated with a reflection on ethical practices in economics.

The distinction between positive and normative ethics is based on what Black (1970) called the guillotine of Hume[1]. This distinction goes back to Hume's *Treatise of Human Nature* wherein he presents the proposition that "we cannot deduce what ought to be from what is", that descriptive affirmations can only lead to or imply other descriptive affirmations and never norms or recommendations. He thus establishes a difference between the domain of facts and the domain of values.

Max Weber voiced a similar opinion when he elaborated on the doctrine of *Wertfreiheit* or the freedom in relation to values. Similarly, the distinction of Sen (1970) between "basic" and "non-basic" value judgements corresponds to the Weberian point of view where the former adopts a rational discourse on value judgements efficiently held by persons. This brings us to consider, in the case of positive ethics, what would happen if individuals do respect ethical norms in their behaviour. *In fine* economic methodology consists in proposing a modelisation of such behaviour. Normative ethics would on the other hand indicate what ought to be done.

One should therefore not have any value judgement on what ought to be done, but rather, make note that individuals do indeed have value judgements, and one should also take these value judgements objectively into account, with the help of suitable methodology for economic analysis.

We are faced here with Nagel's (1961) distinction between judgements characterising value and those which increase value by referring to certain evaluations of the world and their desirable or undesirable nature.

We thus develop a form of positive ethics in economics, where economics deals with a particular methodological approach that aims at taking the behaviour of economic agents and their after-effects into account, without however having any value judgement upon such behaviour.

What characterises this process is the fact that it considers that economic agents act morally. We would thus no longer have to moralise economics, as proposed by normative ethics, but rather, we would have to take into consideration the simple fact that the *homo œconomicus* lives in society. He cannot totally withdraw himself from the others. His relation to others could nevertheless be conceived in various forms. On the one hand, reasoning on the economic agent could be enlarged by the integration of a social constraint i.e. the presence of others. In this case, rational behaviour remains primordial. One has to merely create a maximising pattern of behaviour in the presence of others. On the other hand, the modality of the preceding reasoning could be considered as highly insufficient. Life in society does not limit itself to a rational calculation, which takes the Other into consideration. The individual finds himself immersed in a world where there are pre-existing norms that are more or less internalised by him. This does not however exclude the possibility of egoistic calculation. Feuerbach (1855) for example, by mixing egoism and religion, insists on the "sordid" dimension of religious practice- a thesis also used by Marx in the *Jewish Question* and the *Holy Family*. However, economic analysis cannot exclude from its reasoning the possibility of considering the individual as guided by certain motivations that are determined outside all social context.

The philosophy of human action that we defend here is based upon two focal points: internalisation and adaptation. The individual more or less internalises the norms of the world to which he belongs. He adapts himself to these norms and to the constraints that they impose upon his behaviour by adjusting them through rational calculation. We could thereafter consider **positive ethics in economics as the analysis of economic behaviour or "mores" under moral constraint.** However, the praxis put forward by us could be divided into behavioural practice on the one hand and the practice of conscience (of the Other and of one's belonging) on the other. By following this problematic, we enter into the very core of the positive economical practice of ethics. Economics, in all its various forms, combines these two elements in a practical manner.

This book is however not an attempt to defend a praxeological approach anchored in a historical and methodological perspective, based on an empirical investigation of the studied phenomena. Quite the opposite. The form of positive ethics that we develop here constructs hypothetical modalities of reasoning. This vision is typical of the general conception of economic action where maximisation under constraint is its ultimate representation. The concept of praxeology as developped by us has closer affinities with the thoughts of Lukàcs (1967, 1974) rather than those of his precursor (Espinas 1897) and his followers (Von Mises 1949[2] and Kotarbinski 1960, 1965[3]). We hence develop a concept of praxeology, in the sense of praxis, as a methodology of human action. However, this methodology of human action cannot be elaborated based upon an isolated and egoistic individual.

While considering man as a moral person, positive ethics proceeds to create reasonings and ethical models based on hypotheses that go beyond the simplistic framework of the atomised *homo œconomicus,* isolated from his peers, and purely and simply egoistic. In accepting the fact that man lives in a society, positive ethics formalises such a consciousness. If man is guided by moral motivations, and if these motivations are retranscribed in his daily economic actions such as consumption, savings and transfers, economics could in no way ignore such considerations. Positive ethics specifically concentrates on the study of the practical modalities of the construction of an ethical economic man. This does not imply the denunciation or rejection of economic models, but rather, is an analysis of the broadening or the reconstruction of the analytical and theoretical framework.

We shall highlight through the following chapters that economics develops a positive ethical practice which at times wavers from the philosophical concepts which it borrows, but which always enriches the economic debate. It generates thought on behavioural hypotheses in economics that is far from being well-defined.

2. Positive Ethics in Economics: which way?

Three ways have been created in order to model a theoretical economic framework that takes moral individuals into consideration. These ways include rationality, reason and responsibility respectively, also known as the three Rs. They thus correspond to three practical modalities concerning the integration of ethics into economics. This book is divided into three parts where each part deals with one of these ways of integrating positive ethics into economics.

2.1. Part One: Altruism and rationality

The science of economics has, since of long, been considered to be dedicated, within a market economy, to material riches, without any particular interest for moral considerations. Its founders such as William Petty and most of his followers confirm this moral neutrality. This neutrality is reinforced today by the concept of a "society of nature" without any *a priori* morality. Such moral neutrality helps give free reign to a certain economic opportunism devoid of norms. If ever moral norms do exist, they are either the result or the derivatives of economic opportunism.

It is rationality that is in question here. The science of economics proceeds from a method within which rationality is considered as fundamental. Nevertheless, morality is considered to emanate from belief or conviction and thereby greatly diverts from rationality. In the initial stages of a positive integration of ethics into economics, it thus seems to be of great importance to reconcile ethics and rationality, in conformity with economic methodology.

As such, the consideration of an economic man as a non-atomised individual who is not isolated from his contemporaries and who is obliged to take others into consideration, presupposes the construction of a socially oriented economic man in conformity with economic procedures.

Economic analysis has proposed ways of integrating moral behaviour through the concept of altruism. The first part of this book is a bid to examine such ways and also aims at highlighting some of their limits. The first part is divided into three chapters. The first chapter written by *Jérôme Ballet* and *Augendra Bhukuth* deals with the origins of the concept of altruism. It examines the evolution, through economic theory and practice, of the very meaning of this term. Initially created by *Auguste Comte* in a strictly sacrificial context and under the motto "live for the Other", this concept was immediately contested by authors such as John Stuart Mill and Herbert Spencer who differentiated between altruism and benevolence. Altruism, according to these authors, refers to a calculation on society within a utilitarian context while benevolence is the individual calculation motivated by one's feelings towards other persons. Such a distinction between these two terms brings forth a fundamental error often seen in numerous contemporary works. This error concerns the distinction between personal and social preferences. Paradoxically, as highlighted by the authors, while John Stuart Mill and Herbert Spencer considerably influenced future economic theory, future economic theory in turn assimilated altruism into the notion of benevolence.

A second turning point was the assimilation of altruism by economic theory and through the influence of Alfred Marshall (1890).

Marshall questions the manner and extent to which ethics could be integrated into economics. He recognises that theoretical economic constructions based on a man who seeks, mechanically and egoistically, to gain a pecuniary advantage could not be of great use. According to his conclusion in chapter 11.7 of the *Principles of Economics*, economists study an individual's actions from a social point of view and not from an individual point of view. It could hence be considered normal to introduce altruistic relations into economic methodology.

One would, however, have to respect economic methodology in this integration. Still, Marshall states in chapter III.4 that "Economic laws, or statements of economic tendencies, are those social laws that relate to branches of conduct in which the strength of the motives chiefly concerned can be measured by money price"[4]. Although Marshall, in his preface to the *Principles of Economics*, states that economists cannot shun ethical considerations. He also insists that this integration should be conducted in conformity with the methodology upon which economics is based.

Conforming to the economic methodology "*De Gustibus non est Disputandum*" (Stigler and Becker 1977), the economic analysis of altruism proposes a "neutralised" definition based upon behaviour.

Though this method offers us the considerable advantage of not drastically modifying economic theory, and especially preserving the principle of rationality, it nevertheless presents certain disadvantages.

The second chapter, proposed by *Jérôme Ballet* and *Sébastien Barillot* closely examines the methodological difficulties relating to the way in which altruism could be integrated into economic calculation. Three major obstacles are presented in this chapter. The first lies in the behaviourist stance of economic theory that puts aside the motivations that drive an individual's actions. The second originates from too narrow a vision of rationality where emotions are neutralised. The third, meanwhile, emanates from a reduced consideration of the person, represented simply by a set of characteristics.

However, economic methodology has largely evolved in recent years, especially through the development of evolutionary games. Paradoxically, it is only when economic theory moved away from altruism and towards cooperation that it was brought to seriously consider certain forms of feelings inherent to altruistic behaviour.

The third chapter presented by *Alejandro Caparros*, *Jean-Christophe Péreau* and *Tarik Tazdaït* explores new possibilities that have been opened unto us by this relatively recent methodology.

As highlighted by these authors, there is no need to postulate moral behaviour in order to have a favourable collective outcome. The economic agent has to merely incite the others, through his actions, to do as he does. The cooperation that results from such interaction does not need to postulate for any particular form of altruism. Mere behaviour of alignment or reciprocity would suffice.

Within the context of evolutionary games, each individual's capacity to adapt to the process enables us to achieve a solution of equilibrium. However, this solution is not necessarily a cooperative solution. As soon as errors and disruptions exist, it becomes essential to introduce certain forms of feelings such as generosity, repentance or forgiveness if one is to ensure cooperation. More generally, the integration of pro-social feelings or emotions pushes economic agents to get involved in cooperative behaviour. The status of the *homo œconomicus* is at this point transformed, since it is now enriched with a psychological capital.

As such, paradoxically, we see the emergence of two specific tendencies. The first begins with the consideration, by individuals, of a certain form of altruism and leads to a cold and mathematical conception of human action. The second, founded upon comparative analysis, has the absence of moral behaviour as its starting point. It has led, unlike the first, to the integration of moral sentiments as a guide to human action.

2.2. Part Two: Commitment and Reason

Reason is a central element in ethical reflection. Economic theory has of course attempted to integrate reason to itself. Indeed, this integration should not be accomplished at the cost of rationality. It is of great importance to render reason more compatible with rationality.

The three chapters that form this part examine how economic theory came to take reason into consideration, while at the same time remaining within a methodological framework compatible with rationality. In doing this, economic theory grew closer to a particular concept of altruism as put forward by Auguste Comte, John Stuart Mill and Herbert Spencer. However, economic theory further associated the term commitment into this concept.

The first chapter proposed by *Jérôme Ballet*, *Aurélie Carimentrand* and *Patrick Jolivet* deals with the distinction between compassion and commitment as proposed in most economic literature. Altruism is defined as the "positive internalisation of the Other's well-being into the utility function of the individual"[5]. As such, compassion could be assimilated to altruism. Benevolent acts that result from this feeling positively affect the well-being of the person acting. Commitment, on the other hand, is characterised by actions that do not positively affect this well-being. Moreover, such actions may even incur costs to the individual who decides to act.

Although compassion is compatible with rationality, commitment seems to be less compatible with it. However, various ways in increasing its compatibility have been explored. The authors of this chapter introduce the reader to this literature, while paying particular attention to the approach of Amartya Sen (1974, 1977). They shall then propose a reading of this notion when applied to acts of consumption.

The next chapter, proposed by *Jérôme Ballet* and *Damien Bazin* deals with a specific interpretation of commitment as seen in the concept of the impartial spectator.

The concept of the impartial spectator is already present in the writings of Adam Smith and David Hume. It is an emblematic form of economic reasoning on justice and equity. Apart from the debate on equity, this debate also implies a discussion on the notion of commitment in economics. The procedure consists in constructing the fiction of an individual who does not possess all available information, and to put him in an impartial situation where he could be any other individual. This method gave rise to great debate between John Rawls (1971, 1980, 2000) and John Harsanyi (1955, 1975, 1995), bringing forward the question of commitment associated to reason in economics. Would an individual still continue to respect the principles he followed when in an impartial situation, even after he has left this particular situation? Rawls believes that commitment to principles once acquired, cannot be pushed aside since reason primes above all others. However, as far as Harsanyi is concerned, it is only rationality that counts.

More recently, the concept of the impartial spectator has taken on a new meaning with the writings of Jürgen Habermas (1991). The ethics of discussion proposed by him had a considerable influence upon certain questions relating to economic decision-making. However, when dealing with such fields and as shall be shown later by the authors, the concept of the impartial discussant as presented by Habermas is not very relevant to current methods.

Indeed, reference to the idea of the impartial spectator lies within the framework of post-Kantian thought. Kantian philosophy, however, has long led to numerous attempts of integrating Kantian morality into economic reasoning. The third chapter of this part, presented by *Jérôme Ballet* and *Patrick Jolivet* thus deals with Kantian economics.

The authors divide this relatively heterogeneous set into three approaches. The first, qualified as *ordinary or everyday Kantism*, is associated with the principle of generalisation. The second deals with the unconditionally of action. Finally, the third approach deals with the concept of commitment, but appears as a specific category of this notion. Whatever the approach may be, Kantian economics moves away from Kantian philosophy. Nevertheless, it considerably enriches methodology regarding human action in economics.

These three chapters lead to a better comprehension of certain hypotheses regarding the integration of ethical behaviour into economic theory. They also present us with the limits of such a procedure. We shall highlight two such limits.

Firstly, the bid to integrate commitment is far from satisfactory. As a matter of fact, it presupposes a particularly positive character regarding commitment. It thereby casts aside certain motivations that could lead to acts of violence. Commitment could at times lead to crimes or acts of terrorism. We should thus formulate a broader conception of the term commitment that would enable the integration of an ethics of evil.

Next, the broadening of individuals' temporal horizons and the consideration of future generations directly pose the question of responsibility. Commitment, after all, is nothing more than a manner of dealing with the problem of the responsible individual within the framework of economic theory. However, there still remain numerous aspects that need to be closely examined.

2.3. Part Three: Responsibility in Economics

The principle of responsibility remains greatly unexplored in economics. The majority of developments deal with problems of redistribution (Roemer 1996, Fleurbaey 1996). Though the principle of responsibility is not new to philosophy, it has undergone great developments in the field of contemporary moral philosophy. Emmanuel Levinas (1979, 1981, 1990) and Hans Jonas (1984), in particular, have contributed, though in diverse ways, to transcending the framework of Kantian philosophy.

Emmanuel Levinas not only refers to, but also amplifies Dostoïevki's problematic of the Karamazov brothers: "We are all responsible for everything before everyone, I more than the others". According to Levinas, responsibility as the founding structure of the subject goes beyond liberty itself Responsibility precedes choice and the individual concerned does not have the freedom of choice. It is no longer freedom that founds responsibility, but rather, it is because I am responsible that my choices reveal my freedom. Moreover, I am directly responsible for my actions because others impose themselves upon me.

Hans Jonas highlighted the limits of Kantian morality when attempting to insert the theory of responsibility into a dynamic perspective. According to Jonas, the ethics of the categorical imperative is barely interested in the consequences of the maxim of action on the empirical world. However, the foundations of ethical theory are disrupted when moving on to what Jonas defines as the technological civilisation that introduces the element of cumulative irreversibility through the transformation of nature that it implies: the conditions determining the actions of tomorrow's humans would no longer be the same as those of today.

These two analyses highlight the role of responsibility in moral philosophy. They show us the extent to which moral man is also, and most importantly, a responsible man. We should then reflect on the perspectives of formalisation of this responsibility in economic analysis.

The three chapters of this part together offer a positive analysis of the notion of responsibility in economics. The first chapter written by *Jérôme Ballet* and *François-Régis Mahieu* argue in favour of such positive analysis. The authors' initial hypothesis states that normative ethical analysis in economics is essentially a result of the primacy of individuals' rights. Within this framework, responsibility is, at its most, the counterpart of individuals' rights. The authors thus propose two approaches. They first insist upon the importance that positive ethical analysis could have, and then, they move on to insist that responsibility could be conceived through duties. For this, they highlight the importance of religion or the ethics of Just when faced with the actions of persons.

The second chapter proposed by *Jérôme Ballet* and *Damien Bazin* is an extension of this reflection. It begs the question: "what is the status of the person in economics? The reasoning of economic theory, greatly influenced by utilitarianism, is not based on the person but on the individual. The latter's status is that of a quasi-object. This implies that choices, considered as rational, are carried out between objects, in their full meaning of consumption, and between quasi-objects represented by individuals. Here, one could substitute the other.

In the eyes of the authors, this manner of dealing with choices is highly unsatisfactory, since they ignore the fact that our economic actions, just like all other actions, are dependent on the moral rules that guide us. It is hence important to consider the person as responsible. However, there are two possible and complementary ways of reasoning. The first focuses on the meaning of the person, while the second stresses that the person acts in a responsible manner. Although these two methods of reasoning are complementary, they could also produce different approaches regarding human action.

The third and final chapter proposed by *Jérôme Ballet*, *Vinca Bigo*, *Jean-Luc Dubois* and *François-Régis Mahieu* presents the reader with some reflections on the integration of the positive ethics of responsibility into economics. These reflections are divided into three parts. Firstly, if the individual is not an atom independent from the rest of society and if he is above all a being who is caught up in a set of relationships, it is then these relationships that imply his responsibility. But these relationships are numerous. The individual is not merely responsible for one single person, but is simultaneously responsible for many. One must then reflect on the choice of responsible action and the given priorities. The authors shall examine how alterations could be made to responsibility. They highlight that these alterations presuppose the rationality of choice. Moreover, it is equally important that these choices seem reasonable. Finally, they question the meaning of happiness given that the individual is a responsible person. Happiness would then no longer be the maximisation of individual utility. Rather, it shall be closely linked to responsible action.

Notes

1. For more details about this distinction see M. Blaug (1982).
2. Von Mises (1949), see especially ch.XV, interprets this term in the very broad sense through "human action". He insists upon an *a priori* conception of action. His disciple Rothbard (1967) enlarges the scope of application of economics to the theory of hostile action and to the game theory. Without

adhering to their whole doctrine, we shall nonetheless borrow the teleological conception of these two authors and not merely the causal conception of praxeology.
3. Kotarbinski, (1960, 1965). We shall not make use of the narrow vision developed by this author concerning the adaptation of praxeology to the theory of organisation bent towards cybernetics.
4. 1966 edition, p.27.
5. Rapoport (1998, p.246).
6. Minani (1989, p.20).

References

Black, M. 1970. *Margins of Precision. Essays in Logic and Language*. Ithica: Cornell University Press.

Blaug, M. 1982. *Economic Methodology*. Cambridge: Cambridge University Press.

Espinas, A. V. 1897. *Les origines de la technologie.* Paris: Alcan.

Fleurbaey, M. 1996. *Théories économiques de la justice*. Paris: Economica.

Habermas, J. 1991. *Erläuterungen zur Diskursethik.* Suhrkamp Verlag: Frankfurt.

Harsanyi, J.C. 1955. “Cardinal Welfare, Individualistic Ethics and Interpersonnal Comparison of Utility”. *Journal of Political Economy*, 63, 309-321.

Harsanyi, J.C. 1975. “Can the maximin principle serve as a basis for morality? A critique of John Rawl’s theory”. *American Political Science Review,* 69 (2), 594-606.

Harsanyi, J.C. 1995. “A Theory of Prudential Values and a Rule Utilitarian Theory of Morality”. *Social Choice and Welfare*, 12, 319-333.

Jonas, H. 1984. *The Imperative of Responsibility. In Search of an Ethics for the Technological Age.* translated by H. Jonas with the collaboration of D. Herr. Chicago and London: The University of Chicago Press.

Kant, I. 1997. *Lectures on Ethics*. New York: Cambridge University Press. Translated by P. Heath.

Kant, I. 1785. *Foundations of the metaphysics of morals*. Chicago: University of Chicago Press. 1950.

Kotarbinski, T. 1960. “The concept of actions”. *The Journal of Philosophy*, 57 (7), 215-222.

Kotarbinski, T. 1965. *Praxiology, An Introduction to the Science of Efficient Action*. Oxford, Pergamon Press. Translated from Polish by Olgierd Wojtasiewicz.

Levinas, E. 1979. *Totality and infinity: an essay on exteriority*. Translated by A. Lingis. Boston: M. Nijhoff Publishers.

Levinas, E. 1981. *Otherwise than being: or, Beyond essence*. Translated by A. Lingis. Boston: M. Nijhoff.

Levinas, E. 1987. *Time and the Other*. Translated by R. Cohen. Pittsburgh: Duquesne University Press.

Levinas, E. 1990. *Nine Talmudic readings*. Translated and with
an introduction by A. Aronowicz. Bloomington: Indiana University Press.

Levinas, E. 1998. *Between us, thinking of the other.* Translation by M.B. Smith and B. Harshav, Columbia: Columbia University Press.

Lukàcs, G. 1967. *History and Class Consciousness*. Translation by R. Livingstone. Merlin Press.

Lukàcs, G. 1974. *Soul and Forms*. London.

Marshall, A. 1890. *Principles of Economics*. New York: MacMillan.

Minani, P. 1989. *L'Autre dans la pensée d'Emmanuel Levinas*. Rome: Pontificia Universitas Urbaniana, Dissertio ad Doctorum.

Nagel, E. 1961. *The Structure of Science. Problems in the Logic of Scientific Explanation*. London: Routledge and Kegan.

Rapoport, H. 1998. "Coordination, altruisme et développement". In Mahieu F-R. and Rapoport H. (eds.). *Altruisme, analyses économiques*. Paris: Economica.

Rawls, J. 1971. *A Theory of Justice*, Harvard: Harvard University Press.

Rawls, J. 1980. "Kantian Constructivism in Moral Theory". *Journal of Philosophy*, 77, 515-572.

Rawls, J. 2000. *Lectures on the History of Moral Philosophy*. Harvard: Harvard University Press.

Rothbard, M.N. 1967. "In Defense of Extreme Apriorism". *The Southern Economic Journal*, 23 (3), January, 314-20.

Roemer, J.E. 1996. *Theories of Justice*. Cambridge Mass: Harvard University Press.

Sen, A.K. 1970. *Collective Choice and Social Welfare*. Oxford: Elsevier Science Publishers.

Sen, A.K. 1974. "Choice, Ordering and Morality". In Körner S. (ed.). *Practical Reason*. Oxford, Blackwell.

Sen, A.K. 1977. "Rational Fools: A Critique of the Behavioural Foundations of Economic Theory". *Philosophy and Public Affairs*, 6, 317-344.

Stigler, G.J. and Becker, G.S. 1977. "De gustibus non est disputandum". *American Economic Review*, 67 (2), 76-90.

Von Mises, L. 1949. *Human Action, A Treatise of Economics*. London: W. Hodge and Co.

PART ONE

Altruism

On the Concept of Altruism[1]

Jérôme Ballet
Augendra Bhukuth

The term "altruism" is attributed to either Andrieux (professor of Auguste Comte at the Ecole Polytechnique) or to Auguste Comte himself in his "*Positive Catechism*". Nonetheless, the latter systemized the term in his writings. From now on, the term is defined in economic theory notably since Kolm (1966), Hochman and Rodgers (1969), as the positive integration in the utility function of an individual 'i' of an argument representing the consumption or the well-being of other individuals 'j', with j≠i. In other words, altruism is defined by the positive internalisation of the well-being of others in the utility function.

This definition is actually common in economic theory. However, it deviates totally from the original concept meaning as it was proposed by Auguste Comte. In this paper, we shall propose to go back to the origin of the term throughout the controversy, which happened between Auguste Comte, John Stuart Mill and Herbert Spencer. We extract some elements of thoughts towards the actual definition. The assumption that we uphold is as follows: the concept of altruism, as it is seen originally, implies a social dimension in accordance with the actual notion of social preference. Hence, it moves from the actual definition based on an individual dimension and personal preferences. We understand that the word altruism in its origin implies an account on society and it cannot be reduced to a simple inter-individual theory, which refers to the notion of benevolence.

We support this assumption by three stages. In the first stage, the point of view of Auguste Comte will be exposed and the critical reaction of two of his contemporaries: John Stuart Mill and Herbert Spencer. In a second stage, the point of view of Mill and Spencer on altruism will be briefly developed. In a third stage, we shall characterize the difference between altruism and benevolence by different authors. Finally, we will conclude on the abusive interpretation of the contemporary concept of altruism.

1. Altruism by Auguste Comte and its Critics

Auguste Comte develops the term altruism with reference to the law of solidarity, a central law in his work. This law is connected to the notion of humanity and links individuals to the past. Humanity is the whole human-being past, future and present submitted to an interdependence formulated by solidarity. According to Comte, living-beings are necessarily more and more governed by the dead. Each person belonging to humanity knows two successive lives. A first temporary life, which constitutes the actual life, is qualified as objective life. A second life, a subjective one beginning only after death, is formed by the imprint left by everyone. The proportion of dead over livings is always increasing in a way to prevail the first over the followers.

The law of solidarity was developed in reality before Comte. Laurent (1991) makes us go back to the solidarity tradition of the beginning of the XIX century. The change over of the semantic meaning of the adjective "solidary" from its legal origin towards the qualifying utilisation of the interdependence relation of human-being, was the act of Mirabeau since 1789 and Châteaubriand in 1802. Yet it occupied an entire place in the social philosophy from the writings of Pierre Leroux (1840). The contribution of Comte consisted in giving it a real ethical dimension through the association of duties and altruism.

The argument that Comte used in other respects was directed at economic elements such as the division of labour. The law of solidarity, which unites members of humanity, takes on an economic form under the division of labour. As this division increases, cooperation becomes increasingly necessary. But intensification of this division of labour favours personal instincts over social moral. To avoid all forms of halt or even regression in social progress, which are due to the dissolution of solidarity, the social moral must be imposed to all individuality. It becomes a superior reference to individual moral. The true social moral implies that everyone is born with obligations towards their predecessors, their contemporary and their followers. Comte insists on "the irrevocable substitution of duties to rights" (Cingolani 1992). He withdraws the idea of right with its individual reference to substitute it with the notion of duty, which translates concrete solidarities of work in society: "positivism never admit rights by everyone to others. Because his point of view, which is always social, cannot include any notion of right based constantly on individuality" (Comte 1852, p.297)[2].

Altruism takes an extreme form under the formula "live for others", which reflects genuine compatible feelings with duties towards others. In this framework, the artificial order instituted by the government consists to improve the natural order formed by the spontaneous participation of individuals to the law of solidarity. Freedom consists, as a matter of fact, in the subordination of personal feelings to altruistic feelings. Individual freedom, which is used to devote absolute individualism, is only "a result of modern anarchy", which will disappear with individual subordination to social order. Each individual is seen constrained to sacrifice his personal interests to duties resulting from social solidarity.

Beneficence is linked to selfishness and solidarity to altruism. Meanwhile this altruism is extreme in its benevolent form since a precept as "treat others as you would like to be treated" according to Comte (1852) is merely reduced to a personal calculation. It corresponds to an indirect form of stimulation of selfishness. Pure altruism is translated by personal sacrifice for the gain of others.

This notion of solidarity will experience a great success with Bourgeois (1896, 1902), who ensures the link between the social ethic of solidarity and the principles of political action. To this solidarity, in term of duties, opposes a concept (Nozick 1974, Rothbard 1982) founded on individual right to ownership and in the first instance, the right to ownership of oneself. This libertarianism leans on the virtue of selfishness (Rand 1964). Altruist-collectivist thought, to use the word of Rand, is based on the fact that humans are responsible of each other and that the misfortunate of them is a "mortgage" on the others. In this sense, the notion of duty is a priority. The notion of right is excluded from the argument. The foundations of thought are to overthrow according to libertarianism. Only rights have a moral value.

The same argument was used by John Stuart Mill and Herbert Spencer to oppose the cardinal rule of moral as they perceived it in Comte's work, since this one is "live for others". Comte not only considers that individuals must give priority to requirements of general wealth over their selfish tendency, but also states that each of them should search for the slightest defect he could bring to their personal interests. The argument of Mill and Spencer on "rights" is opposed to that of Comte, based on "duties". This notion of right is closely linked to that of Justice. Yet, the aim of Justice, and by consequence of rights, is to assure the highest possible amount of happiness. Thus, the law of solidarity is rejected since Humanity can probably obtain the highest amount of happiness when each individual pursues his own interest, under the condition of submitting himself to the rules established to respect others' goods. The rules to respect by each other towards everyone concern equality and the inviolability of rights. Beneficence, as opposed to Justice, creates no rights. It can be that an individual does not need the kindness of others, but the rights that he possesses are, on the other hand, always necessary.

Without directly quoting Comte, Mill (1861) too forwards a criticism. He reproaches him for not distinguishing generosity from Justice, by making entire humanity a holder of rights, and making present individuals debtors towards the former: "He (the moralist, and by implication Comte) is well obliged to say that our efforts, to all possible extent, are due to our fellow creatures assimilating our efforts to a debt (Mill 1861/1988, p.133). Yet for Mill, there is a type of altruism up to which we all must be required to rise and beyond which there is no obligation but shall be considered as meritorious (Mill 1865/1890, p.144).

The personal sacrifice imposed by duties, is moreover for Mill (1861), only a virtue in a "very imperfect state of social arrangements" and probably unnecessary in a perfect state of society. In November 1829, in a letter addressed to Gustave d'Eichthal, he was praising, just as enlightened interest or caution, certain categories of impulsion that were non representative of principles of morality. Justice is the moral principle by excellence. It is based upon the notion of individual rights. Having a right implies possessing an element guaranteed by society, because of its indispensable nature that helps reach the highest general utility as possible.

The analysis of Mill and Spencer in terms of rights joined in the criticism of Comte. This is quite distinct regarding women's rights. When Comte supported the subordination of women to men in a compatible way with the notion of social duty, Spencer in *Justice* and Mill in *Subjection of Women* voiced their favour towards the equality of rights of men and women. Fairness according to Spencer, requires that women not be penalized. Just as men, they have the right to physical integrity, ownership, freedom of belief and the right to speech, etc. However, in a couple, for example, rights are qualified in function of family responsibilities. The distribution of rights depends on the distribution of responsibilities. The system of status is substituted to the system of contract. However, as opposed to Mill, fervent defender of the suffragettes, he seems to consider that there is no urgency in England to give more rights to women. Whereas Comte sees a form of elevated altruism in marriage, where the devotion of women is merely the counterpart of plain altruism by men who provide to their needs, Mill considers the family as often being, for its head, the occasion to express a refined selfishness, whose sacrifices simply take on one particular form. He could, in this way, sacrifice the happiness of other members of his family to satisfy his "slightest preferences". The quest for the greatest happiness implies that the relationships between individuals must not be established according to subordinate relationships. Similarly, Mill opposes himself to the paternalist vision of Comte on relationships between the richer and the poorer or the working class (de Bry 1998). The manifest opposition of ideas defended by one or the other eventually leads to a breakdown in their correspondence (Ballet 1998, cf. note p.147).

Spencer (1891), as Mill, makes rights the principle of Justice. Once the pacific state is achieved, where men are perfectly adapted to social life, the sacrifice of someone to the profit of the group or species no longer have any meaning. We leave the area of "relative morality" associated with the conflicting phase, and enter into an area of "absolute morality", which only deals with the principles of Justice in a peaceful society, where living-beings are perfectly adapted.

Justice includes two elements: One positive element represented by the right of everyone to free activities, and to the fruits of these activities; a negative element, in presence of others, since it imposes limits to the freedom of everyone, by giving others similar rights. The negative element associated with the right of others gives its ethical character to Justice. This limitation to individual action differs from limitations of private behaviour imposed upon certain individuals under the form of acts of beneficence. Justice deals only with limits that should be maintained to assure the harmonious cooperation between individuals.

Spencer acknowledges the law of cooperation in society, but the conditions of this cooperation move away from the position held by Comte. Indeed, what is the fairest distribution of advantages obtained as a result of cooperation for individuals who submit themselves? Cooperation produces an excess in relation to non-cooperation. However, the advantages extracted by cooperation do not comply with Comte's rule of "live for others", which implies a form of large redistribution, but rather, comply with the rule of Justice which establishes itself in function of rights. Justice simultaneously takes on a form of equality and inequality. It is equalitarian by the rights accorded to each other for freedom of activity and for the fruit of that activity. It is unequalitarian because it does not imposes any principle of redistribution on the fruits of the activity obtained through association. Thus, the maxim "treat others like you would like to be treated", a particular form of selfish calculation for Comte, becomes a vague idea for Spencer. This imperfectly implies the equality of rights, but on the other hand, runs the risk of leading to abusive interpretations. This is mainly because it does not present any reasons which can justify inequalities. Indeed, Mill (1861) adds that equality in the importance of everyone insofar as global utility is concerned, requires that each one has the means to achieve happiness, within the limits imposed by the general interest. Beyond this, all social inequality, which does not contribute to general interest can be considered as unfair[3]. Yet for Spencer, reducing the inequalities constitute a trangression of everyone's right to the results of free activity and therefore infringes the equality of rights.

The use of rights in the place of duties condemns the concept of altruism as presented by Comte. Mill and Spencer proposed a vision of "rational" altruism in opposition to Comte's altruism which may at times be considered "sacrificial" (Ballet 1998).

2. Altruism by J.S. Mill and H. Spencer

For Mill as for Spencer, the opposition to Comte is manifest. Whereas the latter makes altruism an extreme form of benevolence, based on devotion and veneration, the two former conceive altruism as Justice. Justice limits itself to the respect of rights, the first of which is freedom. For Spencer, they form the necessary basis to maintain the peaceful society in an evolutionist logic. These rights are justified by Mill through their particular utility for society. His defence for liberty is clear in *On Liberty*. It is the principal source of happiness and its suppression will be the origin of harm for humanity. The restriction of liberty leads man to seek power. Yet, as highlighted by Bentham, power is a pleasure, but its absence is not a harm. According to Mill, the supremacy of freedom can be imposed without any difficulty. It is all the more necessary since love for power and love for freedom are in an eternal antagonism (Mill 1869).

The right to freedom is based on rational behaviour. Individuals have objectives, which, in order to be accomplished, require freedom. Is rationality sufficient to define this right of freedom? According to Williams (1985), mere rational deliberation is not sufficient, it does not permit to achieve the impartiality that is required to define rights. We can follow its reasoning through the following example: Agent A hopes to earn money. To achieve this aim, he needs freedom. This individual then stipulates: I should not let others infringe upon my freedom. This prescription Pa is reasonable according to A. But agent A also admits that another agent B can similarly aim to earn money. Agent B then states: I should not let A make an attempt against my freedom. The principle of universalization involves that A assumes that prescription Pb is reasonable because Pa is. In other words, Pb is reasonable because like A, B is rational. But this signifies in no means that A could be rational by accepting Pb, if, by accepting it, he commits himself not to make an attempt against the freedom of B, since he can probably gain more money by, for instance, stealing from B.

A first solution to this problem resides in commitment. According to the categorical imperative of Kant "behave only according to the maxim which implies that you can wish while it, at the same time, becomes a universal law". Rational liberty then presupposes ethical considerations so that it leads to an already committing freedom (Williams 1985). However, according to utilitarianism, the Kantian solution is seen as insufficient. In spite of the misunderstanding between Spencer and Mill on the limitations of the law drawn by rights, their position regarding the Kantian principle is similar. This principle does not guarantee the highest amount of happiness. Rights, and therefore the maxim of Kant, must be formulated in a rational consequentialistic logic: " If we are to give a meaning to the principle of Kant, it should be interpreted as follows: we must guide our conduct according to a principle which all reasonable human-being could adopt for their general interest" (Mill 1861/1988, p.137); "Kant expresses a priori a requirement and abstracts all beneficial ends, whereas for me, in the conduct of a social state, only conformity to this demand can a priori ensure the achievement of these ends" (Spencer 1893/1895, p.313). The solution proposed by Mill and Spencer is based on a broad rational calculation. Altruism becomes rational. Impartiality and rationality are themselves based on a feeling of Justice.

The feeling of Justice is a particular altruistic feeling. This feeling involves acts having useful social consequences. It is the combination of a selfish feeling and extended sympathy. Whereas Mill notices the existence of sympathy without searching for its origin, Spencer (1855), on the other hand, tries to explain the apparition through an evolutionist logic. This attempt permits him to reconcile the evolutionist theory of moral feelings with the theory of utility. Sympathy begins with group life. It develops into an evolutionist rule of safeguarding the group. Although there are three direct reasons for the existence of sympathy, the association of members of same species or of a same group, the union of male and female or of man and woman, and the union of parents and children, the essential condition of its extension is "intelligence".

For the two authors, the feeling of justice is only a combination of selfishness and sympathy rendered compatible by the intelligence. According to Spencer (1904), Smith in the *Theory of Moral Sentiments* produces beneficence by the help of sympathy. As for Spencer, he wishes to go further and make Justice, just as benevolence, a mixed feeling. From 1843, in his letters (cf. Spencer 1904), he describes the components of this composition. It concerns sympathy and concept of personal rights. Justice then becomes sympathy for the personal rights of others.

The principle of sympathy, largely used by Smith, does not differentiate itself completely from an utilitarian vision (Dupuy 1992). In joining up with rational altruism, it differs from perfect sympathy or from pure altruism, for whom the happiness of others is the aim that guides everyone. In fact, Spencer (1880) notes the paradox of utilitarianism conceived as pure altruism. If everyone experienced pleasure in giving pleasure, the genesis of altruistic pleasure for each individual depends on the pleasure testified by others. To summarize, this principle reflects like a game of infinite mirrors, without a definite solution. At least one of the members of the society must not be a pure altruist.

Sympathy can only have minimum selfishness as a base. The impartial spectator of Smith becomes a calculating spectator, for whom the respect of necessary rights to his life is just as necessary for the life of others.

An individual living in a society where the members have common interests will soon become conscious, through his intelligence, that any attack against his community would also threaten his own security. Thus Spencer underlines, the English protest with vehemence against infractions to parliamentary procedures since such infractions, although they could not affect their interests directly, can confer power to an authority which will impose non desired restrictions and could touch them indirectly. At this level the feeling of Justice is purely selfish. In order to become altruist, we require a feeling of sympathy. Therefore, according to Spencer: "all altruistic feeling presupposes the corresponding experience of selfish feeling. Sympathy for other's pain can only be felt by those who have experienced pain…" (Spencer 1893/1895, p.35).

Sympathy itself can be raised through selfishness. The selfish feeling of Justice is not moral. It becomes altruistic and moral thanks to the extent of sympathy. Selfishness associated, through intelligence, to sympathy towards all human-beings in general or the community in particular, enables us to carry out an individual and ethical calculation. What is good for an individual is good for all other individuals of the community. Selfishness and altruism are "coessential". The opposition with Comte is obvious. Comte's concept of altruism "live for the other" which involves a personal sacrifice, moves towards an altruism where the other's happiness depends closely on one's personal conception of happiness. In this sense, it does not reject personal sacrifice, but does not require it at all. The replacement of duties by individual rights is then only a rational form of ethics based on selfishness and the extent of sympathy; these rights are being considered as essential for the highest happiness of the individual and the collectivity. Sacrificial altruism gives way to rational altruism, in other words, to rationality extended through sympathy towards the other.

3. The Distinction between Benevolence and Altruism

The terms "altruist" and "altruism" by their definition present, in the expression used by Spencer (1855), an opposition to the terms "selfish" and "selfishness", which is far more clear than the terms "benevolence" and "beneficence". The notion of benevolence which we find before Comte refers directly to a subjective and personal situation. For instance, Bentham uses benevolence in his division of pleasures and pains. He splits them into two categories. One category is constituted of purely personal pleasures and pains. The other category refers to pleasures and pains in relation to others. This category includes the pleasures and pains of benevolence and malevolence. The pleasures of benevolence correspond to pleasures felt by an individual when considering the happiness of other persons. These pleasures can be restricted to a close circle of individuals or extended to entire humanity. Benevolence expresses personal pleasures in relation to others. In return, altruism, as it is presented by Comte refers to a situation or to a social state.

A crucial point which interests us in the debate between Comte, Mill and Spencer resides in the distinction between benevolence and altruism. There seems to be a consensus between the three authors regarding this distinction, even though each of them perceives it differently.

Comte begins the distinction in his *Physique Sociale* with the degree of relationship to others. These degrees depend on the level of analysis of society. Although this study is restricted to the level of the individual, while firmly rejecting selfishness, Comte (1830) believes that the individual in general wishes for others what he desires for himself. At this stage, public interest could not have sense without individual interest. The suppression of personal instinct, as opposed to moral improvement, could moreover provoke a mere degeneration of altruism to a vague, undetermined and rather ineffective form of benevolence, under the form of a "sterile" action of charity and beneficence. At the family level of society, on the other hand, sympathy tends to dominate over selfishness. Finally, as we go through the study of the society in general, we see the emergence of the law of solidarity or corporation which unifies all people to each other, regardless of their will. This law covers to all operations both material and moral. Society constitutes a social organism inside which the law of solidarity unites all the elements. The individual is then preoccupied with the direct consideration of economics in general.

With the help of three levels, Comte distinguishes the actions linked to "enlightened interest", the actions of beneficence and those of solidarity; given that first the individual then the family instincts are being subordinate to the highest form of moral. The social morality resulting from the law of solidarity is distinguished from beneficence which is judged sterile. The latter would moreover be a "so-called benevolence", a made up form of benevolent action linked to envy (Comte 1852).

According to Mill, a certain kind of moral sensitivity is useful. As he has written to Gustave d'Eichthal in May 1829, the superiority which permits a nation to take out the best possible parts of its productive and commercial resources is connected to the worst defect, which is the tendency to sacrifice everything to the accumulation of wealth and to this exclusive and bitter selfishness which accompanies it. However, this commercial spirit risks bringing with its happier consequences a "certain dose of harm". To avoid this, we must set the nation free from moral indifference and insensitivity. But although this moral sensitivity is necessary, it is not the private and spontaneous beneficence and momentum of heart which, on the contrary, could be harmful to society. Indeed, as Mill (1869/1990, p.174) underlines it: "As for charity, it is a subject matter where the immediate effect on the persons we want to assist, and the consequences on general welfare are always radically in contradiction with each other".

Following Bentham, Mill supposes that acts of charity, if they are to be useful, must be subject to social calculation. Nevertheless, Mill does not suppose that acts of charity should be in charge of the state. Simply, while benevolent acts of charity result from individual calculation on an individual state, desirable moral calculation must be executed on a social state.

Spencer (1893), distinguishes acts of Justice from those of beneficence. Justice involves the recognition of others, the right to the freedom of activity and the outcomes of this activity. Beneficence, furthermore, involves efforts to increase the other's happiness. He divides beneficence into two distinct categories. Negative beneficence which is characterised "by the passivity in words or in actions when action could ensure certain advantages or enjoyments of selfish order" (Spencer 1893/1895, p.21) and positive beneficence which "embraces all actions which involve sacrifice of a good possessed actually or virtually on behalf of others: at times, it may involve the sacrifice of an effort which we could have spared, of a product already obtained, or of the future result of an effort already accomplished in the past" (ibid., p.22). Negative beneficence is linked to passivity, whereas positive beneficence is linked to activity. He makes use of the reasoning of Mill and pushes it even further. Charity imposed by law cannot be reconciled with Justice. Moreover, what is not fair ceases to be a form of beneficence. However, justice is essential to social equilibrium and results from public interest. Benevolence, on the other hand, is not necessary for this equilibrium and only affects private interests.

Altruism is differentiated from benevolence in reference to the level at which the calculation is carried out. Benevolence corresponds to a calculation on an individual state, a personal and subjective calculation. Altruism, on the contrary, is situated at the level of social calculation *vis-à-vis* an ethical reference.

Whereas benevolence does not refer directly to ethics or to morality, altruism corresponds to them.

4. What Conclusion on the Concept of Altruism

Whether in Comte, Mill or Spencer, benevolence is clearly distinguished from altruism. The distinction these authors make support those proposed by Harsanyi (1955) between subjective preferences and ethical preferences. Ethical preferences express the preferences of an individual only in function of social and impersonal considerations. Subjective preferences, on the other hand, express an individual's real preferences. The latter depend on their simple personal interests or on other criteria such as benevolence towards others.

The structure of preference thus established forms a separation between what a person considers to be good from a social point of view and what he considers to be good in his own point of view. Sen (1974, 1977), through the introduction of a meta-ranking, has gone beyond this structure. A particular moral can then be considered from a moral ranking in the set of feasible actions, and moreover, from a moral ranking of the sets of actions. Sen calls this ranking of rankings a meta-ranking. The possibility of maximisation in cascade is then opened. A first ranking maximisation will focus on social or ethical preferences. Meanwhile, a second ranking maximisation will focus on subjective preferences.

Benevolence appears at an inferior level of preference rankings. Subjective preference for a type of action based on benevolence does not necessarily correspond to the ethical preference. If we follow the argument of Comte, Spencer or Mill, it can be contradictory. Generalised benevolence is then, not always desirable. It can even be fatal to the community.

What appears paradoxical about the contemporary use of the term altruism is that it refers to an individual calculation, whereas the original analyses of Comte, Spencer or Mill have explicitly made altruism a form of social calculation. In this sense, altruism corresponds to ethical and social preferences, whereas benevolence corresponds to subjective and personals preferences. This shift in meaning is probably due to an abusive interpretation of Comte's writings, in which altruism is assimilated to an extreme form of benevolence without realising that the change of term proposed by Comte also corresponds to a change in the level of argument. Returning to the original sense of the term is especially difficult, since the contemporary sense has become so common. Still, it is extremely important to recognize this transformation, to highlight it, and not to reject analyses which offer a different sense to it[4].

Notes

1. This text has been inspired by a previous text: Ballet, J. 1998. "Altruisme sacrificiel et altruisme rationnel". In Mahieu F.-R. and Rapoport H. (eds.), *Altruisme, analyses économiques*, 139-159. Paris: Economica.
2. All quotations of A. Comte, J.S. Mill and H. Spencer are extracted from french editions of their books. See references for editions.
3.This principle makes us think of the principle defended by Rawls, since he considered inequalities as admissible as long as they are to the benefit of the less fortunate, especially the logic of the just savings.
4. According to Mahieu (1998), the meaning taken by the term in the contemporary sense is not neutral since it makes altruism a concept full of values, which is automatically positive because it is associated to benevolence. It simultaneously forbids a more philosophical interpretation of altruism as an a priori neutral concept, which can take on positive or negative values by being associated to benevolence or malevolence. It then becomes possible to talk about "malevolent altruism".

References

Ballet, J. 1998. "Altruisme sacrificiel et altruisme rationnel". In Mahieu F.-R. and Rapoport H. (eds.), *Altruisme, analyses économiques*, 139-159. Paris: Economica.

Bourgeois, L. 1896. *Solidarités*. Paris: Armand Colin.

Bourgeois, L. 1902. *Essai d'une philosophie de la solidarité*. Paris: Alcan.

Bry de, F. 1998, "Le paternalisme entrepreneurial, égoïsme éclairé ou altruisme rationnel?. In Mahieu F.-R. and Rapoport H. (eds.), *Altruisme, analyses économiques*, 161-189. Paris: Economica.

Cingolani, P. 1992. "L'idée d'humanité chez Auguste Comte, solidarités et conduite". In CURAPP, *La solidarité: un sentiment républicain?*, 42-54. Paris: PUF.

Comte, A. 1830. *Cours de philosophie positive, Physique sociale, leçons 46 à 60*. Paris: Hermann 1975.

Comte, A. 1844. *Discours sur l'esprit positif*. Paris: Vrin 1995.

Comte, A. 1852. *Catéchisme positiviste ou sommaire exposition de la religion universelle en treize entretiens systématiques entre une femme et un prêtre de l'Humanité*. Paris: Leroux.

Comte, A. 1975. *Correspondance générale et confessions*. Paris: Mouton.

Dupuy, J.P. 1992. *Le sacrifice et l'envie*. Paris: Calmann-Lévy.

Harsanyi, J.C. 1955. "Cardinal Welfare, Individualistic Ethics and Interpersonnal Comparison of Utility". *Journal of Political Economy*, 63, 309-321.

Hochman, H.M. and Rodgers, J.D. 1969. "Pareto Optimal Redistribution". *American Economic Review*. 59, 997-1002.

Kolm, S.C. 1966. "La production optimale de justice sociale". Conférence de l'AISE. In *Economie publique*. Paris: CNRS.

Laurent, A. 1991. *Solidaire, si je le veux*. Paris: Les Belles Lettres.

Leroux, P. 1840. *De l'Humanité, de son principe et de son avenir; où se trouve exposée la vraie définition de la religion et où l'on explique le sens, la suite et l'enchaînement du mosaïsme et du christianisme*. Paris: Perrotin.

Mahieu, F.-R. 1998, "Altruisme et ingérence, modalités de l'altruisme dans l'analyse économique". In Mahieu F.-R. and Rapoport H. (eds.), *Altruisme, analyses économiques*, 113-137. Paris: Economica.

Mill, J.S. 1859. *On Liberty*. In The Collected Works of John Stuart Mill, J.M. Robson (ed.). Toronto and London: University of Toronto Press, 1963-1991. French translation, Paris: Gallimard 1990.

Mill, J.S. 1861. *Utilitarianism*. In The Collected Works of John Stuart Mill, J.M. Robson (ed.). Toronto and London: University of Toronto Press, 1963-1991. French translation, Paris: Flammarion 1988.

Mill, J.S. 1865. *Auguste Comte and Positivism*. In The Collected Works of John Stuart Mill, J.M. Robson (ed.). Toronto and London: University of Toronto Press, 1963-1991. French translation, Paris: Alcan 1890.

Mill, J.S. 1869. *The Subjection of Women*. In The Collected Works of John Stuart Mill, J.M. Robson (ed.). Toronto and London: University of Toronto Press, 1963-1991. French translation, Paris: Avatar 1992.

Mill, J.S. 1873. *Autobiography*. In The Collected Works of John Stuart Mill, J.M. Robson (ed.). Toronto and London: University of Toronto Press, 1963-1991. French translation, Paris: Aubier 1993.

Mill, J.S. 1898. *Correspondance inédite (1828-1871)*. Paris: Alcan.

Nozick, R. 1974. *Anarchy, State and Utopia*. New York: Basic Books.

Rand, A. 1964. *The Virtue of Selfishness*. New York: Objectivist Newsletter.

Rothbard, M. 1982. *The Ethics of Liberty*. Atlantic Highlands: Humanities Press.

Sen, A. 1974. "Choice, Ordering and Morality". In Körner S (ed.), *Practical Reason*. Oxford: Blackwell.

Sen, A. 1977. "Rational Fools: A Critique of the Behavioural Foundations of Economic Theory". *Philosophy and Public Affairs*, 6, 317-344.

Spencer, H. 1850. *Social Statics: or the Conditions essentials to Human Happiness specified, and the first of them developed*. London: Williams and Norgate.

Spencer, H. 1855. *The principles of Psychology*. French translation, Paris: Germer Baillière 1875.

Spencer, H. 1880. *The Data of Ethics*. French translation, Paris: Germer Baillière.

Spencer, H. 1891. *The Principles of Ethics. Part IV Justice*. French translation, Paris: Guillaumin 1893.

Spencer, H. 1893. *The Principles of Ethics. Parts V and VI*. French translation, Paris: Guillaumin 1895.

Spencer, H. 1904. *Autobiography*. Paris: Alcan 1907.

Williams, B. 1985. *Ethics and the Limits of Philosophy*. London: William Collin Sons and co.

Methodological Aspects of Altruism in Economics

Jérôme Ballet
Sébastien Barillot

Currently, altruism is commonly considered as a concept of economic analysis. However, the way it is dealt with remains specifically-linked to this field. The approach usually privileged is that of social interaction. In such a framework, the behavioural aspect is the only one to be taken into account. Therefore, the question of the Other refocuses on issues such as external effects or social costs, which must be endogenised by the most efficient organisational form (Manski 2000). Although the approach does not exclude the existence of a variety of motivations at the origin of individual actions, it does not clearly establish a link between these motivations -pushed into the background- and the economic agent's final behaviour.

Therefore, referring to moral philosophy allows us to assert that the economic process does not seriously consider moral motivations. Since motivations are neutralised, any action is the direct result of a rational calculus constrained by the presence of others, and it does not allow us to judge whether the maximising individual is morally disposed in relation to his/her environment. Indeed, an action considered as "moral" cannot be directly connected to an individual's benevolent motivation.

In a reductive way, morality therefore becomes a calculus domain among others, relegated to the same level as substitution between people and goods: by helping others you do them a favour which is a substitution to a consumer good used as numerary. In other words, charity is not the result of a strong emotion facing indigence, but rather due to a rational choice which fills its author with personal satisfaction.

Although a certain advantage lies in this reasoning, when it comes to analysing individual behaviours in a specific context, there are also obvious limits to it since it overlooks the nature of the links binding the protagonists of a social action, and consequently, the prevailing moral principle. The problem posed is therefore that of the status of others, followed by the problem of economic choices constrained by morals. This questioning shows that the analysis of altruism in economics currently remains unsatisfactory, because it only gives a minimal valuation of the impact of interpersonal relations on individual decisions.

Thus, in order to best identify the difficulties linked to the modelling of altruism in economics, we will proceed in three stages. First of all, we will go deeply into the opposition between behaviour and motivation. Then, we shall examine how economic analysis neglects the delicate issue of morality as a prerequisite to the decision. Finally, we will conclude on standard economic methodology's inability to deal with that kind of problem.

1. Behavioural vs. Motivational Altruism

All economic modelling is based on a certain number of hypotheses. Indeed, a particular postulate deeply marked the consumer theory: the "axiom of revealed preferences". The consistency condition of the axiom gave rise to sharp debates which defined a weak axiom and a strong axiom[1]. We will deal with this debate here, but we will simply study the axiom, in its general meaning, alongside the consequences it has on the economic analysis of altruism.

1.1. Revealed Preferences and Behaviour

The axiom of revealed preferences first appeared in Samuelson's work (1938). He points out that observed choices reflect consumer preferences. Consequently, there is no point in knowing the structure of individual tastes to understand individual rational behaviour. The observation of choices must only be done according to certain logical criteria. More specifically, if a set of goods y can be bought by an individual, bearing in mind his/her budget, but the individual instead buys a set of goods *x*, then it is assumed that he/she has revealed his/her preferences for *x*, as compared to *y*. Of course, for this individual, preferences dictate choices, but from an observer's point of view, the choices made by the individual reveal his/her preferences. The economist, who cannot meddle in the "secret garden" of individuals, does not directly know their preferences, but can deduce them from the observation of their choices. This idea is extremely well explained by Hicks (1956, p.6) when he writes: "the econometric theory of demand does study human beings, but only as entities having certain patterns of market behaviour; it makes no claim, no pretence, to be able to see inside their heads". There is an essential virtue to this axiom, which, according to Samuelson, is (1938, p.71): "to develop the theory of consumer behaviour freed from any vestigial traces of the utility concept".

Through this axiom, economic analysis is completely behaviouralist, since behaviour supersedes motivation in the study of decision-making processes. Elements only relating to consumer psychology are then referred to as a "black box".

The postulate applies to selfish as well as altruistic behaviour. In such a case, being altruistic simply means behaving in an altruistic way, i.e. positively integrating others as a source of utility. Such a point of view is understandable, especially when there are numerous motivations and that a particular kind of behaviour cannot be inferred from a particular kind of motivation (Ballet 2000). For example, altruistic behaviour can be the result of many things: an ethics of sharing or of reciprocity of gifts (Hirshleiffer 1985), a search for a social status which can sometimes lead to a competition of generosity, or even to a real war of gifts (Mercier-Ythier 1993), but it can also result from individual pleasure such as the "warm glow" produced by the act of giving (Andreoni 1989), etc. Given the diversity of motivations which can lead to altruistic behaviour, it is tempting to present a neutralised definition of altruism (Koulibaly 1998). For instance, Becker (1981/1994, p.279) clearly asserts that "I am giving a definition of altruism that is relevant to behaviour - to consumption and production choices- rather than giving a philosophical discussion of what really motivates people"[2].

However, motivations undoubtedly enhance the vision that we may have of economic behaviour. For lack of being able to decipher the "black box", it is still possible to postulate these motivations, just as Becker (1974) with a theory of social interaction and the case of the "rotten kid": facing an altruistic parent (hypothesis), the rotten kid, only prompted by his/her personal interest, behaves in accordance to his/her father's expectations, i.e. in an altruistic manner, so as to obtain money transfers from him. As long as the child's motivation is not integrated into the reasoning, it is possible to talk about behavioural altruism. In the opposite case, it is also possible to imagine situations in which a child, prompted by altruistic motivations, behaves in a selfish, or even malevolent, manner.

It is undeniable that bearing in mind motivations makes it possible to enrich the analysis, but above all, to obtain a more comprehensive conception of the individual than the one suggested in the theory of revealed preferences. This theory implies a disembodiment of the individual, reduced to a sum of physical characteristics, deprived of any moral depth. Regarding this topic, Samuelson (1938) uses the expression "individual guinea-pig" which precisely reflects the dullness of the notion of the individual imagined through this approach. The human being, just like animals, is a guinea-pig put through behavioural experimentation.

1.2. Resurgence of Moral Motivations

In the same way, Sen (1973) believes that explaining choices by merely referring to behaviour is sheer rhetoric and that the theory of revealed preferences gets its meaning from at least one hypothesis on the psychology of individuals: the search for personal interest. Sen's criticism came prior to the large development of models including a hypothesis of altruism, and therefore could not attack them. Nonetheless, even in those models, the conception of the individual is extremely poor. The idea of altruism mainly seems to be a "holdall" in which all non-selfish motivations can be put away. This idea has already enriched research in economy[3], but it also has its own limits. Therefore, is it equivalent to link an altruistic motivation to any value judgement with no distinction whatsoever (compassion, will to commit oneself, an ideal, or a religious belief)? However, our aim is not to examine all various possible motivations. It will be done in the following chapters[4]. Here, we would merely want to point out that taking motivations into account is a crucial wager of economic research.

This opinion can be strengthened by considering the concept of action. If acting is considered as an ability shared by all human beings and by other organised beings, considering human action as a mere behavioural form, actually comes down to creating a non-human economy, in which the human being can easily be replaced by a laboratory rat. Regarding this topic, Magee's (1993) typology of interpersonal relations is eloquent.

		The agent's behaviour in relation to his/her environment	
		Positive	Negative
The agent's behaviour in relation to him/herself	Positive	Cooperation	Selfishness
	Negative	Altruism	Cruaulty

According to this typology, others' happiness is a means to obtain maximum satisfaction, and it is not an apriorism. Indeed, happiness can be obtained in two ways: either by compromising, which enables the individual to indirectly take advantage of his/her own acts of kindness (cooperation), or by adopting a behaviour of renouncement (altruism). However, suppressing one's own desires is a mere constraint that has to be met in order to reach a selfish well-being. Therefore, moral motivation can not be used to justify altruistic behaviours, since rats can also behave in an altruistic or cooperative way, if circumstances make it a necessity for survival!

This observation shows how difficult it is to clarify the causes of an action. The behavioural option seems to simplify the methodology, but has proved to be unsuitable when it comes to taking mixed situations where moral judgement intervenes into account. Although all human beings are not constantly prompted only by moral motivations, the latter still remain essential for the analysis of altruistic behaviour, and having resort to ethology becomes specious. Indeed, it is more than doubtful to confer to a rat a feeling other than that of belonging to a group, whereas the individual is often able to accept or reject others as members of his/her social environment (Ballet et Barillot 2004). Therefore, showing kindness corresponds to a global conception of others, with no distinction among people, and it is considered as a moral motivation.

Nonetheless, it is impossible to directly deduce altruistic behaviour from this motivation. According to the paradox of sympathy (Smith 1759) a human being can consider deviant behaviour as morally desirable. Let us take three individuals: the acting individual who carries out an action, the observer who has a moral judgement on this action and the third individual, recipient of the action's consequences. The reasoning can be divided into four stages. First of all, the observer identifies the acting individual and the third individual. Secondly, the acting individual acts, producing consequences on the third individual's living conditions. Thirdly, the observer valuates these consequences and decides if they have worsened or, on the contrary, improved the third individual's life. Finally, the observer concludes by giving a final judgement on the acting individual or more specifically on the reasons of his/her acts. Therefore, even if the observer thinks the reasons or the intentions were kind, if the consequences turn out to be negative, he/she will show no leniency towards the acting individual. By applying this reasoning to the set of feelings the observer might feel for the third individual, we obtain the following table in which the corresponding feelings of the observer for the acting individual are written in each box.

Such a result allows us to understand, for instance, why the death penalty still exists in some countries. The prisoner under the sentence of death is responsible for his/her own fate, because of his/her behaviour. This situation comes under the last box in the table, at the bottom right.

<table>
<tr><td colspan="2"></td><td colspan="2">Consequences of the acting individual's
Actions on the third individual*</td></tr>
<tr><td colspan="2"></td><td>Good</td><td>Bad</td></tr>
<tr><td rowspan="2">Observer's feeling towards the third individual</td><td>Sympathy</td><td>Esteem, thankfulness, gratitude (affection and thankfulness)</td><td>Disgust, resentment
(revenge blow for blow)</td></tr>
<tr><td>Antipathy</td><td>Indifference</td><td>Esteem, thankfulness, gratitude</td></tr>
</table>

*According to the degree of affection of the observer for the third individual

The observer (the Nation) believes the action is positive, because he/she has a negative value judgement on the third individual (the prisoner). This explains why the acting individual's (the court) action is justified, even though it has a very negative impact on the third individual. By a converse reasoning, anybody sympathizing with the prisoner will disapprove of the court's decision. Herein lies the delicate problem of liability, which corresponds to the way the reasons of others' misfortune or happiness are judged. Positive moral motivations might then produce negative behaviour.

1.3. Externalism vs. Internalism

Economics studies the preceding dilemma by expurgating from the reasoning any element which could make interpersonal relations more complex. We therefore believe that the classic distinction between internal motivations and external motivations remains the most pertinent one, since it clearly indicates whether the economic model is referring to a form of behavioural or motivational altruism. Internal motivations refer to motivational altruism whereas external motivations refer to behavioural altruism.

The words "internalism" and "externalism" are commonly used to designate two concepts regarding the relation between ethics and motivation[5]. According to externalism, the motivation to act is not the result of ethical principles or moral judgements themselves. There must be an additional psychological sanction so that the motivation to act complies with ethical principles. According to this conception, as Nagel (1970/1978, p.9) explains: "claims about what we should do simply are on this view claims about what we have a certain sort of motivation for doing"[6]. Nonetheless, externalism does not exclude the existence of various motivations. It simply points out that the presence of such motivations does not follow from moral judgements, but is guaranteed by a fact external to ethics which comes prior to ethical behaviour.

Hobbes's ethical system is certainly one of the best examples of externalism. Rational individuals prompted by a universal desire for self-preservation cooperate in such a way that the motivation to cooperate follows from this desire for self-preservation. The resulting ethical cooperative system is in fact only the consequence of a non-ethical fundamental motivation; of course, only if we assume that the desire to preserve one's own life is not an ethical principle. In this case, the theory of motivation comes before ethics. More recently, Buchanan (1994, p.68) defended an externalist position in economics by asserting that: "If we look at social interaction in this way, we get a different interpretation of the origins of ethical constraints. Such constraints do not emerge from a rational choice calculus on the part of the person whose behaviour is constrained, as is the case with both the self-control and the contractarian models sketched out above, but, instead, from the rational choice calculus of others with whom the person to be constrained is expected to interact in the social nexus. In a sense, this model that locates the origins of ethical constraints into the rationally self-interested calculus of others than the acting individual is both simpler and more strictly economic than either of the alternatives".

Contrary to externalism, in the case of internalism, an ethical proposition can not be asserted if there is not at least one motivation to act in accordance with this proposition. We can not act morally unless there is at least one moral motivation in keeping with the action we are about to carry out. In other words, according to internalism, the presence of a motivation to act morally is guaranteed by the ethical proposition itself. When a person thinks it is morally required to do something, then he/she has the motivation to do this thing. However, motivations referred to by internalists are varied, ranging from kindness, to benevolence or even the approval of others. According to internalists, ethical motivations, even at the most fundamental level, are directly and closely linked to ethics. Therefore, Kant gives the impression of being an internalist. Indeed, when he formulates categorical imperatives as a base for morality, he also stipulates that these imperatives cannot be determined by any factor external to morality. Morality is not the consequence of something external to it. It directly follows from ethical principles themselves.

These two conceptions of the relation between motivation and ethics obviously differ in the way they apprehend altruistic behaviour in economy. On the one hand, externalists assume altruism follows from social interactions, without individuals needing any altruistic motivation whatsoever. On the other hand, internalists postulate that the altruistic behaviour is a direct result of an altruistic motivation. Both concepts are of scientific interest, but they are clearly not based on the same vision of the world and of the individuals living in it.

2. Neutralization of Moral Motivations

As mentioned in the previous section, altruism is, most often behavioural, in economics. This way of solving the question of moral motivations is a considerable reduction of human behaviour. Therefore, emotional altruism will be treated in the same way as strategic altruism. However, economic analysis recently suggested attempts to integrate emotions, therefore allowing for an in-depth analysis of motivations. We will emphasize, in this section, that these attempts do not take internalism seriously into account and that their effect is mainly to neutralise moral motivations.

2.1. Cost of Culpability

Becker's (1996) work on culpability and love is a good illustration of this type of analysis. According to Becker, most people avoid approaching beggars so as not to feel guilty. By a converse reasoning, it is possible to feel some kind of happiness when meeting a beggar. By merely comparing his/her situation to the beggar's, the observer is then convinced to be lucky or develops a sense of superiority.

The modelling of this phenomenon uses a classic cost-benefit analysis, by postulating culpability as the source of an individual psychological cost. Therefore, the individual's real ability to do a money transfer towards the person in need has no influence on the sense of culpability, which is to say on the attaching cost. The latter only integrates with the individual's utility function and generates a negative external effect. Consequently, the budget constraint does not interfere with the potential donor's feeling. Thus, if the walker does not have enough money with him/her in order to satisfy the beggar's request, he/she feels guilty about it. So as to reduce this cost, the walker will decide to change pavements or even to take another street. Let us note that a road being a public good with no obligation of use, the individual will bring the psychological cost down to nothing, by avoiding the area during his next walks. At this stage, we might consider that the individual is facing a subjective toll, made up of the psychological cost and his/her marginal predisposition to pay. Therefore, the decision to take the road depends on the sign and on the absolute value of this psychological cost. If, generally, the cost of culpability does not exceed the profit resulting from the use of road A, the individual will be able to take this road without risking a negative final profit. In the opposite case, the individual will choose road B. This arbitrage is based here on the sense of culpability and on the external effect it generates.

Thus, even if this methodology seems interesting, since it is a way of analysing the behaviour of donation, it remains very reductive insofar as the study of motivations is concerned. At most, it tackles the relation between the donor and the beneficiary as a game in which the donor tries to avoid the beneficiary, while the beneficiary tries to meet the donor. It considers that ethical considerations are objects of calculus among others. Indeed, Becker (1996, p.18) says: "However, I do not believe that higher-order rankings are either necessary or useful in understanding behaviour since ethics and culture affect behaviour in the same general way as do other determinants of utility and preferences. In particular, considerations of price and cost influence ethical and moral choices -such as whether to act honestly- just as they influence choices of personal goods".

But does the distinction of motivations have a real influence on the final choice (road A: donation, road B: no donation)? As an answer, we suggest two criticisms of the previous approach.

2.2. Criticisms of Behavioural Rationality

The first criticism can be found in Elster's (1998, 1999) work. Let us suppose an individual wants a book, but that he/she does not have enough money to buy it and that having resort to theft will make him/her feel guilty. The cost-benefit analysis weighs the cost of culpability against the profit resulting from theft (pleasure of reading…). Let us now imagine there is a pill that can cancel culpability and is available at a very low cost. In this case, any rational person would buy and take the pill and then steal the book. Nevertheless, this result downplays the sense of culpability. Indeed, culpability mainly follows from moral or social norms which are internalised by individuals. These norms forbid me to steal the book, just because theft is considered as a deleterious act. Seeking amorality (moral neutrality) by taking a pill is on the same level as the immorality of theft. If the act of stealing is done in one stage (without the pill) or in two stages (with the pill), the consequences remain the same. As Elster emphasizes, the individual would feel guilty before buying the pill and consequently would not buy it. The cost-benefit analysis cannot be used in this case since culpability can not be the direct object of an economic calculus.

The second criticism that can be made about Becker's analysis follows the previous logic. As we just mentioned, culpability is closely related to social and moral norms. However, in certain cultures or religions, it is a duty to give to beggars; an imperative that individuals must submit to, all the more so, if they have integrated these norms. Hamzetta (2003) developed this point of view in his analysis of begging in Mauritania. Passing a beggar certainly provokes culpability since it is a duty to give, but internalised norms annihilate any rational calculus. If culpability is at the origin of certain behaviours, it is certainly not the object of a calculus and directly concerns a system of norms internalised by the individual.

2.3. Internalisation of Norms and Intergenerational Calculus

These two criticisms defend an internalist point of view, whereas Becker's analysis does not take this point of view seriously into account. His position aims at neutralising moral motivations by reducing them to the object of a calculus. According to this type of analysis moral motivations do not infer a specific behaviour. They are themselves the object of a calculus whose result depends on the other objects considered in this calculus. It comes down to saying that moral motivations are not treated distinctly. In that case, we refer to the neutralisation of morality since morality is itself the object of a calculus.

However, such a position could be accused of being a bit too radically critical since Becker (1996), himself, developed an analysis that endogenises culpability. He suggested such an analysis in the parent-child relationship. In his model, parents try to teach their children culpability, in order to be able to take advantage of this culpability when they are old. In teaching their children culpability, parents know that when they get older, their children will care for them. Therefore there is an inverse relation between the culpability felt by the children and their contribution to their parent's well-being. We join up with standard economic analysis, because parents invest in culpability to make a future profit out of it. Elster (1998, 1999) has already suggested a detailed criticism of this model. Here, we will develop another criticism: the model's vacuity as soon as several generations exist.

If parents invest in their children with the sole selfish aim of securing their future life, they also do it as a result of being driven by affection and responsibility, because they feel morally obliged to do so. But taking these other possible motivations into account changes the reasoning.

In Becker's model, parents invest in their children because they are rational. In return, the children, who are overwhelmed with culpability, feel obliged to provide for their parents' needs.

Therefore, there is an asymmetry of treatment between the parents and the children. Do the children behave like their own parents, when they become parents themselves? That would seem quite strange given that they have internalised culpability, which still holds in their relation with their own children. Once it has been internalised, it seems unlikely that culpability could be a feeling only used towards older generations, whereas the present generations would adopt a purely calculating behaviour towards future generations. Culpability is likely to be valid for all generations, or otherwise completely absent. As a conclusion, Becker's model can be validated only in comparative statics, but it does not fit into intergenerational reasoning.

Moreover, the relation between culpability and rationality remains quite ambiguous in Becker's model. Parents justify their investment by their rationality, while their children are not yet rational and thus not aware of their parents' strategy. If it is possible to admit that young children are not aware of their parent's strategy, what about when they grow up? They are then confronted with the same situation as their own parents, and they become aware of this strategy. In such a case, it is unthinkable that these individuals could decide to provide for their parents' needs, since they have integrated the manipulation they underwent. It is even likely that in return, as a kind of revenge, they take no further interest in their old parents. Once more, Becker's reasoning turns out to be fallible.

As a conclusion, Becker's model aims at depicting culpability as the product of a rational calculus, and it is then confronted with the limits of his approach. He reduces moral motivations to a cost-benefit calculus. The model is no longer valid as soon as several generations exist. Moral motivations are not the object of a calculus, because they modify the calculus itself by forcing themselves on individuals. His approach corresponds, at its best, to weak internalism. But it seems in many respects more adequate to refer to a stronger internalism. It does not mean that parents expect nothing from their children, but that it is an *ex-post* expectation of behaviour after having searched for moral or affective reasons, and not an *ex-ante* expectation which is at the origin of the decision to invest. Parents may consider it normal that their children play a role in their well-being when they are old, since they did the same before. Children might feel guilty if they do not look after their parents, because they know their parents devoted a lot of money and affection to them when they were younger. They might feel guilty, even if they know their parents tried to manipulate them. But this culpability is the result of internalised norms that constrain economic calculus.

3. Substitution facing Ethics[7]

The way of tackling altruism in economy is in accordance with the general methodology according to which the individual optimizes a preference or utility function under constraint. In such a case, altruism internalises an externality, which is to say, other people. To represent this externality, in keeping with methodology, a characteristic representative of other people is generally introduced into the individual's preference function. The individual then optimizes under constraint from arguments that are his/her own (his/her consumption) and from arguments representing others (their consumption), just as if he/she optimizes for two different consumption sets. But is such a methodology really adapted to the analysis of altruism and ethics?

3.1. Economic Tradition faced with the Dilemma of Ethical choice

In order to pose the problem, let us take the following example. A house is burning: only two things inside can be saved; either a painting by a famous artist or a child. What should be done? Should we save the work of art that represents an incomparable collective heritage or should we save the child, even if he will turn out to be an undesirable individual, a miserable being, contributing no good to society? From a casuist point of view, there is absolutely no doubt that the child should be rescued. This illustration indicates a decision for the protection of life (real and potential). Jonas (1984) points out that, in this kind of dilemma, the decision solves itself morally because the work of art cannot pose the question *What have you done to me?*, whereas the child is justified in reproaching my conscience. If we take a purely economic view, we can evaluate in monetary terms the value of a painting, its price at an auction, as well as the price of a human life (sale of a slave in Africa, organ selling -voluntary or forced, etc…). The notions of price and value indicate a correspondence between two goods, a relation of exchange. Expanded to individuals, this amounts to treating people as commodities.

The example shows that economic methodology does not take ethics seriously into account. From a moral point of view, or at least from an internalistic point of view, the aim is not to optimize between a bit less child and a bit more painting, by saving for instance the painting and the child at the same time, while still knowing both will be damaged; but of course to give the absolute priority to the child.

However, economic theory often uses the idea that the characteristics of the other can be substituted for those of the individual who must optimize his/her choice, and it is in that sense that the individual is altruistic. This methodology is derived from a long tradition, although it seems to be in contradiction with ethics.

This tradition was largely influenced by Marshall (1890). He defined a programme of integration of ethics with economy while trying to respect the principle of continuity. In the preface to the first edition of the *Principles of Economics*, Marshall asserts that continuity is an essential element in his approach and that he will put it into practice in the field of ethics, like in other economic fields. This principle leads to treating a person like a good.

Marshall (1890) wonders how, and within which limits, ethics can be integrated with economics. He affirms in his preface that economists cannot escape taking ethics into account. According to the conclusion to his chapter II.7, economists study individual actions from the perspective of social life and not from that of individual life. It then seems normal to bring altruistic relations into consideration. Integrating altruism with economics requires a monetary measurement of people's motives of action. Marshall does not exclude any motives from economic analysis, but he is only interested in them if they are quantifiable; that is, if they can be represented by a price. Of course, this does not mean that money is the only goal, or even the principal goal, of human action, but simply that money is the only way of measuring human action in economic analysis. The Kantian categorical imperative is cited as one motivation among others. However, Marshall underlines many times in chapters II and III that the motive of action in itself, the state of mind, be it altruistic or selfish, is not measurable, but indirectly, a measurement could be envisioned through the effects or actions produced by different motives. Integration of ethics and economics can only be pictured through a behavioural point of view.

However, our first example clearly shows that priorities must be set and that people cannot be treated like objects. Of course, one could say it is an example with no real economic dimension to it and that in economic life the problem would be different. Yet, this objection does not hold much ground. There are many examples of the same kind and with an economic dimension attached to them. Let us suppose a baby has been in a coma since birth or that a dozen miners are blocked at the bottom of their mine. Why should vast sums be spent to save the baby or the miners, whereas the same amount of money could be used for the development of a prenatal prevention system or for the improvement of safety conditions for all miners, thus avoiding many additional disasters (Hausman and McPherson 1996)? Except that there is an immediate priority due to the situations and it relates to ethics!

To give another example, I might openly talk about my vegetarian convictions, either because I feel compassion towards animals, or because I believe it is an appropriate way of resolving some existing environmental problems, or even for other reasons. Once more, ethics does indeed imply priority. I will not accept a consumption set which would include meat, be it a lot or very little meat. I am not ready to substitute vegetables for meat.

3.2. Priorities and Economic Calculus

More generally, if the individual establishes his/her economic habits (consumption, production, savings, transfers,…) according to his/her social environment, he/she more or less internalises certain norms. These norms, according to the human being's behaviour, may become material constraints. They then imply priorities in the granting and the distribution of resources. For example, I will give money to my children in priority, rather than increasing my own consumption.

If ethics impose priorities, it is not in accordance with the economic methodology used for the representation of altruism, which on the contrary postulates substitution. However, "can we place into the same utility function the arguments of the 'Other' (society, values, social obligations, friends, etc.), even when specifically considering its characteristics (consumption, revenue…), and the arguments treating individual goods or commodities? In other words, can the choice of one's moral code and that of one's favourite kind of cheese be placed within the same framework?" (Ballet, Bazin and Mahieu 2001).

Other methodologies exist in economics and have already been used. The lexicographic principle is one of them. This principle means a good is absolutely favoured to all other goods. Therefore, in the Olympic Games' country classification, a gold medal is absolutely favoured to any other combination of silver and bronze medals. This principle thus implies absolute priorities, but it can be made more flexible. Admitting hierarchy does not imply abandoning all forms of substitution, but it can confine, in keeping with morals, the substitution between goods and people.

"One critique of microeconomics (marginalism) is that it reduces the intrinsic value in favour of an instrumental value, and this in an almost systematic manner. This is ethically inconceivable. Nevertheless, we would reduce everything to an instrumental conception (without finality), which would not permit us to do as we please. From this point of view, we could thus see that free substitution could be criticized. Admitting an intrinsic value means accepting that we cannot dispose of it in an arbitrary manner and that we cannot replace it by any other equivalent" (Ballet, Bazin and Mahieu 2001).

Economic methodology representative of altruism is problematic from that point of view. Morals forbid me to sacrifice people for material goods or animals. Therefore I cannot answer "the painting" in the example of the burning house.

Notes

1. For the debate, see the pioneering work by Samuelson, P.A. 1938. "A note on the pure theory of consumer's behaviour". *Economica*, 5, and "A note on the pure theory of consumer's behaviour: an addentum". *Economica*, 5, and the articles Samuelson, P.A. 1948. "Consumption theory in terms of revealed preference". *Economica*, 15; Little, I.M.D. 1949. "A reformulation of the theory of consumer's behaviour". *Oxford Economic Papers*, 1; Hicks, J.R. 1956. "The measurement of income". *Oxford Economic Papers*, 10; Houthakker, H.S. 1950. "Revealed preference and the utility function". *Economica*, 17.

2. Becker, G.S. 1981, quotations from the 1994 edition, p.279.

3. It is the case for articles on child labour. The altruism hypothesis allows us to solve certain questions regardless of the exploiter behaviour some parents

might have. For a recent survey, see for example Bhukuth, A. 2004. "Le travail des enfants: une revue de la littérature économique récente". *Ethics and Economics*, 2, http://Ethique-economique.org.
4. Chapter 4 and the following ones detail these distinctions.
5. For such a distinction, see Falk, W.D. 1947. "Ought and Motivation". *Proceedings of the Aristotelian Society* ; Frankena, W.K. 1958). "Obligation and Motivation in Recent Moral Philosophy". In A.I.Melden (ed.), *Essays in Moral Philosophy*. Seattle.
6. Nagel, T. 1970. *The Possibility of Altruism*. Oxford: Clarendon Press; quotation form the 1978 edition, p.9.
7. This section is based on two former articles: Ballet, J. and Mahieu, F.-R. 1998. *La continuité pour quoi faire?*. Société Canadienne de Sciences Economiques, 38ième congrès annuel, Québec; Ballet, J.; Bazin, D., Mahieu, F.-R. 2001. *Continuity and Ethical Economics*, Mimeo: University of Versailles Saint-Quentin.

References

Andreoni, J. 1989. "Giving with Impure Altruism: Application to Charity and Ricardian Equivalence". *Journal of Political Economy*, 97(6), 1447-1458.

Ballet, J. 2000. "Altruisme et biens collectifs: une revue de la littérature". *Revue économique*, 51(4), 789-811.

Ballet, J. and Mahieu, F.-R. 1998. *La continuité pour quoi faire?* Société Canadienne de Sciences Economiques, 38ième congrès annuel, Québec.

Ballet, J.; Bazin, D.; Mahieu, F.-R. 2001. *Continuity and Ethical Economics*. Mimeo: University of Versailles Saint Quentin.

Ballet, J. and Barillot, S. 2004. *Club discriminant et disposition morale à coopérer*. Mimeo: University of Versailles Saint-Quentin.

Becker, G.S. 1974. "A Theory of Social Interactions". *Journal of Political Economy*, 82(6), 1063-1093.

Becker, G.S. 1981/1994. *A Treatise on the Family*. Cambridge Mass: Harvard University Press.

Becker, G.S. 1996. *Accounting for Tastes*. Cambridge Mass: Harvard University Press.

Buchanan, J.M. 1994. *Ethics and Economic Progress*. Norman: University of Oklahoma Press.

Elster, J. 1998. "Emotions and Economic Theory". *Journal of Economic Literature*, 36(1), March, 47-74.

Elster, J. 1999. *Alchemies of the Mind. Rationality and the Emotions*. Cambridge: Cambridge University Press.

Hamzetta, B. 2003. *La mendicité: une forme de pauvreté ou une opportunité sociale pour la constitution de capabilité?* 3rd Conference on Capability

Approach, From Sustainable Development to Sustainable Freedom, September 5-7, Pavia, Italy.

Hausman, D.M. and McPherson, M.S. 1996. *Economic Analysis and Moral Philosophy*. Cambridge: Cambridge University Press.

Hicks, J.R. 1956. *A Revision of Demand Theory*. Oxford: Oxford University Press.

Hirshleiffer, J. 1985. "The Expanding Domain of Economics". American Economic Review, 75(6), 53-68.

Jonas, H. 1984. *The Imperative of Responsibility. In Search of an Ethics for the Technological Age*. trans. Hans Jonas in collaboration with D. Herr, Chicago: University of Chicago Press.

Koulibaly, M. 1998. "Solidarité internationale, altruisme et sous-développement africain". In F.-R. Mahieu and Rapoport H. (eds.), *Altruisme, analyses économiques*, 263-294. Paris: Economica.

Lévinas, E. 1998. *Ethique comme philosophie première*. Paris: Payot/Rivages poche.

Magee, S.P. 1993. "Bioeconomics and the Survival Model: The Economic Lessons of Evolutionary Biology". *Public Choice*, 77, 117-132.

Manski, C.F. 2000. "Economic Analysis of Social Interaction". *Journal of Economic Perspective*, 14(3), 115-136.

Marshall, A. 1890. *Principles of Economics.* New York: MacMillan.

Mercier-Ythier, J. 1993. "Equilibre général de dons individuels". *Revue économique*, 925-950.

Nagel, Th. 1970. *The Possibility of Altruism*. Oxford: Clarendon Press, edition 1978.

Samuelson, P.A. 1938. "A note on the pure theory of consumer's behaviour". *Economica*, 5.

Samuelson, P.A. 1948. "Consumption theory in terms of revealed preference". *Economica*, 15.

Sen, A.K. 1973. "Behaviour and the Concept of Preference". *Economica*, 40, 241-259.

Cooperation and Reciprocity

Alejandro Caparros
Jean-Christophe Pereau
Tarik Tazdaït

The topic of cooperation is one of the richest and most enthralling of social sciences since it crosses disciplinary borders. Anthropologists, economists, psychologists, sociologists as well as political scientists have studied it. In general, social sciences analyse cooperation based on a static and simultaneous game: the prisoner's dilemma (PD). However, this game leads to a paradox since self-interest favours the non-cooperative solution whereas collective interest recommends the cooperative solution. Several options have been proposed to overcome this dilemma, but reciprocity is probably the most satisfactory one, since it is based on conditional cooperation and credible threats.

This article proposes to analyse reciprocity as a solution to the PD paradox. We will analyse the properties of cooperative behaviour and the process that is at its origin. To do so, we need to take into account (i) the conditions of emergence of cooperative behaviour, (ii) the way in which it extends within the population and (iii) the elements which guarantee its stability and make it a norm[1]. Selected literature has in common to be based on individualism, which is not necessarily synonymous of selfishness. Individualism should be understood as the possibility for agents to individually express choices which are, above all, their choices. This is at the origin of the denomination "rational choice". In what follows, we shall speak indifferently about rational choice model or *homo œconomicus*.

In this article, we study two methodological concepts: the rational choice model, where agents are supposed to be rational (i.e. acting according to their own interest), and an alternative framework where the assumption of rationality is relaxed: the evolutionary game theory approach.

The structure of the article is as follows. Section (2) presents the problems related to the PD. In section (3) we introduce "reciprocity" in order to study its characteristics in the context of the rational choice model. We complete the analysis by integrating intentions. Section (4) continues, to a certain extent, the analysis in section (3) but supposes that individuals are characterized by a slow learning process. This implies to assume that they have no rationality and permits to study the process of generalization of reciprocity.

1. Problems

Cooperation has been, and continues to be, a major subject of study since individual logic seems to preclude any collective action. In Boudon's foreword to the French version of Olson´s (1987), *Logic of Collective Action*, he wrote: "All the political philosophy of the eighteenth century, all the economy of the end of the eighteenth century and the nineteenth… turned around the paradoxes of collective action. Hobbes's Leviathan, the social contract of Rousseau, the paradox of Condorcet, the "invisible hand" of Adam Smith all boil down to the paradox of collective action". As shown, he clearly states that common action is controlled by paradoxes. In fact, the rest of the article will be devoted, to a certain extent, to clarify this point of view.

It is generally accepted that the prisoner's dilemma[2] (PD) clearly describes the type of situation confronted by individuals when they need to cooperate. This game was introduced by Merrill Flood and Melvin Dresher at the Corporation RAND in 1950 or 1951, and called prisoner's dilemma by Albert Tucker at a game theory seminar organized at the psychology department of Stanford (Straffin, 1980; Raiffa, 1992). The PD describes a situation where each player has the choice between two strategies: to cooperate (C) or to defect (D). The history behind this game is related to the arrest of two accomplices. Since hard evidence is not available the judge needs one of the suspects to testify against the other, so he decides to interrogate them separately. The offer made by the judge implies that the situation where both cooperate is preferred to the one where both denounce each other, whereas the situation where one speaks while the other keeps silent is paying. The normal form below describes the utilities associated with this game.

		player 2	
		C	D
player 1	C	3,3	0,5
	D	5,0	1,1

Figure 1: prisoner’s dilemma game (formulation 1)

The conventional representation (figure (1)) assumes the existence of a scale of utilities (for each individual) according to which freedom has a utility of 5, the worst outcome a utility of zero and the intermediate outcomes, with a penalty of say 1 and 3 years a utility of 1 and 3 respectively. Of course, the numbers can be changed without necessarily changing the paradox. In fact, the paradox can be defined by a system of two inequalities, following Rapoport and Chammah (1965):

		Player 2		
		C	D	
Player 1	C	x_1, x_1	x_2, x_3	$x_3 > x_1 > x_4 > x_2$
	D	x_3, x_2	x_4, x_4	$2x_1 > x_2 + x_3$

Figure 2: prisoner's dilemma game (formulation 2)

The first inequality implies that strategy D dominates C, since it is the best option whatever the choice of the other player. The second inequality prevents the strategy where each player defects one turn (sharing profits) in a repeated PD[3]. An additional and fundamental assumption, although seldom evoked, is that players cannot avoid the game. Without this last assumption, the paradox can be avoided (Vanberg and Congleton 1992; Stanley et al. 1994).

In order to base our reasoning on figure (1), let us examine how a rational player will act. Quite simply, by betraying. This choice will be adopted whatever the action of the other player. To show this, let us analyze the game from the point of view of player 1. Faced with a player 2 who cooperates, player 1 obtains a utility of 5 by defecting and only a utility of 3 while cooperating. Faced with a player 2 who defects, his utility would be 1 if he also defects and zero if he would cooperate. Thus, non-cooperative behaviour proves to be the best strategy for player 1. Given that the second player is also rational, he will follow the same reasoning. Consequently, both players will obtain a utility of 1 (i.e. individual interest prevails on collective interest), whereas mutual cooperation would yield a utility of 3 (i.e. collective interest would yield a higher level of utility). Although both would benefit from cooperation, individual rationality recommends enjoying, at the expense of the other, the benefits of his cooperation. This is known as free-riding. For social contract theorists, like Hobbes (1651) or Gauthier (1986), this reasoning is that of insane persons who cannot be accepted in society without vigilance. Along the same lines, Sen (1993) sees in the *homo œconomicus* a "*rational fool*".

The equilibrium of this game is thus (D, D), which constitutes an equilibrium in dominant strategies, although (C, C) is strictly preferable. In addition, the latter is a Pareto optimum, i.e. it is not possible to increase the level of utility of one of the players without deteriorating that of the other player. On the contrary, starting from (D, D) both utilities can be improved (reaching (C, C)). There is a variety of problems that can be interpreted as a PD[4]. Among them, the funding of public goods (Olson 1965), competition in oligopolies (Marks 1989; Dixon et al. 1994), or international trade (Krugman and Obstfeld 1992). The PD can also be used to clarify the limits of class behaviour in Marx's sense. Although a worker can find that a "proletarian" government is beneficial, he will not be in the front line of a revolution, since it is more interesting to let other workers risk their lives. This questions the idea of the "logic of class" itself and may explain why Marxist revolutions were always organized by a small elite in times of weak governments and social disorganization (Olson 1965). All these situations are identified with social dilemmas. The term "social dilemma" refers to a large number of situations in which individuals make independent choices in an interdependent situation and where the maximization of short-term self-interest yields outcomes leaving all participants worse off than feasible alternatives (Hardin 1971). The PD or other famous paradoxes like the trust game fall into this classification (Kreps 1990).

In general, if the PD results in an ineffective solution, we are in a situation where "for a player who is not entirely ensured of the peaceful intentions of his partner, the use of the aggressive strategy is the best one given his individual interests" (Moulin 1981)[5], and this although collective interest supports a solution which is better for both players. We could object that communicating agents could agree on the cooperative solution.

Admittedly, but this oversees the fact that nothing prevents them from reconsidering their word.

Another way out is to admit the intervention of a third party charged of arbitrating between the players and convincing them to adopt the cooperative outcome. This can be done by signing a contract at the beginning and letting an institution (justice) to control the players in case of betrayal. But this solution is partial: why should individuals who are not able to cooperate spontaneously agree that a third party control their relation? How was this institution set up? The same critique can be formulated against the solution suggested by Schelling (1960), the delegation to an agent who becomes an additional player.

As shown, leaving the dead end of the PD is not an easy matter. Nevertheless, there is a solution which is relatively satisfactory: reciprocity. We will now study this alternative.

2. Stabilizing Properties of Reciprocity

2.1. Bases of Reciprocity

There are multiple definitions of reciprocity, and this obviously makes the task more difficult. Kolm (1984) confirms this point of view: "Other disciplines have dealt with these subjects, reciprocity and social and psychic aspects of economic systems: anthropology and sociology. Reciprocity is even one of their preferred subjects. But what they said is too vague, their concepts are too fuzzy". However, Gouldner (1960) gave reciprocity all its dimension, and subsequent developments have evolved around this proposal. Thus, there is a common base to all definitions which appeared thereafter. Kolm for example, provides an extremely broad representation: "One can call, more specifically, reciprocity a set of interdependent gifts in the sense that some influence others (but not that each one necessarily influences each other). The set of independent gifts, i.e. where none influences another, can be excluded from this definition, or included as an extreme case (in this last case, a single gift can, still, be excluded or included as an extreme case)... A central feature is that a gift of a person depends on gifts received from others..."[6].

This representation coincides to a certain extent with the definition of Keohane(1986), for whom reciprocity refers to exchanges of relatively equivalent value where the actions of each part depend on the former actions of the others, so that positive produces positive and negative, negative. These exchanges are often mutually beneficial and can be founded on self-interest or on rights and duties. Finally, the value exchanged can be comparable or not.

A priori these two configurations seem to diverge. Kolm regards donation as a type of reciprocity, whereas Keohane does not. Generally, donations are seen as an "altruistic behaviour", i.e. the agent who gives the gift incorporates in his objective function the welfare of others. Kolm's definition can appear excessive compared to Keohane's , since it is much broader: the gift is a confuse form which is not exclusively related to reciprocity. However, the divergence is only "*a priori*" since no fundamental differences can be found. For Blau (1964), and within the reciprocity framework, actions (considered) depend on the behaviour adopted by the others in return, and this exchange relation ceases when the expected reactions do not take place. Consequently, reciprocity underlies a conditional action founded on the equivalence of benefits: conditional since it presupposes a reaction and equivalent because this reaction must be equitable. These fundamental characteristics of reciprocity can be found in the different definitions proposed. Moreover, the precise details in the definitions correspond to the interpretation of the idea of *equivalent conditional action.*

These explanations favour, according Kolm, considering donations as an engagement towards reciprocity, at least in certain instances. But this form of reciprocity does not correspond to the simple gift, because agents discounted a specific reaction, in fact an equivalent reaction ("... so that the positive answers the positive"). If this reaction does not appear, agents answer "negative by negative". On the contrary, an altruistic gift is an unconditional voluntary act. However, unconditional is the opposite of reciprocity. Although the altruistic gift may be followed by a positive reaction, it was not the goal. This attitude does not impose any obligation in response to the benefits offered.

2.2. The Analogy Reciprocity-Tit For Tat

The concept of reciprocity that we will finally retain is concise and clear, while it preserves the criteria of conditionality and equivalence which constitute its basis: "People should meet smiles with smiles and lies with treachery" (Gouldner, 1960)[7]. This also follows the Tit For Tat strategy, studied by Axelrod (1980) via computer contests. This strategy consists in playing C at the beginning of the game and then to answer C vis-à-vis C and T vis-à-vis T[8]. Admitting a relation of equivalence between reciprocity and Tit For Tat, it is possible to show that reciprocity increases the chances of cooperation, in particular when one passes from a static PD to a repeated PD[9]. Supposing a PD is repeated a given number of times, players can communicate by showing their strategies. Thus, they can use threats and make them credible by repetition. Cooperation contracts can now be concluded since a player can use the following stages of the game 'to punish' defection. However, the repeated PD limits us to two extreme schemes: (i) the game is repeated indefinitely and a great number of situations are possible due to Folk's theorem[10], or (ii) the game is repeated only a given number of times and the 'backward induction'[11] argument (Selten, 1965) brings the possibilities of cooperation back to the static level.

Let us consider the case where the PD is repeated N times. We will analyze the behaviour of the players in the different stages of the game according to the information that they have on the number of repetitions. Neyman (1999) shows that uncertainty on this number does not prevent the emergence of cooperation. In the same way, each individually rational solution of a one shot game can be approximated by a (perfect) equilibrium in the game repeated in finite horizon. If agents think that the number of repetitions is equal to L, to obtain cooperation we need to suppose that the probability of the event L=N is common knowledge of high degree[12]. The intuition is based on the idea that given the long-term repetition, both agents think that treason will take place, but very tardily in the game. Thus, nothing prevents agents from cooperating in the first stages of the game.

If the length of order R is mutually known, players choose (T, T) in the R last stages in any equilibrium of the repeated PD. To see it, suppose that we are at the last stage N. Each player knows that this is his last movement; thus, both are interested in adopting D (their best option). As stated above, we have used here the common knowledge about the length of the game of order 1. Suppose now that we are at stage N-1. Each player knows that the other knows that the game finishes at the following stage; therefore, both know that the other will play D at the following and last stage. Consequently, no player benefits from cooperation and both play their best response D at stage N-1. We now have used the common knowledge of order 2. By increasing the degrees of common knowledge until R, we can conclude that both players will choose D in the R last stages. However, at the N-R-1 stage nothing can be concluded as to the choices of the players, since there is no common knowledge of order R+1 about the length of the game[13].

In a model with a PD repeated in finite horizon, Renault (2000) shows that if each player knows the upper bound of the number of repetitions and both allot a positive probability to the fact that his interlocutor over-estimates this number, then cooperation can be the equilibrium of the game, under the condition that the game is sufficiently long. By generalizing to the game where the length is common knowledge, the author shows that the only equilibrium will consist in playing D at all stages and this for both players. However this result is to be put into perspective. When the length of the game is infinite[14], equilibria containing phases of cooperation can be observed. In one of these equilibria, both agents play C as long as the other does as much and punish deviation by playing D long enough to cancel the profit of the deviation[15]. An analytical representation of reciprocity under the angle of the Tit For Tat strategy confirms, under certain conditions, the stabilizing properties of cooperation.

The major difficulty of the reciprocity principle relates to the concept of equivalence. To determine a level of equivalence between two actions is not an easy matter. Although this implies balanced benefits, the measurement is subjective or even impossible. This balance is even harder for topics such as international relations. Keohane (1986) recalls that the requirement of an approximate equivalence means that most real-world political relations are not reciprocal. Consequently, setting up degrees of equivalence plays a paramount role, since any deviation (or non-respect) of an equivalence ratio undermines the existence of reciprocity. This remark deserves attention since "claims of reciprocity may be fraudulent, hiding domination and exploitation". That contributes to restrict the possibilities of reciprocity. Thus, reciprocity, although suggesting a solution to the problem, still suffers from limitations.

2.3. Intentionality as a Source of Reciprocity

Up to now, we considered reciprocity within the axiom of rationality: the individual is supposed to act according to his own interest. However, this approach does not explain the origin of this behaviour. What reformulation of *homo œconomicus* could enrich this framework? Behavioural economics (or economic psychology) tries to answer this question. This approach tries to provide a better comprehension of the human cognitive system and its consequences: *homo œconomicus* is enriched by motivations, or intentions. This enables to analyse certain properties of reciprocity.

Economic psychology[16] analyses the diversity of motivations of the individual. Individuals are not supposed to form a homogeneous population. This diversity can be apprehended in two ways: either it arises from the existence of different individuals, who form a population whose composition is stable, or it is the fact of the individual himself, who has contradictory feelings. However, these two interpretations meet in the main question: the coherence of the individual.

Rabin's (1993) model, which analyses reciprocity, belongs to this category. For this author the intentionality of an action can favor cooperative behaviour. Intention relates here to a concern about the fairness of a sharing rule (of reciprocity). Since each agent judges that intentions lead the action of the others, the benefit for an individual i from his action (a_i) will be related not only to his own actions but also to his beliefs on the strategies of the others (b_i) and to his beliefs on the beliefs of the others on his own strategy (c_i). Since intentions propose the impact of beliefs, they require the definition of a new class of equilibrium: the *fairness equilibrium*.

To clarify this concept, we have to introduce some details about the characteristics of the agents. Let us consider a game with two players, 1 and 2. Each individual is supposed to have a kindness function, $f_i\ (a_i, b_j)$ with $i \neq j$. The kindness of i towards j is given by:

$$f_i\ (a_i, b_j) = \frac{U_j(a_i, b_j) - U_j^e(b_j)}{U_j^{max}(b_j) - U_j^{min}(b_j)} \quad .$$

$U_j^{max}(b_j) = \text{Max}_{a_j} U_j(a_i, b_j)$ and $U_j^{min}(b_j) = \text{Min}_{a_j} U_j(a_i, b_j)$ indicate, respectively, the highest and the lowest benefit that agent j can obtain. The term $U_j^e(b_j)$ is the "equitable payoff":

$$U_j^e(b_j) = [U_j^h(b_j) + U_j^l(b_j)]/2,$$

knowing that $U_j^l(b_j)$ (respectively $U_j^h(b_j)$) represents the weakest (respectively highest) benefit that j could obtain among points that are Pareto-efficient. This point of reference enables us to evaluate the generosity of I towards j.

The beliefs of player i on the intentions of the player j are defined by the function $\tilde{f}_j(b_j, c_i)$ which, by construction, is formally equivalent to the function $f_j(a_j, b_i)$:

$$\tilde{f}_j(b_j, c_i) = \frac{U_i(c_i, b_j) - U_i^e(c_j)}{U_i^{max}(c_i) - U_i^{min}(c_i)}.$$

The preferences of each individual are then characterized by a function of utility $U_i(a_i, b_j, c_i)$, which includes the material benefits $U_j(a_i, b_j)$ and the two preceding functions:

$$U_i(a_i, b_j, c_i) = U_i(a_i, b_j) + \tilde{f}_j(b_j, c_i)[1 + f_i(a_i, b_j)].$$

This function expresses the arbitration that agent i makes between the satisfaction obtained from material benefits and that obtained from the appreciation of the behaviour of agent j. The preferences so defined reflect certain behavioural specificities. Indeed, if player i thinks that j treats him badly, case where $\tilde{f}_j(.) < 0$, i will pay j back by choosing an action a_i so that $f_i(.)$ is sufficiently weak or negative. On the other hand, if player j treats i kindly, $\tilde{f}_j(.)$ will be positive and i will also be kind, in return, with j. However, this does not prevent both agents from outbalancing their wish of reciprocity and their search of material welfare.

Rabin defines a fairness equilibrium by analogy to a Nash equilibrium (condition (1)), with the only difference of the additional condition which requires that beliefs correspond to an effective behaviour (condition (2)). According to condition (1), given the beliefs of i on the fairness of j, i will play his best answer a_i^*: $a_i^* = \arg\max_{a_i} U_i(a_i, b_j, c_i)$. Since beliefs and effective behaviour must correspond at equilibrium, the couple (a_1^*, a_2^*) will constitute a fairness equilibrium if:

$$a_i^* = \arg\max_{a_i} U_i(a_i^*, b_j, c_i^*)\ i = 1,2.$$

This is summarized in the following definition.

Definition 1. Fairness Equilibrium

Let S_i be the set of potential strategies of player i, i = 1,2. $(a_1^*, a_2^*) \in (S_1, S_2)$ is a fairness equilibrium if, for i = 1,2, $j \neq i$:

Condition (1): $a_i^* \in \arg\max_{a_i \in S_i} U_i(a_i, b_j^*, c_i^*)$.

Condition (2): $c_i^* = b_i^* = a_i^*$.

Introducing psychological elements into individual preferences determines the way in which individuals allot a cause to events and the way in which it affects their behaviour. Thus, based on the concept of fairness equilibrium, it becomes possible to explain cooperative behaviour in the PD.

Let us come back to the PD described in figure (1). If 1 defects, the highest profit that he can obtain is 5 while the weakest is 1. Thus:

$$U_1^{max}(D) = 5 \quad \text{and} \quad U_1^{min}(D) = 1,$$

which implies $U_1^e(D) = 3$. On the other hand, if 1 cooperates we have:

$$U_1^{max}(C) = 3,\ U_1^{min}(C) = 0 \ \text{ and } \ U_1^e(C) = 1{,}5.$$

For agent 2, we obtain:

$$U_2^e(T) = 3 \text{ and } U_2^e(C) = 1{,}5.$$

The kindness functions are:

$$f_1(C,C) = f_2(C,C) = 1/2 \qquad f_1(D,D) = f_2(D,D) = -1/2$$

$$f_1(C,D) = f_2(D,C) = 1/2 \qquad f_1(D,C) = f_2(C,D) = -1/2.$$

The psychological benefits for each agent are:

$$f_1\left(1+f_2(C,C)\right) = f_2\left(1+f_1(C,C)\right) = 3/4$$

$$f_1\left(1+f_2(D,D)\right) = f_2\left(1+f_1(D,D)\right) = -1/4$$

$$f_1\left(1+f_2(C,D)\right) = f_2\left(1+f_1(D,C)\right) = 1/4$$

$$f_1\left(1+f_2(D,C)\right) = f_2\left(1+f_1(C,D)\right) = -1/2.$$

Introducing the impact of intentions related to fairness into the PD, the transformed game can then be described through the following matrix.

		player 2	
		C	D
player 1	C	$3+\frac{3}{4}\alpha,\ 3+\frac{3}{4}\alpha$	$-\frac{1}{2}\alpha,\ 4+\frac{1}{4}\alpha$
	D	$4+\frac{1}{4}\alpha,\ -\frac{1}{2}\alpha$	$1-\frac{1}{4}\alpha,\ 1-\frac{1}{4}\alpha$

Figure 3: prisoner's dilemma with intentions

The parameter α gives the value of the psychological benefits (in relation to material benefits). For $\alpha = 0$ (i.e the situation where intentions do not play any role), we have the standard PD. More precisely, for all $\alpha \in [-4,2[$, the fairness equilibrium is (D, D), which is not the case when $\alpha \geq 2$, where both equilibria (D, D) and (C, C) are obtained.

The intuition of this result is obvious. When it is common knowledge that players will choose (C, C), both know that the other agrees to sacrifice his own material welfare to help the

other. Thus, both are encouraged to show reciprocity (while playing C) as long as the material benefits resulting from D can be compensated with the psychological benefits. In addition, if it is common knowledge that agents are inclined to play (D, D), both know that the other does not agree to sacrifice his own benefit and none obtains the cooperative benefit, resulting in a reciprocal behaviour of hostility. The relevance of the solution (D, D) is explained by the fact that players are satisfied twice: by carrying out their desire to punish the other and by the defense of their personal interest.

To obtain a situation of multiple equilibriums is, to a certain extent, a step forward compared to the standard analysis of the PD. This gives cooperative behaviour all its sense, without forsaking the feasibility of the non-cooperative solution. However, we find a new handicap: it is impossible to make any prediction. Indeed, for a given situation, which behaviour is likely to be the outcome? Which solution will agents favour? The answer could only be given after the game is played. With this framework, we cannot do better than providing an ex-post justification. We could possibly eliminate the least plausible solution, but that requires the introduction of ad hoc selection criteria, weakening the scope of the analysis.

However, this equilibrium concept is actively used in experimental economy, i.e. the branch of economics that uses experimentation by reproducing in laboratory (stylized) economic situation to test theoretical models[17]. Nevertheless, to obtain a solution, in particular in sequential games, it is always necessary to refine the concept. Those are interpreted as defining particular forms of preferences. Thus, an analysis in terms of fairness returns, to a large extent, to specify the preferences corresponding to the behaviour that one seeks to study.

3. The Evolutionary Approach

Since the approach based on the *homo œconomicus* explains the stability of reciprocity but not its emergence, we need to redefine a framework for this task. With this intention, we abandon the assumption of rationality and work within the theory of evolutionary games[18]. Due to the absence of rationality, reciprocity no longer studied exclusively from a theoretical point of view, since simulations now play an important role. However, we will not really be able to explain the emergence of the Tit For Tat strategy since we will need to assume its existence. Therefore, evolutionary game theory should be seen rather as complementary to non-cooperative game theory than as a substitute. Their basis being non-cooperative, the complementary character reinforces both. Even more, in spite of certain differences between both approaches there are a high number of games where predictions agree.

3.1. Some Methodological Elements

Friedman (1998) defines an evolutionary game as a formal model of strategic interaction that goes on in time and where: (1) strategies which are accompanied by the highest benefits tend to replace those whose benefits are weak, but (2) the elimination of the least profitable strategies is marked by a certain inertia, in the sense that the change does not occur suddenly but gradually, and (3) agents do not try to systematically influence the future actions of their partners (as in the rational choice model). Other authors (for example Van Damme, 1991; Weibull, 1995) propose a more restrictive definition by imposing additional conditions: the population must be very large, individuals have a reduced rationality, meetings between agents are random and strategies are observable. Nevertheless, Friedman (1998) judges these restrictions useless when studied problems are associated to economic situations.

The major concept of evolutionary game theory is that of an evolutionarily stable strategy proposed by Maynard Smith and Price (1973). Such a strategy is robust to the evolutionary pressure exerted by the environment, a term that includes all available alternative strategies (the term of mutant strategies is also used): a population playing such a strategy cannot be invaded by any other strategy. The intuition of this concept is as follows. Let us suppose that individuals composing a large population are repeatedly randomly matched by pairs to play a symmetrical two player game. Suppose that initially all individuals play a certain strategy, pure or mixed, noted x (this is called a monomorphic population). Now let us consider a small group of individuals who use the same alternative strategy, pure or mixed, noted y. The strategy in place is then evolutionarily stable if, for each alternative strategy y, an entrance barrier exists so that if strategy y does not exceed this threshold, then x yields a higher benefit than y. More precisely, strategy x is evolutionarily stable if it resists all alternative strategies y because: (1) they yield a lower benefit, or (2) they yield a benefit identical to x, but with a lower benefit if they become too numerous.

The evolutionary approach is probabilistic and induces, in certain cases, nonlinearity. Therefore, it is sometimes impossible to use deductive mathematics to determine the consequences of a given model. The problem has been solved via simulations, which show the dynamic paths as well as the equilibrium points.

The first analysis of a repeated PD by the simulation of contests was done by the political economist Axelrod (1980, 1981, 1984). He twice invited game-theorists to propose programs which should answer C or D to other players, remembering preceding duels. Deterministic as well as (partially) random strategies were accepted. The simulated contest was articulated on a PD repeated 200 times, with the structure of benefits of figure (1). In the first tournament, 14 strategies (programs) were proposed, plus a fifteenth added by Axelrod, which answered C or D randomly (Hazard). This last strategy was included as a "non-strategy": if a strategy cannot do better than Hazard, it is rather bad (Dawkins, 1976). The 15 strategies matched made up for 225 distinct duels. At the end of the 200 shots, the benefits obtained by each strategy were calculated to determine the winner. The strategies were proposed by specialists in the PD coming from various scientific horizons: psychology, economy, political sciences, mathematics and sociology. The winning strategy was Tit For Tat, proposed by Anatol Rapoport, psychologist at the University of Toronto. As surprising as that can appear, this strategy contains the lowest number of instructions: 5 against 24 on average, one of them having as much as 77 program lines. At the beginning of the second tournament, the results of the preceding one were made available to participants, who were 62 this time (Axelrod still added Hazard). Tit For Tat won again. According to Axelrod, its capacity to support a cooperative equilibrium is related to its three properties. It always begins a duel by cooperating, i.e. it is never the first to betray. Nevertheless, it betrays if its adversary tries to benefit from it. However, its behaviour never results in a tough resentment since it preserves the possibility of bringing cooperation back. Thus, it is at the same time nice, touchy and indulgent, and these three qualities guarantee its robustness.

Taking into account the success of Tit For Tat, Axelrod tested the resistance of this strategy in an ecological tournament. This consists of a sequence of instantaneous simulations, where at each stage, the environment is determined by the results of the preceding simulation. "Ecological" means that simulations relate to the evolution of a predetermined set of strategies, and not to an evolution where new strategies could appear. In other words, the relevance of a strategy in the following generation is proportional to the score obtained in the preceding generation. By repeating this process over several generations, the proportions change, highlighting the robustness or weakness of the strategies. The results show that Tit For Tat prevails in the long run. The population, after having tried out several strategies, retains that which checks the properties of a norm.

Nevertheless, Nachbar (1992) posted some reserves, even serious critiques, concerning the reliability and interest of this result. It is known that in a repeated PD with finite horizon the equilibrium implies that all players betray. Thus, no simulations are needed to show which strategy will survive if all are present in the initial population. Nachbar concludes that Axelrod's results are, in fact, determined by the initial composition of the population. As Binmore (1994) pointed out, Axelrod made his simulations inadvertedly with a finite horizon repeated PD. That does not invalidate the results, since the strategies suggested were not elaborate anticipating the end of the game: nobody took into account the fact that the non-cooperative solution was the equilibrium of the game. The proof is that no one proposed systematic defection. The "spirit" of Axelrod's contest implied agents answering step by step.

Nachbar (1992) considered an ecological tournament based on the dynamic replicator model, including the strategy of permanent defection. The PD is repeated six times and, in addition to permanent defection, strategies more or less close to Tit For Tat are available. The game has 700 periods and, at the initial stage, all strategies appear in the same proportions within the population. Two results are obtained. Firstly, as the analytical treatment of the finite horizon PD shows, the equilibrium is mutual treason (Luce and Raiffa, 1957). However, this strategy needs a lot of time to impose itself: it represents 99% of the population only at the 650th generation. In fact, all strategies have, successively, their fifteen minutes of fame, starting with the most cooperative and moving towards the less cooperative. The second result shows that, based on a situation of relative cooperation, the population does not manage to maintain this behaviour: it is invaded by an increasing number of agents playing defection. Thus, a certain type of behaviour is needed to protect oneself from non-cooperative attitudes. Social sanctions seem to be able to play this role and to constitute a fundamental safeguard for society.

Although Nachbar's results are in conformity with theory and, therefore, contradict those of Axelrod, Linster (1992) validated Axelrod's approach to a certain extent. Taking once more the 63 strategies of the second tournament of Axelrod to test them in an infinite horizon repeated PD, he arrives to a conclusion similar to that of Axelrod. However, in Linster′s simulations, it is not a strategy but a set of strategies that survives, including Tit For Tat. The latter is the most important, but it is adopted only by one participant out of six.

How does one explain this result? For that, we need to go back to theory. Theory shows that Linster simulations must converge towards one of the multiple Nash equilibriums of the game 63x63. In fact, when the population considered starts the game with each one of the 63 strategies available (in equal proportions), Linster's simulations show that the system converges towards a Nash equilibrium, more precisely, a Nash equilibrium with mixed strategies in which Tit For Tat is played with a probability of 1/6. By systematically studying all the initial conditions, i.e. by modifying the proportion of the strategies available, Linster showed that the highest probability with which Tit For Tat is played is around 1/4.

3.2. Evolutionary Learning and Noises

If the PD is disturbed by random noises, does Tit For Tat support cooperation? Kandori et al. (1993) and Young (1993) initiated the systematic study of noises. Although both models are formally similar (defining a non-disturbed game and introducing noise), use similar mathematics (Markov's chains) and obtain similar result, they have some structural differences. Young assumes a single population made up of homogeneous agents whereas Kandori et al. use two types of populations. However, the latter game could also be defined with a single homogeneous population. The major difference is the learning process. In Kandori et al. players learn observing the behaviour of all the members of the population in the preceding stage. In Young's approach, players learn from the behaviour of the population in a certain number of preceding stages. Thus, memory is more important in this approach. However, both models lead to the same result[19]: noises make it difficult to maintain cooperative behaviour.

To illustrate this, let us consider an alternative to the model of Kandori et al. (1993) developed by Van Damme (1994). The game described in figure (4) is in discrete time (t = 1,2,…) and concerns the members of a population of finite size N. At the beginning of period t, both agents choose an action that they will use while playing against any one of the N-1 remaining agents. The members of the group are randomly associated per pairs, and adjust their strategies progressively.

		player 2	
		a_1	a_2
player 1	a_1	2,2	0, v
	a_2	v, 0	1,1

Figure 4: game with noises

We pose the following constraint: $0 < v < 2$. This matrix results from a repeated PD with a_1 for Tit For Tat and a_2 for systematic defection.

Calling z the number of agents that adopt strategy a_1 at time t, the equation of replication is:

$$\dot{z} = Z\,(1\text{-}z)\,[(3 - v)\,Z - 1].$$

Consequently, if the initial proportion of cooperators is higher than z (v) = 1/(3-v), the system will converge towards a state where all agents choose a_1 . In the opposite case, the system will converge towards the state where all agents choose a_2 .

Let us now introduce a noise into the system, in the form of an error in the behaviour of the agents. When an agent wishes to play one strategy he will play the opposite strategy with a weak probability ε . The probabilities of the errors are supposed to be independent. For ε sufficiently weak, the system undergoes fluctuations from one extreme state to the other (i.e. from a state where all cooperate to one where all defect). Abandoning a situation where all agents cooperate is only possible if a proportion of the population at least equal to (1 - Z (v)) suffers a simultaneous mutation. In the same way, abandoning a state where all defect requires a simultaneous mutation of a proportion Z (v) of the population.

3.3. Alternative Solutions with Tit For Tat

Many studies have shown the vulnerability of Tit For Tat to noises. However, there are as many studied developing solutions to this problem, redefining new variants of Tit For Tat or constructing alternative strategies. In general, this work insists on the arbitration between resistance to exploitation and capacity to maintain cooperation with errors.

According to certain authors (Kraines and Kraines, 1993; Nowak and Sigmund, 1993), the best strategy to improve Tit For Tat is Pavlov´s, whose principle is to change a strategy if it fails. In the simulations by Nowak and Sigmund (1993), random probabilities of mutations are introduced every 100 generations. After 10^7 generations, less than 8,3% of the population uses Tit For Tat and Generous Tit For Tat (GTFT). GTFT allows a percentage of agents to betray before adopting treason. The 91,7% remainders of the population use a strategy relatively similar to Pavlov's. However, Pavlov supports mutual cooperation. To see it, let us consider a monomorphic population of Pavlov players. Unilateral defections due to a noise will lead to mutual defection for one stage, but afterwards, players will cooperate to improve their score. Thus, noise does not prevent Pavlov players from converging towards mutual cooperation.

If we come back to the terms of figure (2) with Pavlov's eyes, to win is to get x_1 or x_3 and to lose is to get x_2 or x_4. The recommendation of this strategy is simple: never change a winning strategy and modify any behaviour leading to a failure. On the other hand, we should not fear the other player's reactions to our own treasons and benefit if he does not react.

Although more robust than Tit For Tat, Pavlov does not resist some variants of Tit For Tat. One of them was proposed by Sugden (1986). This strategy is Contrite Tit For Tat (CTFT): for a given player i, CTFT consists in playing C with a certain probability when the other players played T against the treason of i. Wu and Axelrod (1995), Boyd (1989) and Harrington and Axelrod (1995) studied the properties of this strategy. The analysis of Wu and Axelrod takes the original second tournament of Axelrod and redefines it in an environment with noise. They analyze four additional strategies: Pavlov, GTFT, CTFT and Generous Pavlov (GP). This last strategy acts as Pavlov with the only difference that it cooperates a given percentage of times even when it should play T. In addition, a 1% noise is introduced, i.e., for each deliberated choice, there is 1% chance of choosing the opposite strategy.

Initially, each one of the four new strategies is confronted in a duel form with the other 63. GTFT obtains a better score vis-à-vis each one of them. CTFT also obtains good scores, except against five of the original strategies. Pavlov exceeds only 8 strategies and GP obtains better scores than 15 of the original strategies.

To evaluate the impact of various levels of noise, four new strategies were added to the other 63, and the tournament was played with noises ranging from 0,1% to 10%. The results obtained are rather explicit: for all levels of noise, GTFT and CTFT yield good results, while Pavlov and GP fail. GTFT does slightly better than CTFT for low levels of noise, whereas for levels higher than 1% the opposite is true.

A third test was done within the framework of an ecological simulation, where the 67 strategies are divided into equal proportions in the population. The tournament is over 2000 generations. The most powerful strategy in the first generations was classified eighth in the 1984 original tournament. However, it declines thereafter. CTFT becomes leader after generation 1000 and continues to grow until accounting up to 97% of the population in generation 2000.

Comparing these experiments, we can make the following remarks. Pavlov and CTFT recover rather quickly from a noise when playing against themselves. When two Pavlov agents meet and one betrays due to an error, both agents betray for one stage but later go back to cooperation. The same is true if two CTFT agents meet, if one betrays by error he will change his behaviour at the following stage while the other betrays. However, both will cooperate at the following stage. However, the weakness of Pavlov is that, vis-à-vis another type of agent, its predisposition towards cooperation after a mutual treason creates an incentive for systematic defection in the other player. Therefore, the introduction of noise, while reducing the range of Tit For Tat, rehabilitates it at the same time, through its variations. In other words, when Tit For Tat adopts a form of repentance, with a lower degree of generosity, it becomes a strategy likely to prevail in an environment with noises.

This approach with noises is attractive because it permits more realistic long term predictions. However, as Bergin and Lipman (1996) underline, these predictions can only be taken with restrictive conditions on the form of the noises. That raises an important issue concerning the representation of noises, since isolated or cumulated noises can have different consequences. Foster and Young (1990) introduce stochastic shocks on the basis of a process of Wiener, and Fudenberg and Harris (1992) suppose that objective functions suffer cumulated shocks.

Kandori et al. (1993), for their part, suppose that agents make errors in the choice of their strategies, and these errors take place following a fixed probability. Thus, future research should try to clarify the types of noises that are more reasonable.

4. Conclusion

Taking into account our discussion on the PD, we can state that the interdependence of choices does not favor cooperation. Individuals, fearing to lose with the exchange, prefer to avoid any risk by renouncing to any exchange. However, reality shows that cooperative behaviour take place within families, companies, associations or nations.

Perhaps the problem is that cooperative behaviour is not well represented through the game theory. Admitting that cooperation is, to a certain extent, "unconditional" (like morality or altruism) implies admitting that this choice is more a personal affair than a strategic consideration. Choosing independently from the behaviour of others, the agent no longer follows a group effect, which is, now, a consequence and not a necessary condition of cooperation. However, it is difficult to accept such a representation since social rules to guarantee cooperative behaviour generally imply sanctions. To be set up, these sanctions must precede cooperation, which leads us to a dead end. Indeed, if cooperative behaviour is a personal affair, cooperation is already present when individuals conform to it.

Reciprocity, summarized as the Tit For Tat strategy, constitutes an innovation. It is defined as behaviour capable of being determined by individuals and not as a morality imposed from outside. This strategy guarantees the stability of a cooperative solution, although it is a conditional cooperation. Only after playing both, cooperation and punishment, does cooperation emerge. However, this is only true under certain conditions. The framework needed for the emergence of cooperation implies a particular context, leaving the door open to other forms of behaviour and consequently permitting the diversity of attitudes observed in reality.

Notes

1. A norm describes a rule sanctioned and followed by all the members of a group (Axelrod, 1986; Elster, 1989; Jordan, 1991). Thus, norms are constraints accepted by agents before maximizing their objective functions.
2. Poundstone (1992) shows all alternative games which also lead to a paradox in the sense of non-emergence of the cooperative solution.
3. The repeated PD describes a framework where agents act simultaneously at each stage. Their choice at the current period takes into account the option chosen by the other player at the preceding period.
4. For Dawkins (1976), life is formed by games of the form of the repeated PD, including humans, animals and flora.
5. We know that defection is an (individually) optimal strategy in a one game shot within the rational choice model, and this does not permit considering the influence of intentions. However, widening the framework (intention-action-gains), one can imagine that peaceful intentions on both sides will lead to a result different from non-cooperation. Rabin (1993) shows this: incorporating intentions in the basic model, the cooperative solution arises as an equilibrium, as well as non-cooperation. See below.
6. Altruism is a form of unconditional generosity, and thus different to reciprocity: altruism is not offered as an answer to received altruism (Fehr and Gächter, 2000).
7. Sugden´s (1984, 1986) version for the funding of a public good is different, since it is reduced to the principle whereby the individual should not adopt a free-riding behaviour when others contribute to the public good. This design of reciprocity is a more weak version of the Kant's categorical imperative.
8. According to Elster (1987), this strategy had been partly formulated by Descartes, i.e. well before the appearance of game theory. The argument of Descartes is that prudence requires one to help others, which is even truer in repeated interactions where one can expect a favour in return.
9. The repetition of a game results in a superset where strategies are continuations of actions and individual payments the sum of instantaneous payments.
10. The 'Folk' theorem shows that in an infinitely repeated game, any solution guarantees each player at least his equilibrium maximin payoff.
11. The resolution of the dynamic game is carried out by backward induction. The solution is found by iteration starting from the end of the game. That makes it possible to eliminate Nash equilibriums based on non-credible threats, i.e. threats which will never be rendered effective even if the players

were able to do it. Thus, one can then deduce a perfect equilibrium (Selten, 1965).

12. An event E is common knowledge of order 1 when "each one knows E", it is common knowledge of order 2 when "each one knows that each one knows E". One can continue until order K: E is mutual knowledge of order K when "each one knows (reiterated K times) that E".

13. According to Rapoport and Chammah (1965), observation shows that ordinary players are not able to imagine that treason is the only rational strategy, and this intellectual insufficiency avoids loss.

14. Obviously, humans cannot play an infinite horizon game. However, the infinite horizon models a sequence of interactions for which participants do not have any reason to think that the current interaction will be the last one.

15. In general, all possible individually rational strategies can be supported by a Nash equilibrium in the *ad infinitum* repeated PD. Thus, systematic defection is a Nash equilibrium.

16. Following the seminal article by Geanakoplos et al. (1989) several authors developed that research area. Even Pareto (1906), in his time, supported that psychology is at the base of political economy and, in general, of all social sciences.

17. One of the main results of experimental economics concerning the PD is the existence of various types of individuals. Andreoni and Miller (1993), for example, observe that within the framework of the finite horizon repeated PD, some agents always cooperate, while others either never cooperate or play a mixed strategy. Weimann (1994) and Isaac et al. (1994) also identify three types of agents in experiments relating to the funding of public goods, according to the different amounts of the contribution and the duration of the contribution.

18. Evolutionary games were initially introduced into biology to study the behaviour of animal species. However, applications in economics required a somewhat different framework to represent human learning.

19. However, this is not always the case. By applying the two models to other games, Jacobsen et al. (1999) show that the results can be completely different.

References

Andreoni, J. and Miller, J.H. 1993. "Rational Cooperation in the Finitely Repeated Prisoner's Dilemma: Experimental Evidence". *Economic Journal*, 103, 570-585.

Axelrod, R. 1980. "Effective Choice in the Prisoner's Dilemma". *Journal of Conflict Resolution*, 24, pp. 3-25.

Axelrod, R. 1981. "The Emergence of Cooperation among Egoists". *American Political Science Review*, 75, 306-318.

Axelrod, R. 1984. *The Evolution of Cooperation*. New York: Basic Books.

Axelrod, R. 1986. "An Evolutionary Approach to Norms". *American Political Science Review*, 80, 1095-1111.

Bergin, J. and Lipman, B.L. 1996. "Evolution with State-Dependent Mutations". *Econometrica*, 64, 943-956.

Binmore, K. 1994. *Playing Fair: Game Theory and the Social Contract I*. Cambridge Mass.: MIT Press.

Blau, P. 1964. *Exchange and Power in Social Life*. New York: Wiley.

Bolton, G.E and Ockenfels, A. 2000. "ERC: A Theory of Equity, Reciprocity and Competition". *American Economic Journal*, 90, 166-193.

Boyd, R. 1989. "Mistakes Allow Evolutionary Stability in the Repeated Prisoner's Dilemma Game". *Journal of Theoretical Biology*, 136, 47-56.

Dawkins, R. 1976/1989. *The Selfish Gene* (2nd ed.). Oxford: Oxford University Press.

Dixon, H.; Wallis, S.; Moss, S. 1994. "Axelrod Meets Cournot: Oligopoly and the Evolutionary Metaphor. Part One". Discussion Papers in Economics 94-8. University of York.

Elster, J. 1987. *Le Laboureur et Ses Enfants. Deux Essais sur les Limites de la Rationalité*. Paris: les Editions de Minuit.

Elster, J. 1989. *The Ciment of Society*. Cambridge Mass: Cambridge University Press.

Fehr, E. and Gächter, S. 2000. "Fairness and Retaliation: The Economics of Reciprocity". *Journal of Economic Perspectives*, 14, 159-181.

Foster, D. and Young, H. P. 1990. "Stochastic Evolutionary Game Dynamics". *Theoretical Population Biology*, 38, 219-232.

Friedman, D. 1998. "On Economic Applications of Evolutionary Game Theory". *Journal of Evolutionary Economics*, 8, 15-43.

Fudenberg, D. and Harris, C. 1992. "Evolutionary Dynamics in Games with Aggregate Shocks". *Journal of Economic Theory*, 57, 420-441.

Gauthier, D.P. 1986. *Morals by Agreement*. Oxford: Oxford University Press.

Geanakoplos, J.; Pearce, D.; Stacchetti, E. 1989. "Psychological Games and Sequential Rationality". *Games and Economic Behaviour*, 1, 60-79.

Gouldner, A.W. 1960. "The Norm of Reciprocity: A Preliminary Statement". *American Sociological Review*, 25, 161-178.

Hardin, R. 1971. "Collective Action as an Agreable N-prisoners' Dilemma". *Science*, 16, 472-481.

Harrington, J.C. and Axelrod, R. 1995. "Tit For Tat with Contrition is an Evolutionarily Stable Strategy in the iterated Prisoner's Dilemma with Noise". Working Paper.

Hobbes, T. 1651/1971. *Léviathan*. Editions Sirey.

Isaac, R.M.; Walker, J.M.; Williams A.W. 1994. "Group Size and the Voluntary provision of Public Goods". *Journal of Public Economics*, 54, 1-36.

Jacobsen, H.J.; Jensen, M.; Sloth, B. 1999. "On the Structural difference between the Evolutionary Approach of Young and that of Kandori, Mailath, and Rob". Working Paper: University of Copenhagen, Denmark.

Jordan, J.S. 1991. "Bayesian Learning in Normal Form Games". *Games and Economic Behaviour*, 3, 60-81.

Kandori, M.; Mailath, G.; Rob, R. 1993. "Learning, Mutation and Long-Run Equilibria in Games". *Econometrica*, 61, 29-56.

Keohane, R.O. 1986. "Reciprocity in International Relations". *International Organization*, 40, 1-27.

Kolm, S.-C. 1984. "Théorie de la Réciprocité et du Choix des Systèmes Economiques". *Revue Economique*, 35, 871-910.

Kraines, D. and Kraines, V. 1993. "Learning to Cooperate with Pavlov an Adaptative Strategy for the Iterated Prisoner's Dilemma with Noise". *Theory and Decision*, 35, 107-150.

Kreps, D.M. 1990. "Corporate Culture and Economic Theory". In J.E. Alt and K.A. Shepsle (eds.), *Perspectives on Positive Political Economy*. Cambridge: Cambridge University Press.

Krugman, P.R. and Obstfeld, M. 1992. *Economie Internationale*. Bruxelles: De Boeck Université.

Linster, B. 1992. "Evolutionary Stability in the Repeated Prisoners' Dilemma Played by Two-State Moore Machines". *Southern Economic Journal*, 58, 880-903.

Luce, R.D. and Raiffa, H. 1957. *Games and Decisions*. New York: Wiley.

Marks, R.E. 1989. "Breeding Hybrid Strategies: Optimal Behavior for Oligopolists". In J.D. Schaffer (ed.), *Proceedings of the Third International Conference on Genetic Algorithms*. Morgan Kaufmann.

Maynard Smith, J. and Price, G.R. 1973. "The Logic of Animal Conflicts". *Nature*, n°246, 15-18.

Moulin, H. 1981. *Théorie des Jeux pour l'Economie et la Politique*. Paris: Hermann.

Nachbar, J.H. 1992. "Evolution in the Finitely Repeated Prisoner's Dilemma". *Journal of Economic Behaviour and Organization*, 19, 307-326.

Neyman, A. 1999. "Cooperation in Repeated Games when the Number of Stages is not Commonly Known". *Econometrica*, 67, 45-64.

Nowak, M. and Sigmund, K. 1993. "A Strategy of Win-Stay, Lose-Shift that Outperforms Tit for Tat in the Prisoner's dilemma Game". *Nature*, n°364, 56-58.

Olson, M. 1965. *Logique de l'Action Collective*. Paris: PUF, edition 1987.

Pareto, V. 1906. *Manuel d'Economie Politique*. Genève: Droz, edition 1966.

Poundstone, W. 1992. *Prisoners's Dilemma: John von Neumann, Game Theory and the Puzzle of the Bomb*. New York: Doubleday.

Rabin, M. 1993. "Incorporating Fairness into Game Theory and Economics". *American Economic Review*, 83, 1281-1302.

Raiffa, H. 1992. "Game Theory at the University of Michigan, 1948-1952". In E.R. Weintraub (ed.). *Toward a History of Game Theory*. supplement to vol. 24, Duke University Press, 165-175.

Rapoport, A. and Chammah, A.M. 1965. *Prisoner's Dilemma*. Ann Arbor: University of Michigan Press.

Renault, R. 2000. "Privately Observed Time Horizons in Repeated Games". *Games and Economic Behaviour*, 33, 117-125.

Schelling, T.C. 1960/1986. *Stratégie du Conflit*. Paris: PUF.

Selten, R. 1965. „Spieltheoretiche Behandlung eines Oligopolmodelles mit Nachfrageträgheit". *Zeitschrift für die Gesante Staatswissenschaft*, 12, 301-324.

Sen, A. 1991/1993. *Ethique et Economie*. Paris: PUF.

Stanley, E.A.; Ashlock, D.; Tesfatsion, L. 1994. "Iterated Prisoner's Dilemma with Choice and Refusal of Partners". In C.G. Langton (ed.), *Artificial Life III*. Addison-Wesley, 131-175.

Straffin, P. 1980. "The Prisoner's Dilemma". *UMAP Journal*, 1, 101-103.

Sugden, R. 1984. "Reciprocity: The Supply of Public Goods Through Voluntary Contributions". *Economic Journal*, 94, 772-787.

Sugden, R. 1986. *The Economics of Rights, Co-operation and Welfare*. Oxford: Basil Blackwell.

Vanberg, V.J.; Congleton, R.D. 1992. "Rationality, Morality and Exit". *American Political Science Review*, 86, 418-431.

Van Damme, E. 1991. *Stability and Perfection of Nash Equilibria*. Second Edition. Berlin: Springer-Verlag.

Van Damme, E. 1994. "Evolutionary Game Theory". *European Economic Review*, 38, 847-858.

Weibull, J.W. 1995. *Evolutionary Game Theory*. Cambridge Mass: MIT Press.

Weimann, J. 1994. "Individual Behaviour in a Free Riding Experiment". *Journal of Public Economics*, 54, 185-200.

Wu, J. and Axelrod, R. 1995. "How to Cope with Noise in the Iterated Prisoner's Dilemma". *Journal of Conflict Resolution*, 39, 183-189.

Young, H.P. 1993. "The Evolution of Conventions". *Econometrica*, 61, 57-84.

PART TWO

Commitment

Beyond Altruism: Commitment?

Jérôme Ballet
Aurélie Carimentrand
Patrick Jolivet

Since Howarth S. Becker's article (1960), the concept of commitment has become common in sociology, to such an extent that commitment sociology has been developed. In economics, however, there is much less work referring to the concept, although A. Sen's article (1977) gave an impetus in the field. Some articles by economists now refer to commitment, but they remain rare. Yet, there is no doubt that committed behaviour accounts for the major part of the reflection conducted on ethical practices of individuals.

This chapter aims at widening the economic perspective on commitment, still bearing in mind these ethical practices. In a first part, we shall recall how the notion of commitment is formulated in economic theory. It is characterised by its opposition to compassion. The concept also gave rise to a formalisation that we will present. The first part ends with the presentation of the critical overview, given by standard economics, to the concept.

In a second part, we try to go beyond the opposition that exists between compassion and commitment, and which seems characteristic of economic theory, by using the ethics of care. We show that the opposition between compassion and commitment is very formal and that it may not be put forward in concrete cases such as the consumption of fair trade goods.

1. Commitment

The concept of commitment appeared quite recently in economic theory. It is characterised by an opposition, now classic, to compassion. A. Sen (1977) offered a formulation of it, which was officially formalised by C. Arnsperger (1998). The first criticisms made about this formulation are also quite recent (G.S. Becker 1996).

1.1. Compassion and Commitment: a Classic Distinction

The distinction between compassion and commitment is now well known. It was first developed through Collard (1975) and Sen's (1977) articles. We will not dwell at length on this distinction, but just succinctly mention it.

Collard, like Sen, finds the origins of this distinction in Edgeworth's work published in 1881 and entitled *Mathematical Psychics*. According to these two authors, an individual shows compassion, or *sympathy* (in Smith's words, 1759) when the well-being of other individuals has a direct influence on his/her own well-being. The act of worrying for others affects our own well-being. On the contrary, commitment sets a distance between personal choices and personal well-being. To take up Sen's example, if acts of torture make you ill, they therefore affect your own well-being which means you are in compassion. If you consider these same acts as reprehensible, without being affected by them, but really just because you consider them reprehensible, you are ready to do something to fight these acts, you are then dealing with a case of commitment.

Finally, compassion classically corresponds to the presence of an externality, whereas commitment is different and cannot be merely apprehended as an externality. According to economic formalisation, compassion is synonymous with altruism. Indeed, altruism is often formalised by inserting an externality which is representative of the well-being of other economic agents, into the utility function of the economic agent. The concept of commitment is more demanding. It implies going beyond usual formalisation and therefore overcoming the altruistic frame as it is defined in economics. The formalisation of commitment must take into consideration the fact that the individual's effective choice no longer simultaneously reveals his/her preferences and his/her well-being.

In accordance to this condition of formalisation, Sen does not put ethical concerns and considerations of individual well-being on the same level, thus wandering away from a strictly utilitarian philosophy. According to Sen, it is the uniqueness of the set of preferences that should be questioned, as a unique ranking of all feasible actions by an individual, illustrating all his/her motivations.

Let us suppose that there is a plurality of motivations, each of which ranks feasible actions into a set of specific preferences. Sen (1974, 1977) offers to define a new set of preferences, which would introduce a ranking over traditional preferences. This technique, called meta- ranking, allows us to introduce the individual's morals, ethics, etc., as an element structuring the set of preferences and the choice. It therefore consists in expressing preferences *over preferences* (saying for example: "I want individual choices to lie within the scope of this political priority").

The technique of preferences over preferences, or of ranking of rankings, is a way of integrating, into the analysis, different types of individual motivations, each of which carries out a ranking of feasible actions. Faced with a consequentialistic idea of rationality that assesses choices as individual utilities, without any other considerations over behaviour rules, Sen suggests assessing the rules before the consequences of acts. Commitment, understood as a product of a meta-preference, is the expression of rationality over rules, but without, for all that, considering it irrational regarding the internal consistency of choices. The action, chosen in the end by the agent, depends first of all on the rankings made by each of his/her preferences, but also on the actual ranking of motivations, which illustrates his/her individual behaviour ethics.

Therefore, the technique of meta-ranking is a way of integrating commitment into economic theory. Now, A. Sen's article can no longer be ignored and recent approaches explicitly refer to it (Schiell and Rush 2003, Igersheim 2003). Arnsperger's theory (1998) is undoubtedly among the most accomplished attempts coming in the wake of the previous formulation. He suggests a modelling of the idea of commitment which continues A. Sen's article but also develops its own specificities.

1.2. An attempt to Formalise Commitment: the Interpretation of Sen by Arnsperger

The topic of Arnsperger's article (1998) is the representation of moral commitment through a process of individual optimization. The author gives an operational form to the idea of meta-preferences suggested by Sen, by separating the behaviour rule representative of individual ethics, from the choice of action which ensues from it. Here, we will follow the formalisation suggested by the author to deal with both elements.

The reflection tackles the ranking made by the preference relation. Let *Ai* be the set of *P* actions feasible by an individual *i*, with p = 1, …, P: $A_i = \{a_1^i, ..., a_P^i\}$.

The first new point introduced by Sen is the break with the assumption that there is a uniqueness of ranking defined by the preference relation within the set of feasible actions, since a sole order of actions can not exhaustively reflect the various motivations of individual choice.

Sen's suggestion (1974, 1993) may be explained in the following way: to the set A_i of actions, feasible by an individual *i,* correspond as many particular sequencings as there are individual behaviour motivations. This suggestion means that the set A_i is not ranked by a unique relation, but can be classified according to various considerations, be it personal well-being or other motivations. Let us suppose there are *L* distinct motivations, that we will write ϕ_l, with $l = 1, ..., L$, the individual interest ω_i being one among others. The issue of ethical choosing, in this case, requires working within two sets:

- The set of feasible actions $A_i = \{a_1^i, ..., a_P^i\}$
- The set of different possible rankings, each of them corresponding to a type of individual motivation: $E = \{\omega_i, \phi_1, ..., \phi_L\}$

We may suppose that the set A_i will not be ranked identically if we choose, as action guide, personal well-being, the respect of a philosophical or religious norm, the will to abide by a community's values, etc. If we also suppose that the individual acts according to a certain ethical concept, he/she can then rank the sequencings of feasible actions following his/her ethics, which is to say expressing preferences over other preferences. This meta-preference is a way of ranking A_i according to the various interests ω_i and ϕ_l, but also of classifying[1] the actual set of rankings $E = \{\omega_i, \phi_1, ..., \phi_L\}$ according to individual ethics. Commitment comes in, since ranking according to ω_i is not considered by the individual as having priority over *all* other rankings ϕ_l. We may, in particular, represent ethical choosing as a lexicographic process stemming from meta-ranking.

Let E_i^* be the ranking of all or part of E corresponding to the ethical idea of the individual i. For instance, let us take $E_i^* = \{ \phi_2, \phi_3, \omega_i, \phi_1 \}$, which means the individual ranks motivation ϕ_2, as "the highest" from a moral point of view, then ϕ_3, and finally ω_i and ϕ_l. The lexicographic process implies that the individual first chooses, in A_i, actions that fulfil his ideal ϕ_2; let us write $P_i^{\phi_2}(A_i)$ the set of actions which are morally possible for the individual i, once the ideal ϕ_2 has been fulfilled. The restriction caused by this new set according to A_i depends on the constraint due to the respect of the ideal which has priority in the lexicographic order[2]. The individual then maximises the ideal ϕ_3, which determines a new set of possibles $P_i^{\phi_3}(A_i)$, restriction being imposed by the respect of ϕ_3 within the set $P_i^{\phi_2}(A_i)$[3]. The individual then selects the action(s) which maximise his/her personal well-being ω_i, then the ones which fulfil ϕ_l within the new set $P_i^{\omega_i}(A_i)$.

Introducing the meta-sequencing E_i^* implies the individual is not trying to reach, within the set of feasible actions, a particular sequencing representing his/her well-being, but his/her meta-sequencing of morally feasible actions ranked following a lexicographic order of ethical priority.

The process of fulfilling individual preferences represented by ω_i takes place in our example in the set $P_i^{\phi_3}(A_i)$, and no longer in the set of possibles A_i. We must therefore distinguish between:

- The ranking of action guides (the different sets of preferences illustrating the motivations ω_i or ϕ_l) according to individual ethics;
- The maximising action itself.

The restriction which occurs when going from A_i to $P_i^{\phi_3}(A_i)$ does not reveal an exogenous cause of irrationality, but allows us, on the contrary, to introduce the individual's ethical values in the model: in the end, commitment boils down to the same thing as a voluntary limitation of the space of choice, since the individual no longer maximises in the set of feasible actions but in the set of *morally* feasible actions. The set of morally feasible actions cannot be directly obtained from a ranking of A_i; it is understood as a meta-ranking of actions coming from a ranking of sets of actions according to personal ethics, but *also* of the actions themselves inside each set.

The distance between the choice of a committed action and personal well-being is only visible when the respect of an ideal that has priority deletes, from the set of morally feasible actions, one or several elements of A_i which would have been ranked by ω_i. Here, therefore, the committed action does not necessarily imply, contrary to Sen's writings (1977), a choice *contrary* to preferences. Arnsperger (1998, p.200) specifies that "this idea of moral commitment is far too restrictive", since the adoption of a priority action guide by the individual (as mentioned above) is sufficient to define the responsible act, seeing that the meta-ranking of morally feasible actions is not conditioned by the lone personal well-being ω_i. Responsibility (commitment) is: being able to rank several sets of preferences, each reflecting a particular motivation, and to then progressively narrowing down the set of morally feasible actions (following a lexicographic order of ethical priority), in order to determine a meta-sequencing of the actions on which the fulfilment of preferences has an influence. Thus, *a priori*, nothing prevents the meta-sequencing of morally feasible actions from ranking actions which would have been chosen, using as unique guide, individual well-being: it all depends on the restriction which is imposed by priority ideals over the set of feasible actions.

Therefore, Arnsperger distinguishes dichotomous ideals (for example "you will not throw your trash on the streets") that often allow a wide range of actions, from consequentialist ideals (as "the most eco-friendly action must be chosen") that noticeably narrow down the set of morally feasible actions. Let's suppose the perfectly informed individual. Respecting a consequentialistic ideal could leave him/her with only one morally feasible action. Let us take up our example of a moral view represented by $E_i^* = \{ \phi_2, \phi_3, \omega_i, \phi_1 \}$. If ϕ_2 and ϕ_3 are two consequentialistic ideals, there can only be a very low, even *nil*, number of morally feasible actions left over when ω_i[4] is fulfilled.

This conception of commitment allows us to oppose, to a certain extent, non-consequentialistic ideals, like Kant's morals, to consequentialistic ideals. When it comes to it, Kant's morals appear to be relatively flexible and to not totally narrow down the range of feasible actions. However, this type of formalisation does not confine itself to this moral theory, which *a contrario* is only a particular case.

1.2. A Criticism of the Notion of Commitment: G. Becker's Point of View

Gary S. Becker suggests an interpretation of commitment which is very different from the one mentioned above. Indeed, he directly chooses to criticise the approach initiated by A. Sen. In the 1996 book's first chapter, it is written (p.18): "In this book, moral and cultural judgments affect choices by influencing the personal and social capital included in a single extended utility function. Second-order meta-preference rankings may help to articulate the moral judgments that underlie behaviour, which appears to be Sen's purpose in introducing them. However, I do not believe that higher-order rankings are either necessary or useful in understanding behaviour since ethics and culture affects behaviour in the same general way as do other determinants of utility and preferences."

And further, in chapter 7 (p.153): "Economists have too narrow a perspective on commitments. Manipulating the experiences of others to influence their preferences may appear to be inefficient and fraught with uncertainty, but it can be the most effective way available to obtain commitment".

Becker then suggests two commitment models using manipulation. The first one deals with the parent-child relationship. Parents, who feel concerned about their own future well-being, when they are old, and about the financial support they might then get from their children, try to instil in them a sense of guilt, of obligation and of duty. It is a way for the parents to ensure that their children will really commit themselves to helping their parents when they are old. This model was already the subject of a critical debate in chapter 2 of this book; we will therefore not deal with it again.

The second model tackles social class relations. Higher social classes create norms in order to influence other social classes' preferences. According to Becker, religious norms are favoured by higher social classes who want to protect themselves against risks emanating from the poorest, such as rebellion, revolt, theft or other forms of aggression. In other words, religious norms pacify the poorest so that the richest maintain their power and domination over others. A criticism of this model can be found in Elster (1998, 1999). We are not questioning the relevance of Becker's model, but are merely trying to understand the meaning that it brings to the notion of commitment.

Through these two examples, he tries to consider commitment from a perspective that is very different to the one suggested by A. Sen. Nonetheless, these two approaches are not as opposed as they seem to be. In fact, they do not deal with the problem from the same perspective or on the same level. Manipulating preferences does not prevent the formation of a structure of preferences as defined by Sen. Even if it is obvious that the individual's conception, behind each analysis, is very different, it is not absolutely impossible to combine both. The first conception deals with the process of formation of norms while the other deals with the structure of preferences once norms have been interiorized. Clearly, those are two different stages of reasoning.

Becker's theory does not question Sen's proposition. These two approaches are methodological options apprehending a same phenomenon but on different levels.

In the following part, while adopting Sen's interpretation, we will suggest a critical vision which aims at overcoming the over-caricatured opposition between compassion and commitment.

2. Compassion and Commitment: a Strongly Exaggerated Distinction

In this section, we would like to show that the opposition between compassion and commitment is very excessive and that commitment cases may also originate in a certain form of compassion. Firstly, we defend this point of view by drawing on the ethics of care, an ethical trend which was given an impetus by feminist movements. Then, we reinforce the idea by an example on committed consumption. In his 1977 (1982, p.94) article, Sen wrote "I think one should immediately agree that for many types of behaviour, commitment is unlikely to be an important ingredient. In the private purchase of many consumer goods, the scope for the exercise of commitment may indeed be limited and may show up rather rarely in such exotic acts as the boycotting of South African avocados or the eschewing of Spanish holidays. Therefore, for many studies of consumer behaviour and interpretations thereof, commitment may pose no great problem". On the contrary, we think that consumption is a breeding ground for applications of commitment and that, although committed consumer behaviour is not a majority, they are neither marginal. Indeed, since the beginning of the 1990s, supply of "ethical" products, as they are called, has grown, therefore allowing more boycott actions. Moreover, campaigns to heighten consumer awareness of social and environmental issues, linked to production conditions and to international trade rules, have taken on new dimensions. Take the example of campaigns to eliminate child labour, campaigns against the use, in agriculture, of genetically modified organisms (GMO), or finally, campaigns in favour of fair trade between North and South. We illustrate our point of view with the consumption of fair trade products, a concept which encourages the selection of consumer goods by positively discriminating products derived from fair trade practices with Southern underprivileged producers, through debate, transparency and respect.

This kind of committed consumption is based on a relational theory which calls for a certain form of compassion.

2.1. Ethics of Care

Carol Gilligan's work, presented in her best-seller entitled "In a Different Voice"[5], has made a great contribution to the development of a concept known as the ethics of care. The concept, which was initially suggested from a feminist perspective as opposing Kohlberg's thesis of moral development[6], is becoming widespread, in many fields.

Care for others is at the heart of this analysis, which especially deals with a certain number of fundamental issues found in our society, such as isolation, oppression and suffering. Ethics of care is characterised by care, compassion but also solidarity towards others. Moral sensitivity counts above all, and not the use of great principles of justice which are disconnected from specific contexts.

According to this approach, moral considerations cannot be merely based on the rights acknowledged to each of us, but they require the acknowledgment of the specificity of individual needs in specific circumstances. Impartiality, based on equity in rights, and non-interference with the obtaining of these rights are both far from being sufficient. On the contrary, each case requires a specific analysis of the situation. Therefore, ethics of care applies quite as much to circumstances defined by close relations between people, in which other's specific needs and traits are well defined and acknowledged, as to circumstances characterised by an absence of knowledge of those needs and traits. Thus ethics of care cannot be demolished by anonymity and distance between people. According to its defenders, even when it comes to people suffering from hunger on the other side of the world, ethics of care is more capable of defining what type of action is needed than any theory based on abstract principles of justice. Moral sensitivity applies to close relations as well as to anonymous ones. The aim is not to deny the usefulness of principles or rules of justice, but simply to highlight their inadequacy.

Principles of justice build a vision of the world based on equality, where everybody, even oneself, is treated in the same way and where equity and justice rule. Ethics of care establish a vision of the world in which interdependent relations imply the fulfilment of everybody's needs and from which nobody is left out.

Moral dilemmas are no longer in keeping with these conditions: how can one impose the respect of rights, other's rights and one's own too, while leading a life made of obligations towards oneself and towards others. In a more simplified way, we have on the one hand a vision of the world based on obligations and, on the other hand, a vision of the world built on rights.

This opposition means that principles of justice suggest a moral reasoning organized by concepts of "indifference" and non-interference: relationships with others are then, above all, relationships based on rights. The respect of rules is of the utmost importance, regardless of others' individual situation. On the contrary, ethics of care shows a will to pay attention to others. A moral person is a person who helps others. Therefore interdependence among people implies kindness, liking and compassion. It is no longer a matter of interference since interdependence actually implies intervention.

Ethics of care exists in concrete situations, whereas principles of justice establish types of reasonings that are hypothetical, but also disconnected from the context and from History. However, it is indeed through concrete situations that commitment is made possible. As a conclusion, compassion can then become a feeling in favour of commitment, and the opposition between both ideas is greatly exaggerated.

2.2. An Example: the Consumption of Fair Trade Products

A major ethical point is at stake in consumption. Not only does consumption take on a strong symbolic dimension, but it also directly interferes with people's physical aspects such as health. Through everyday consumption acts, anyone can have influence on the many material and symbolic levels of one's own life. However consumption is not only an act that makes sense by itself; it also refers to the logic of collective action. To take just one example, I might regret not having at my disposal a neighbourhood shop, yet by shopping in supermarkets I contribute to the absence of these small shops. Of course, I cannot be entirely blamed for the absence of such small stores, since if I am the only one to shop in supermarkets, small shops will not close down. It is the same type of action carried out by everybody that produces the negative effect, i.e. the closing down of small shops.

Consumption has become a field in which individuals can express their moral beliefs. There are now numerous expressions referring to new forms of consumption, among which we find, to refer to the consumer: the citizen consumer, the responsible consumer, the consum'actor or even the alterconsumer.

Still, the consequences of these new forms of commitment through consumption should not be exaggerated. According to Jolivet (1999, 2001)[7], citizenship of consumption is based on strong and far from realistic assumptions, which define a continuous rationality of consumers. By studying environmental issues, he defines continuous (environmental) rationality when there is a feedback of environmental concerns in the consumers' purchasing act. On the contrary, rationality is discontinuous when the agents' ecological sensitivity does not find expression in their purchasing behaviour, but in other ways. In the case of household waste and their sorting, rationality is rather discontinuous. On the one hand, the citizen's values are in favour of sorting and recycling, on the other hand, the consumer, as an agent, does not feel responsible and therefore does not modify his/her consumer habits: "the interest in a better control of waste does not concern the consumption act, but is rather related to the individual's civic commitment in the city" (Jolivet, 1999, pp.45-46). Households do not consider themselves waste producers and they blame those distributing goods, particularly with regard to packaging.

Nonetheless, we must not deny the progression of commitment in consumption. For instance, the consumption of fair trade products seems to be rapidly increasing. In 2002, 16% of consumers considered fair trade "a means to become a responsible consumer". Moreover, the buying conversion rate of consumer willingness regarding that type of product seems quite high: among people who know about fair trade, one out of three has already bought fair trade products[8].

Carimentrand and Ballet (2004) analyse the consumption of fair trade products according to four different levels of consumer morality. The first level is that of the awareness of the problem. The consumer becomes aware of the importance of expansion and practice problems in fair trade. He is then able to give an opinion on these practices. This is an established fact, clearly shown in surveys. Indeed, a great number of consumers say that they are in favour of fairer trade and that they are ready to consume fair trade products. But this is only the first stage, in which the consumer asserts his/her moral preferences without, however, taking action: once more, this phenomenon is shown in surveys that highlight the difference between the assertion according to which consumers are generally in favour of fairer trade and the fact that they do not take action, on an everyday basis, to encourage fairer trade. Sterckx and al.'s study (2004) on Belgian fair trade product consumers is a good illustration of the problem: it defines separate profiles for potential fair trade product consumers and for those who actually consume these products.

The second level is that of the information on products. At this stage, the consumer is aware of the problem, but needs information in order to make a selection among products that are offered on the market. However, it does not mean that the consumer will really carry out his purchasing act. Two complementary conditions are required for this act to happen.

Firstly, the information obtained must be considered reliable. The consumer must be able to reasonably trust the information he receives. This is the third level[9].

Finally, on a fourth level, in the range of alternative products that he/she has selected, the consumer will only carry out his/her choice if he/she gets information, not on the product itself, but on the repercussions of his/her purchasing act. This level is particularly striking in certain opinion polls. For example, the humanitarian aspect is predominant in the vision French consumers have of fair trade. Indeed, 70% of them answered "humanitarian action" to the question "what does fair trade conjure up for you?" (Lecomte 2003), which tends to show that purchasing a fair trade product, is not thought of as a mere consumption act but as a redistributive act.

The first three reasons mentioned for purchasing fair trade products are: paying a fair price to the producer, a healthy and honest production process, also respectful of people (no child labour…), and the opportunity to restore the dignity and autonomy of southern producers (Sterckx and al. 2004). Those three reasons clearly show that, through consumption, a repercussion on producers is expected. It is therefore no longer a mere purchasing act, but really a committed act whose repercussions are important.

Here, we will not come back to the question of the perception and awareness of the problem, nor will we deal with the availability of information and the trust in available information. We will only take an interest in the role of information in the decision-making process, particularly by studying the repercussion of consumer action on the producer. Indeed, the question is at the heart of the compassion-commitment link.

Information plays an essential role, since it enables consumers to become aware of what is ethically at stake in fair trade, but it also encourages the shift from the awareness or perception of the problem, to the actual purchasing act. Compared to other forms of committed or responsible consumptions, consumption of fair trade products is based on the existence of a direct link between the consumer and the producer. According to Glassman (2001), this direct relation causes a "ladder jump" which enables the consumer to be in the producer's position and to become aware of the difficulties and of what is at stake in production. This ability to identify oneself with others and to develop a sense of empathy for others is made possible through belonging to specific fair trade networks.

It is however to be noted that we can no longer talk about a unified fair trade network, and that we should distinguish between two types of networks: the network of combine chains, and the network of labelled chains. "Combine chains are the historical form of fair trade. They include participants specialising in fair trade activities and are therefore called

Alternative Trade Organisations (ATO)[10]. *A priori*, ATOs have an association or contributory status. They largely resort to voluntary work and to militant processes to handle the various chains" (Habbard et al., 2002). Its outlets are specialised stores, where information on fair trade practices and on the living conditions of partner producers can be found. As for labelled chains, they represent a new type of fair trade, which appeared at the end of the 1980s with the creation of the *Max Havelaar* label in the Netherlands. Such fair trade products are sold through conventional large-scale distribution networks, which need not abide by specific rules to distribute these products. According to Habbard et al., "the entire labelled chain is based on the sole contractual bond between the label licence holder (the importer, the transformer of the conventional sector) and its owner (the labelliser)". In other words, the fair trade network of combine chains seems more in a position to convey relational ethics.

However, the increase in the number of impact assessments of fair trade, carried out for fair trade organisations: FLO[11], Oxfam, Artisans du Monde… very clearly shows the need to know what concrete repercussions the actors' commitment has in the fair trade movement (Schurmann and Van Driel, 1999; Hopkins, 2000; Ciedel, 2002; Ronchi, 2002). This change of scale puts the consumer directly in contact with other's faces. The individual finds himself confronted with the other's face[12].

The impact or the repercussions of their own acts, provide consumers with a concrete understanding of development. They do not act for development in general, which remains a vague concept to them, but for specific producers in a defined area. When they have access to information about the producers' living conditions, consumers are then able to put a face to their action in favour of development. Through consumption, a direct link with the producer is created, and in return it gives a meaning to the consumption act, because the act has considerable effect. Indeed, Sterckx and al.'s study (2004) shows that most fair trade consumers believe that their action has an impact on producers.

They no longer feel as if they are in an anonymous relationship whose effects remain unknown, but fell they are in a face-to-face relationship including a relational dimension, where each act becomes important and where the repercussions of these acts are known, at least partially.

Fair trade, through its operating mode and the principles it is ruled by, leads to the construction of a space, in the geographical sense of the word, where producers are physically materialised and where their living conditions are known by the consumer. Fair trade also favours the creation of a symbolic space where geographical imagination is built (Cook and Crang 1996). Finally, it supplies a material support to the implementation of moral values, in which the fair consumer (Gosseries 2004) easily finds a privileged field for his/her committed acts.

In other words, consumers do not consume only for themselves, but also in order to directly contribute to the development of an area located in a southern country. Therefore, consumption does not have an impact on development in general, but on development in a particular place and related to a specific community of producers. Geographical delimitation and details have a meaning since they give a concrete aspect to the impact of consumption. The consumer acts for somebody in particular, whose economic and social situation, as well as geographical location, are known. Whatmore and Thorne (1997) even define consumers' commitment as corporate sense, since they also become actors of the production activity through consumption. Consumers find themselves in the same situation as people who sponsor the education of children in southern countries: they know the child's name, where he/she lives and his improvements at school. The consumer's action finally has a face. To take up one of Goodman's expressions (2003), to the northern consumer, southern communities of farmers become "near and dear".

This strong relational dimension sends us back to expansive ethics of care (Mansfield 2003) or relational ethics (Whatmore 1997), reducing physical, psychological and cultural distances between the northern consumer and the southern producer. Obviously, fair trade networks strike the chord of compassion. The southern producer is no longer completely unfamiliar to the northern consumer and in a way, for the consumer, knowing that his/her consumption act has an impact on the southern producer, gives a justification for his committing to that kind of consumption. Compassion and commitment are closely linked. But is it finally not the same thing in Sen's torture case? Associations which militate against torture, lead mass media campaigns based on shocking images, which often appeal to compassion. And given that commitment is related to compassion, if this initial compassion leads to awareness, it can also be at the origin of long-lasting commitment in the fight against such practices.

Notes

1. According to Sen and Arnsperger, the ranking does not require checking the characteristics of a simple ordering: two ethical points of view can be incommensurable without it modifying the logic of the analysis mentioned herein. Furthermore, ethical sequencing can only deal with certain action rankings, the others being indifferent.
2. It is to be noted that the word "constraint" must be understood in its extensive meaning, given that ethical commitment is freely consented.
3. We write $P_i^{\omega_i}(A_i)$ in order to simplify the writing, admitting that the respect of ϕ_2 has already been carried out. We would otherwise have to write the set of morally feasible actions $P_i^{\phi_3}(P_i^{\phi_2}(A_i))$.
4. Such a case leads to discuss the "tensions of commitment" and the way to make them acceptable for an individual (for instance by abandoning the lexicographic sequencing of all action guides; see Arnsperger, 1998, pp.203-211).
5. Carol Gilligan, *In a Different Voice. Psychological Theory and Women's Development*, Cambridge, Harvard University Press, 1982. Gilligan's work has given a strong research impetus and was a great success, yet it is based on books written prior to hers, particularly those by Nancy Chodorow, *Family Structure and Feminin Personality*, in M.Z. Rosaldo and L. Lamphere (ed.),

Woman, Culture and Society, Stanford, Stanford University Press, 1974; and those by Jean Baker Miller, *Toward a new Pyschology of Women*, Boston, Beacon Press, 1976.

6. In 1981, Lawrence Kohlberg developed his main thesis, the result of over 20 years of research. He broke the moral development of individuals into 6 stages, all brought together in 3 levels: the pre-conventional level, the conventional level and the post-conventional level. Each level corresponds to a higher degree of moral development, the highest one implying comprehension and application of legal rules, based on individual rights and on equity without bias.

7. Jolivet P. (1999), "Le consommateur responsable? Etude du cas des déchets ménager" ("The responsable consumer? Case study on household waste"), *Humanisme and Entreprise*, n°238, pp.33-46 and Jolivet P. (2001), "Le recyclage des déchets ménagers: une figure de citoyenneté" ("Recycling household waste: a citizenship issue"), *Le courrier de l'environnement de l'INRA*, n°44, pp.29-40.

8. The data mentioned above is from a study on French fair trade consumer demand by Lecomte (Lecomte, 2003), carried out using the following survey: IPSOS October 2000, IFOP July 2001, IFOP January 2002, *Alter Eco*, May 2002.

9. It is to be noted that these first three conditions for a responsible purchasing act are also required if we want the consumer's ecological sensitivity to express itself as a continuous environmental rationality: on the one hand, individuals must express a preference (in the economic meaning of the word) for "green" goods and, on the other hand, reliable information on these goods must be available (which does not seem to be the case in this situation, see Jolivet (2001)).

10. In Europe, ATOs are represented by trading groups such as Oxfam, Solidar'Monde, CTM Altromercato..., distribution networks of stores in the world...

11. Fairtrade Labelling Organizations.

12. Here we are referring to the philosophy of the other developed by E. Levinas. This philosophy insists on responsibility, which becomes the individual's founding structure. Freedom is determined by it.

References

Arnsperger, C. 1998. "Engagement moral et optimisation individuelle". In F.-R. Mahieu and H. Rapoport (eds.). *Altruisme, analyses économiques*, 191-214. Paris: Economica.

Becker, G.S. 1996. *Accounting for Tastes*. Cambridge Mass.: Harvard University Press.

Becker, H.S. 1960. "Notes on the Concept of Commitment". *American Journal of Sociology*, 66, 32-40.

Browne, A.W.; Harris, P.J.C.; Hofny-Collins, A.H.; Pasiecznik N.; Wallace, R.R. 2000. "Organic production and ethical trade: definition, practice and links". *Food Policy*, 25, 69-89.

Carimentrand, A. and Ballet, J. 2004. "Le commerce équitable entre éthique de la consommation et signes de qualité". Congreso internacional ARTE, "*Agro-industria Rural y Territorio*", 1-4 de diciembre del 2004. Toluca, México.

CIEDEL 2002. "Evaluation de l'impact sur les producteurs du Sud de l'action commerce équitable depuis 25 ans". Mimeo.

Collard, D. 1975. "Edgeworth's Propositions on Altruism". *Economic Journal*, 355-360.

Cook, I. and Crang, P. 1996. "The world on a plate: Culinary culture, displacement, and geographical knowledges". *Journal of Material Culture*, 1, 131-153.

Cook, I.; Crang, P.; Thorpe, M. 2000. "Regions to be cheerful: Culinary anthenticity and its geographies. In Cook I.; Crouch, D.; Naylor, S. and Ryan, J. (eds.). *Cultural turns, geographical turns: Perspectives on cultural geography*, 109-139. Harlow: Pearson Education.

Elster, J. 1998. "Emotions and Economic Theory". *Journal of Economic Literature*, 36, 47-64.

Elster, J. 1999. *Alchemies of the Mind. Rationality and the Emotions*. Cambridge: Cambridge University Press.

Gilligan, C.1982. *In a Different Voice. Psychological Theory and Women's Development*. Cambridge: Harvard University Press.

Glassman, J. 2001. "From Seattle (and Ubon) to Bangkok: The scales of resistance to corporate globalization". *Environment and Planning D: Society and Space*, 19, 513-533.

Goodman, M.K. 2003. *Reading Fair Trade: Political ecological Imaginary and the Moral Economy of Fair Trade Foods*. Mimeo, University of California.

Gosseries, A. 2004. *Qu'est-ce qu'un consommateur juste?*. Mimeo: Université Catholique de Louvain la neuve.

Haan, N. 1975. "Hypothetical and Actual Moral reasoning in a Situation of Civil Disobedience". *Journal of Personality and Social Psychology*, 32, 255-270.

Habbard, P.; Lafarge, L.; Peeters, A.; Vergriette, B. 2002. "Etat des lieux et enjeux du changement d'échelle du commerce équitable". Projet Commerce Equitable SOLAGRAL-CIRAD-CICDA-CEDAC, octobre.

Holstein, C. 1976. "Development of Moral Judgment: A longitudinal Study of Males and Females". *Child Development*, 47, 51-61.

Hopkins, R. 2000. "Impact Assessment Study of OXFAM Fair Trade". Oxfam.

Igersheim, H. 2003. *Un modèle de métaclassement des préférences*. Mimeo: BETA, Université Louis Pasteur.

Jolivet, P. 1999. "Le consommateur responsable? Etude du cas des déchets ménagers". *Humanisme and Entreprise*, n°238, 33-46.

Jolivet, P. 2001. "Le recyclage des déchets ménagers: une figure de citoyenneté". *Le courrier de l'environnement de l'INRA*, n°44, 29-40.

Kohlberg, L. 1981. *The Philosophy of Moral Development*. San Francisco: Harper and Row.

Lecomte, T. 2003. *Le pari du commerce équitable*. Editions d'organisation.

Mansfield, B. 2003. "Imitation crab and the material culture of commodity production". *Cultural Geographies*, 10, 176-195.

Ronchi, L. 2002. "The impact of fair trade on producers and their organisations: a case study with coocafé in Costa Rica". Prus Working Paper n°11: University of Sussex, june 2002.

Schurmann, F. and Van Driel, F. 1999. "Evaluation of the impact of the FLO model: an analysis of the significance for coffee farmers and coffee co-operatives". Mimeo: University of Nijmegen, IDS, The Netherlands.

Sen, A. 1974. "Choice, Ordering and Morality". In Körner S. (ed.). *Practical Reason*. Oxford: Blackwell.

Sen, A. 1977. "Rational Fools: a Critique of the Behavioural Foundations of Economic Theory". Reprinted in Sen, A. 1982. *Choice, Welfare and Measurement*, 84-106. Oxford: Basil Blackwell.

Sen, A. 1993. *Ethique et économie*. Paris: PUF.

Shiell, A. and Rush, B. 2003. "Can willingness to pay capture the value of altruism? A exploration of Sen's notion of commitment". *Journal of Socio-economics*, 32, 647-660.

Smith, A. 1759. *The Theory of Moral Sentiments*. Prometheus Books: Loughton (UK), 2000.

Sterckx, E.; Janssen, W.; De Peslmacker, P.; Mielants, C. 2004. *Beliefs, attitudes and buying behaviour of Belgian consummers towards Fair Trade products*. Mimeo: Universiteit Antwerpen Management School, Belgique.

Whatmore, S. 1997. "Dissecting the autonomous self: Hybrid cartographies for a relational ethics". *Environment and Planning D: Society and Space*, 15, 37-53.

Whatmore, S. and Thorne, L. 1997. "Nourishing networks: Alternative geographies of food". In Goodman D. and Watts M. (eds.). *Globalising food: Agrarian questions and global restructuring*, 287-304. London: Routledge.

The Ideal Observer: A Figure of Economic Theory

Jérôme Ballet
Damien Bazin

Economic theory has often elaborated stylistic devices aimed at favouring the integration of ethics within the framework of its mode of analysis. Amongst them, the construction of an ideal observer occupies an important position. This ideal observer is most often compared to the impartial spectator. However, markedly different interpretations have been proposed around this representation. Whatever these interpretations, they are all aimed at constructing a mode of reasoning in which the individual extricates himself from his personal and subjective situation to place himself in a universal perspective, where he finds himself in a position to put himself in the place of others. This procedure enables construction of an economic ethics based on impartiality. As Arnsperger (2001, p.21) points out: "... In a way, contemporary economic and social ethics appears like a hermeneutics of impartiality". This procedure was recently backed by empirical verifications on individuals' opinions.

Taking the example of an opinion poll on the Welfare State, Forsé and Parodi (2002, p.167) argued "that it is not possible to understand these opinions in their entirety if we stick to the idea that they only defend the economic interests or the preferences as to the good life of those who support them, and that in consequence, we must turn towards the broader model of a rational and reasonable actor, who pronounces himself in favour of objectively just solutions to understand and explain these opinions". Thus, the individuals assume opinions, not only for reasons which are only relative to them, which affect either their interests or their conception of good life, but also for neutral reasons, likely to convince the other members of society, even if they do not have the same interests or the same conception of good life.

In this article, several ways of interpretations will be explored. The objective here is to identify the main figures of the ideal observer, even if it means not following ancient texts to the letter, while keeping the spirit at a minimum. Therefore, the perspective chosen rather consists in emphasising how modern economic theory integrates and develops this problem. The article proposes to categorise these figures in view of constructing a certain number of points of reference permitting to distinguish their main forms. To this end, three sections will present different proposals structured around several debates. A first section will draw a comparison between two figures: the impartial spectator and the judicious spectator. These two figures were constructed after A. Smith and D. Hume. The second section will examine the controversy between J. Harsanyi and J. Rawls. This controversy appears as an extension of the opposition between Smith and Hume. It leads to the problem of moral commitment and the conformity of actions with moral judgements. The third section will present a new figure, who, in the tradition of the ethics of discussion, may be described as an impartial discussant. Although this figure is still not used explicitly in economic theory, several avenues of reflection come close to it. A presentation of what this figure could be constitutes a point of reference in this respect.

1. Judicious Spectator or Impartial Spectator

The idea, which raises the figure of the ideal observer may be summed up in one question: how can we neutralise our personal and therefore subjective situation so that we may be able to adopt universally valid moral judgements?

The responses put forward mainly consist in disembodying the individual to make him a kind of spectator who could adopt a point of view of "nowhere" to take up the expression of Thomas Nagel (1970). The construction of such a spectator owes much to Adam Smith and David Hume, thanks to whom the notion of ideal observer asserted itself in economics. Both of them construct a reflection on moral judgements based on sympathy. The ideal observer is above all a person endowed with sympathy. However, divergent interpretations seem to characterise Hume and Smith. A preliminary distinction between sympathy and empathy will first permit a semantic clarification of the question set by the ideal observer. There will then be a presentation of the notion of judicious spectator, which is associated with David Hume. This representation of the ideal observer will permit, by comparison, to bring out that of the impartial spectator, which is now found in modern economic theory.

1.1. Preliminaries: Sympathy and Empathy

Given that the very idea of the ideal observer was constructed on the basis of the concept of sympathy, it is important to present a few explanations on this notion before examining the positions attributed to David Hume and Adam Smith.

It is first necessary to make a distinction between sympathy and empathy. Nancy Eisenberg and Paul A. Miller contrast sympathy with empathy: "We define sympathy as an emotional response stemming from another's emotional state or condition that is not identical to the other's emotion, but consists of feelings of sorrow or concern for another, and we define empathy as an affective state that stems from the apprehension of another's emotional state or condition and that is congruent with it" (p.292). Likewise, Philippe Fontaine underlines the contrast between the two notions: "In sympathy one feels with another, while in empathy one feels into another" (p.292). Therefore, unlike sympathy, empathy is not automatically turned towards the others. Rather, it is analysed as an understanding of others. Ken Binmore (1998) illustrates empathy with an example: "For example, a gunfighter may use his empathetic powers to predict an opponent's next move without losing the urge to kill him" (p.12).

Thus, while sympathy may be understood as altruism towards other individuals and consists in feeling something for these other persons, empathy is, for Martin L. Hoffman (1981), a mixture of altruism and selfishness. Therefore, the concept may give rise to various interpretations. Piliavin et al. (1969), Gaertner and Dovidio (1977) see in it a particular form of selfishness, while others perceive it as a form of specific altruism (Mahieu, 1998). We shall not try to settle this debate here. We only need to retain that empathy is different from sympathy. Empathy may be summed up as the fact of putting oneself into a position to be anyone else in any other situation.

More subtle distinctions are obviously conceivable. Fontaine (1997) proposes, for example, a distinction between two forms of empathy and two forms of sympathy. A first form of empathy corresponds to an "empathetic identification", which presupposes both an imaginative change of circumstances and persons. The individual puts himself into a position to be anybody in any circumstance. A second form of empathy is the "partial empathetic identification". It only implies a change of circumstances; the individual may find himself in any situation, but he is not anybody. In this sense, this second form of empathy is regarded as partial since the individual does not really adopt a point of view of "nowhere". In the same way, the distinction between sympathy as a concernment for the welfare of other individuals and "sympathetic identification" as a recognition of a community of feelings, thoughts and experiences between individuals, may be used.

Yet, the main thing in economic analysis is to make a distinction between sympathy and empathy. As Sugden (2002) underlines it in a critical way: "Within modern rational choice theory, then, the distinction between sympathy and empathy is categorical; and these two theoretical concepts seem to exhaust the possibilities for representing positive relationships between the mental states of different people. From this perspective, arguments which do not recognise a sharp distinction between sympathy and empathy can seem merely confused" (p.69).

This distinction is useful insofar as modern economic theory constructs a concept of the ideal observer in reference to the notion of empathy, while in modern theory, sympathy refers more to the concept of altruism or benevolence[1]. However, David Hume and Adam Smith, the instigator of the figure of ideal observer, readily use the notion of sympathy.

1.2. The Judicious Spectator

The term of judicious spectator was proposed by John Rawls (2000) to explain the way of thinking elaborated by David Hume and to contrast it with Adam Smith, whose lineage has now recognised the term of impartial spectator[2].

For Hume, it deals with finding a place for ethics as a phenomenon of human nature. Everybody's ability to adopt a point of view which is that of a judicious spectator, characterises his approach. This approach is based on psychological principles relating to sympathy.

In section 2 of the second part of book III, Hume constructs an analysis of sympathy resting on a principle of feelings by transference. Sympathy is "a kind of contagion, and even infection, which we contract under the effect of a kind of resonance of our nature through our contact with others" (Rawls, 2000/2002, p.92). This effect of contagion does not come from a direct discernment of the others' mental states, but is inferred from their behaviour and their actions. This means that their behaviour or their attitude are signs revealing the feelings or the emotions, which they undergo, or more precisely, which we consider they feel.

Obviously, this contagion is only possible provided that the experiences undergone by other individuals are also experiences, which we underwent ourselves, or which we think we underwent. The community of experiences is a condition of sympathy by contagion. However, it implies that we sympathise more easily with persons who are close to us or resemble us at least, and with whom we share the same culture, same language... In this sense, sympathy, as it is presented here, is characterised by a certain partiality. The sympathies which everybody feels are very varied, extremely partial, and they depend much on the affinities which bind us to other persons. Yet, in space and time, the circle of persons with whom we shall share these sympathies is quite narrow. It will mostly be limited to the persons stemming from the family or to a few friends.

In such conditions, how can ensure that our moral judgements are consensual and apply to everybody, in a universal way, regardless of the contingencies of time and space? The solution proposed by Hume consists in resorting to the fiction of a judicious spectator.

Everybody has the ability to extricate himself from his present situation in order to adopt firm and general points of view, which constitute a position of judicious spectator. Hume, in section 3 of book III, illustrates this mechanism with a comparison between aesthetic judgements and moral judgements. According to this illustration, a beautiful face, that is to say the pleasure which such a face may bring, and which, on account of this pleasure, may be considered as beautiful, will not give the observer the same pleasure depending on the distance from where he observes it. Yet, we cannot consider this face as less beautiful because we are farther. Therefore, we must momentarily extricate ourselves from our situation to consider the face from a point of view, which would be ours if we were in another situation, i.e. if we were closer to the face. Our present and momentary situation requires corrections, which we are able to carry out by positioning ourselves as if we were in another situation. Moral judgements are like aesthetic judgements, they call for corrections. "Such corrections are common for all our senses, and in fact, it would be impossible for us to ever use the language or communicate our feelings to one another, if we did not correct our present situation" (Hume, section 3, iii, 1). Moral judgements, like the aesthetic judgements, are not only based on our actual feelings, but also on the feelings we know would be ours if we adopted this point of view.

Therefore, we must set for ourselves a firm and general point of view, which is likely to give rise to consensus in our judgements. To take up the example of Hume, we must consider the beauty of the face according to a distance and a point of view, which will enable us to determine in a consensual way whether or not it is really beautiful. It is therefore important to extricate ourselves from our situation. But this does not mean that we should extricate ourselves from our passions. It does not deal with neutralising the individual, but only the circumstances in which he is, while at the same time preserving his passions.

John Rawls (2000) sums up the approach of Hume in five stages. They will be presented below in the form of five principles:

The first principle is a *principle of passion*. The point of view which we adopt depends on a feeling or on a passion. If such were not the case, we would be indifferent and we would consequently be unable to express any judgement.

The second principle is a *principle of economy*. The point of view which we adopt must only bring into play one passion or one feeling. As soon as a point of view involves several passions or feelings, these passions or feelings may turn out to be contradictory; conflicts of passions or of feelings will be frequent and we are unlikely to obtain a consensual judgement. Individuals could be led to express contradictory or hesitant judgements.

The third principle is a *principle of generalisation*. The feeling which is brought into play is such that all the persons who adopt the same point of view express the same judgement concerning the qualities and the pertinence of the action considered.

The fourth principle is a *principle of universality*. The feeling used must be sufficiently universal. Whatever the position of the persons in time or in space, the quality or the action considered must be observed by a same feeling. This principle of universality implies the consensus of the judgements in a universal way.

Finally, the fifth and last principle is a *principle of evaluation*. For moral consensus to be reached, it is necessary to define a criterion of evaluation for the actions or the qualities subjected to our judgement. "This criterion consists in approving or disapproving of these actions and these qualities according to the way they affect the persons subjected to a private or social interaction with the individuals endowed with these qualities or with the authors of these actions" (Rawls, 2000/2002, p.96).

This last principle calls for three comments.

First, this principle of evaluation depends on social interaction between persons whose key is the moral feeling of approval. The action or the quality of a person will be virtuous if it provokes the approval of others with whom this person gets in touch.

Then, from this feeling of approval stems in return a possibility of response to the question as to how to know what urges us to act in compliance with our moral feelings. How is it that we should conform, in our real situation, to the moral judgements which we adopt according to the point of view of the judicious spectator? In other words, should we undertake the respect of our moral judgements? The response here lies in the approval stemming from the actions or qualities which we shall undertake according to the point of view of the judicious spectator. Therefore, the person's commitment mainly lies in the feeling of approval which he expect from others. Here, we deal with a specific interpretation of commitment as a process of social interaction based on approval.

Finally, since approval is a feeling which stems from social interaction, how can we explain the fact that approval may also exist towards persons whose character does not give rise to any benefit? This is the problem of "virtue in rags" raised by Hume. Here again, a comparison with aesthetic judgements sheds light on the problem. Hume illustrates virtue in rags with a man in prison. Now, if this man is regarded as a handsome man, whether he is in prison or not should not change anything regarding the point of view we have on his handsomeness. Even if this handsomeness does not bring any pleasure because it is not visible, as long as the man is in prison, there is no reason to modify this aesthetic judgement. If the external circumstances to make the feeling of approval fully effective are lacking, then this feeling will be obtained thanks to a capacity for imagination, extricating the person from his situation and putting him in more general circumstances.

In this sense, the position of Hume may be interpreted after Mercer (1972) as a projective analysis. According to this analysis, we attribute the fact of being virtuous or vicious to qualities or to actions, without it necessarily corresponding to any empirical observation. These are our emotions projected onto the judged objects, which lead us to such extrapolations. We project ourselves into the others' subjectivity.

We may then understand why Rawls (2000) considers that the explanation of moral judgements proposed by Hume is hypothetical for two reasons. First, because these judgements are not established by our actual feelings of our daily life, but by the feelings we would experience if we adopted the point of view of a judicious spectator. Secondly, because the feelings we would experience as a judicious spectator are those we would adopt if the persons with whom we are in social interaction were situated in normal circumstances, they would then permit the production of the beneficial effects we may expect in these circumstances.

The judicious spectator, as proposed by Hume, more particularly on account of his analysis on social interaction, gives a filiation to the economic theory of altruistic behaviour. However, the emblematic figure of the ideal observer will be characterised by that of the impartial spectator.

1.3. The Impartial Spectator

The origin of the impartial spectator could be found in Adam Smith. While Hume establishes a reasoning based on a mechanism of contagion, Smith describes a cognitive process corresponding to empathy. However, this is a controversial fact. For example, Fontaine (1997) supports Smith's argument of empathy with the following passage extracted from *La théorie des sentiments moraux* (*The Theory of Moral Sentiments*): "When I condole with you for the loss of your only son, in order to enter into your grief I do not consider what I, a person of such a character and profession should suffer, if I had a son, and if that son were unfortunately to die: but I consider what I should suffer if I was really you, and I not only change circumstances with you, but I change persons and characters" (Smith, 1759/1976, p.137).

On the contrary, Sugden (2002), while acknowledging that this passage may be read quite naturally in terms of empathy, considers that it is important to place Smith's whole project in a general perspective again. He considers that Smith should develop a more subtle conception combining sympathy and empathy, but mainly based on affective states. Smith does not reason in terms of preference but in terms of reciprocal influence of the affective states. He uses the term of *fellow-feeling* to represent this affective interdependence. Now, this affective interdependence rests on human psychology and is therefore only a partial feeling. This reading originates from the definition of the impartial spectator.

According to this perspective, Smith's spectator is not that same as described in modern economic theory. He represents, in an idealised form, the correspondence of feelings induced by social interactions. He is based on the mirror of social approval[3]. In this sense, partiality involves systematic biases in relation to the impartial spectator. This position is closely related to that of Boudon (2000), according to which the spectator proposed by Smith would not be mere fiction "but the complex process by which opinions and individual judgements 'biased' under the effect of the interests and the passions of the opinion makers, may, in certain conditions, once aggregated, produce an opinion or a judgement complying with common interest" (p.93-94). The Smithian spectator would be the equivalent of the invisible hand for moral feelings. The aggregation of such behaviour would transform all opinions - biased because they are partial - into opinions complying with common interest.

Be that as it may, the notion of impartial spectator reflecting an empathetic attitude has asserted itself in modern economic theory. The idea of the impartial spectator was used as early back as 1953, and then in 1955, in two articles, by Harsanyi[4]. He defines two kinds of individual preferences, *ethical preferences* and *personal preferences*. Ethical preferences express the individual's preferences according to impersonal considerations;

personal preferences, on the other hand, express the individual's real preferences, whether they depend on his simple personal interests or on other criteria such as benevolence towards others. The structure of the preferences thus established forms a separation between what a person regards as good from the social point of view, and what he regards as good from his own personal point of view. The distinction between these two forms of preferences lies in the information that is available. In the case of personal preferences, all information is available, while in the case of ethical preferences, the individual finds himself in a situation of risk. He will then use an utilitarian reasoning of Von Neumann Morgenstern's type. If the individual does not have any information on his capacities and his social position, and if he consequently acknowledges that he has equal chances of being in any situation, he will then rationally choose a perspective which provides him with the greatest expected utility. Ethics, within this framework, is associated with expected utilitarianism, in such a way that the individual will choose the social system which maximises his expected utility.

With regard to the five principles which may be drawn from the analysis proposed by Hume, the impartial spectator, as it has been described above, considerably simplifies matters. The impartial spectator is a dispassionate spectator. He extricates himself completely from his passions to adopt a perfectly neutralised position. However, neutralised does not imply neutral, since the impartial spectator establishes a calculation in this neutralised position, which gives him the greatest expected interest, or - which amounts to the same thing - the greatest expected utility. Neutralised implies a quest for one's own interest, without knowing the practical forms of this interest, or what will happen. In short, the individual does not have enough information to make a calculation based on his present situation. Therefore, he can make a calculation in his own interest, but not a self-interested calculation.

The impartial spectator may be summed up within this framework according to two principles:

A *principle of universality*: every individual may find himself in such circumstances that he may actually be, strictly speaking, in the place of anybody.

A *principle of generalisation*: everybody is in a position to adopt this point of view, in such a way that, on the whole, the society will be organised on a redistributive principle corresponding to the principle of expected utility.

More recently, Ken Binmore (1998) proposed a different use of the impartial spectator in the game theory. He makes a distinction between two types of games: the *game of life* and the *game of morals*. The game of life represents real human interactions, in which every individual acts according to his own subjective preference. In this case, in accordance with the game theory, an outcome of the game is stable if it is a Nash equilibrium; every individual maximises his own utility by knowing the behaviour of others.

However, the game of life may be confronted with the problem of the selection of an equilibrium if several outcomes are possible. This selection is carried out thanks to a convention. A particular convention consists in selecting the equilibrium for the player of the game of life by adopting the attitude of an impartial spectator. He places himself under a kind of veil of ignorance as described by Harsanyi, that is to say, in the possibility of being any other individual. The imaginary process which enables the adoption of this attitude results in the game of morals. Thus, Binmore and Harsanyi make a distinction between a real domain of the behaviour in which the individuals act according to their subjective preferences, and a moral domain, in which they imagine they act according to a preference for empathy.

Under this form, the impartial spectator evacuates the principle of evaluation present in Hume. A strong controversy between John Harsanyi and John Rawls made this principle arise again in its interpretation of commitment with regard to the principles defined in the position of the impartial spectator. Indeed, like in the analysis made by Hume, we may wonder what urges the spectator to undertake the respect of principles he adopted in this position, once he is aware of the reality of his situation, and why, in certain circumstances, he may obtain greater benefit by not following these principles.

2. Impartial Spectator, Plurality of Persons and Commitment

The cognitive process of the impartial spectator has been the subject of an important criticism, i.e. that it does not really the plurality of persons take into account. This criticism was addressed to Harsanyi by Rawls. The latter proposed a different version of empathy through a "veil of ignorance" recognising the diversity of the partners in an "original position". However, he was also subjected to much criticism, which led him to clarify his position on the conception of the person he contemplated. On this occasion, he had to clarify the person's commitment regarding the principles defined as an ideal spectator, which finally amounts to redefining a principle of evaluation. Within this framework, a positioning with regard to the Kantian philosophy sets Harsanyi against Rawls. If we regard the subject of Kantian philosophy as a being endowed with reason and as the mirror of mankind- a spectator able to follow a will rising up to the level of the universal- then the parallel with the impartial spectator is immediate.

2.1. The Impartial Spectator and the Plurality of Persons

The reasoning supported by Harsanyi leads to define an arithmetic mean of all the levels of individual utility in society. This result was sharply criticised. On the basis of the same reasoning, Weymark (1991) established that to take into account the possibility of being anybody in society leads to a principle which is different from the principle of expected utility[5]. Harsanyi (1977), aware of the problem, actually proposed an argument according to which the individual is not in a position to be anybody, but finds himself in any situation. Then, the reasoning does not turn to a multitude of persons, but to a particular person who may meet with several situations. Harsanyi's conception of the impartial spectator seems extremely restrictive and does not take into account the plurality of persons, on which Rawls takes precisely the opposite view.

Rawls' analysis is immediately opposed to utilitarianism. He points at the tradition of the impartial spectator in this philosophy. According to him, utilitarianism consists in adopting for society the same principle as for the individual, that is to say the principle of rational choice. We thus grant a quite natural place to the idea of an impartial spectator endowed with sympathy, identifying with the others, since "it is this spectator who is conceived as carrying out the required organization of the desires of all person into one coherent system of desire; it is by this construction that many persons are fused into one[6]. This finally amounts to treating all individuals as one. Since the impartial spectator is able to identify himself with others, one fictitious individual, the spectator, represents the desires of all. It deals with a perfectly rational individual who is able to check the intensity of all desires and consequently, attribute to them the values that are necessary for utilitarian calculation. All persons are thus treated as if they were only one. However, according to Rawls, this mode of enforcement of ethics involves a negation of the notion of the person. "Utilitarianism does not take seriously the distinction between persons[7]. Instead of this fiction, he proposes the principle of the "veil of ignorance". It deals with a situation in which the individual is no longer able to identify himself with others, but finds himself in an impersonal situation, which puts him in a position to be anybody else. This slight shift in the concept may look like a sleight of hand. Nevertheless, it really deals with a change in the way of presenting the problem.

Rawls considers individuals as being in an original position, whose main characteristic is the existence of a veil of ignorance on their situations and the particular aims they may expect from their actions. In fact, it deals with invalidating the effects of the particular contingencies which bring men into conflict with one another and inspire them with the temptation to use the social or natural circumstances to their own personal advantage. The individuals are therefore situated behind a veil of ignorance which affects the information available by restricting it. Placed behind this veil, the individuals are not socio-historically aware of the society which determines them, or of their individual position within this society. They are placed in an impersonal situation, that is to say in a situation where they do not know who they will be. The only information available is a general knowledge of human society, an understanding of political affairs and the principles of economic theory, as well as a basic knowledge of social organisation and the laws of human psychology. The individuals, under this limited information, are placed in an initial position of equity. In this initial position, the individuals adopt a series of principles with regard to the organisation of society and the rules of distribution that will become compulsory, once the veil of ignorance is removed.

While the impartial spectator has all the information available on his situation and on the situation of others at his disposal, and is able to identify with others out of empathy, the impersonal position presupposes, on the contrary, a quasi-absence of information. The individual no longer puts himself in the place of others, he may be anybody else because he does not know his situation. The main part of the critical debate concerning this method consists in assessing the degree of information available in this impersonal situation, and calls into question the principles defended by Rawls.

2.2. The Questioning of Rawls' Principles

The debate about the role of information holds a particular place since various principles established by Rawls are contested on this basis. We shall not examine all the criticisms and remarks addressed to Rawls. His book actually created such a stir that criticisms regarding it were indeed very numerous[8]. Here, we shall only take up the criticisms which led to a new formulation of principles and which naturally urged Rawls to clarify his position with regard to Kant's moral philosophy and, consequently, his conception of the person.

The first criticism examined was formulated by Hoffe (1988). He makes a distinction between uncertainty and risk, in the tradition of economic theory. The deliberation proposed by Rawls is not a decision in uncertainty, but a decision under risk. In a situation of risk, we do not know the decisive factors for the decision, but we may attribute certain values of probability to them. However, for decisions in uncertainty, the definition of probability is impossible. Now, Rawls' original position consists in a situation of risk and not of uncertainty. Indeed, under the veil of ignorance, the number of individuals is given since Rawls precisely rejects the idea of a single impartial spectator, in order to admit a plurality of persons. That being the case, if n is the number of members in society, the probability Pi of being in the position of any member in society is $Pi=1/n$. A probability calculus is therefore possible and in this case, we logically come to the result of expected utilitarianism and not that of the principle of difference. Indeed, Rawls himself states that, in the presence of a general knowledge of probabilities, individuals would choose something closer to expected utilitarianism than to the principle of difference. However, the rejection of expected utilitarianism must not consist in an *a priori*, elimination but rather, must result from deliberation (Nagel, 1973).

The second criticism examined deals with the principle of freedom. It led to important changes in the initial formulation proposed by Rawls. This second criticism was formulated by Hart (1973). It concerns the question of the priorities of freedoms between them. The requirement of the principle of freedom is that a freedom be limited only for the growth of another freedom. It is therefore necessary to arbitrate between various forms of freedom. Let us take a simple example. Let us imagine a farmer and a hunter in conflict over the use of a field. The hunter wishes to go through the field belonging to the farmer to exercise his hunting activity, but the farmer refuses. In this case, what is the priority right: the right of property or the right to move? The original position does not provide for any deliberation on this kind of situation, and even if it were so, there is little chance in obtaining an unanimous deliberation. Therefore, there is a strong probability that the social contract entered into in the original position will not be respected in this kind of situation, once the veil of ignorance removed. In fact, the original position does not provide for enough information to settle this kind of situation. Actually, Rawls (1990) asserts that there is no freedom, which, *a priori*, has priority over another one. Yet, without a solution, the social contract will not be respected. The principles set out then constitute an imperfect guide (Mueller, 1980). The proposed solution consists in introducing more information, for example in the case of the farmer and the hunter, the surface area of the land, the population density, etc. In other words, enough information to settle this kind of dispute. But allowing for this information amounts to making a probability calculus possible. Consequently, more information leads us to give up the principle of difference in favour of the principle of expected utility. And as Harsanyi underlined (1975), in the absence of objective probabilities, individuals instinctively apply subjective probabilities, or take decisions as if they were making a probability calculus. They are even unlikely to abstain from doing it in extreme cases, such as mental or physical illnesses. There, Rawls' position is as follows: to drop the constraint of information under the veil of ignorance in order to keep his first principle coherent, but give up the principle of difference or, on the contrary, to keep the principle of difference, but give up his principle of freedom.

The response put forward by Rawls to keep the overall coherence of his theory intact, without introducing more information, was a new formulation of the first principle and a limitation of the number of freedoms by proposing only the freedoms required for the appropriate development of the moral personality. The precise content of each right is not discussed in the original position. Only the form and the general content of the basic freedoms are determined, and the two principles of justice are adopted. The more subtle discussions on the rights are associated with subsequent stages of negotiation. But this type of argumentation is not enough since we may wonder whether the principles established under the veil of ignorance will be respected in subsequent negotiations. On the contrary, we may think that disobedience will rather be the rule.

The third criticism examined here deals with the following question: once the veil of ignorance is removed, will the partners of the original position follow the principles adopted under this veil? The theoretical framework set by Rawls seems to imply that the respect of the principles is guaranteed by the simple fact that the persons accepted it under the veil of ignorance. Once this veil removed, the obligation they consented to is respected. For example, once the veil of ignorance removed, a rich individual may wonder whether his interests have been treated in an equitable manner since, in the absence of information, it has not been possible to establish probabilities on the various possible distributions. The principle of difference asks for more sacrifice from the rich than the principle of expected utility. The rich individuals' refusal to obey is then probable (Nagel, 1973). To this objection, Rawls (1974) responded that the rich are satisfied with their situation by comparing it with the situation of the most underprivileged. The tendency of the rich to assess their own situation by comparing it with the situation of others would lead them to accept the redistribution to the poorest. Nevertheless, this argument is not very effective since problems of obedience may also come from the poorest of persons (Klévorick, 1974). As Arrow (1972), Harsanyi (1975) or Sen (1989) underlined it, the most underprivileged are likely to include mentally or physically handicapped persons beside the poorest individuals. This leads us to define the combination of primary goods according to several dimensions, and this inevitably implies interpersonal comparisons. If all individuals do not have the same place, an unanimous decision is impossible. The problem of the refusal to obey may arise again since those who are not regarded as the most underprivileged, within the framework of the principle of difference, obtain a lower redistribution. For example, in the original position, an individual does not know whether he will suffer from any handicap, and he may rebel if he is struck by one of these handicaps, regarded as the least serious in the original position, but which he himself considers as the worst thing once the veil of ignorance is removed.

These arguments urged Rawls to clarify his position on the notion of obligation and moral person. He then made a return to Kantian theory.

2.3. Veil of Ignorance and Moral Person

In an article of 1975 entitled *A Kantian Conception of Equality*, but mostly in an article entitled *Kantian Constructivism in Moral Theory* from 1980, Rawls expressed himself on his conception of the moral person. Even if we may think that as early as in 1971, his way of apprehending matters was the same, he reformulated it from that date on, according to a perspective which was very close to that of Kant. The parallel between Rawls' *Theory of Justice* and Kantian analysis is already noticeable in the work of 1971. The original position actually reminds us of a positive will for universality, which is specific to Kant, as it is expressed in the transcription: "Act in accordance with the maxim of a will which could, as universal legislator, be at the same taken as an object". If this first indication does not permit to solve the question of obedience or disobedience, a second indication puts us on the right track. Rawls defines "formal constraints" of law, perfectly and clearly explained in the conditions of the contract pertaining to the original position. Among these constraints, we may note the universality of the enforcement of law, and its acceptability by all.

These indications imply a very strong mark of Kantian philosophy in Rawls' analysis. As Canivet (1984) notes it, the original position is much more than a simple self-interested negotiation under the veil of ignorance, it is close to Kantian autonomy. He underlines that to go from the original position to the principles of justice is a short-circuit. "The short-circuit takes place from the moment when, considering the original position, we pay so much attention to what the parties are doing when they have already entered this position, that we forget the essential fact that they choose to put themselves in this position" (p.174).

In his article of 1980, Rawls clearly explains his approach and responds to the criticisms levelled against him. The partners' autonomy in the original position does not merely concern a *rational autonomy*, but also a *full autonomy*, which refers beyond rational to reason. The reasonable presupposes and subordinates the rational. The reasonable prevails over the rational. The rational corresponds to the Kantian hypothetical imperative, to the promotion of particular interests in view of achieving specific goals. The reasonable, on the other hand, is the acceptance of the constraints established in the original position and is therefore associated with the categorical imperative[9].

Individuals are not only rational, they are also reasonable and therefore, they conform to the principles established in the original position. This is not because these principles are given as an external law, but because the individuals have set themselves these principles by committing themselves in the original position, and keeping their commitment in accordance with reason.

On this point, expected utilitarianism obviously departs from Rawls' position. The principle of expected utilitarianism stems from a conception different from moral personality. Harsanyi more particularly refers to Kant several times, but clearly in a different perspective from that of Rawls. It therefore deals with two very different conceptions of the impersonal position occupied by the individuals.

Harsanyi (1958, 1977) rejects the categorical imperative and asserts that only the hypothetical imperative associated with rationality has a meaning in his theory: "... All we can prove are hypothetical imperatives of the form: if you want to act in a way that an impartially sympathetic observer would approve of, then do such and such" (p.62). He then interprets the Kantian criterion of universality as a simple principle of generalisation. In one of his last writings, he actually asserts forcefully that he is opposed to Kant: "I shall argue against Kant that morality is primarily a servant of many other values rather than itself the highest value of human life" (1995, p.319). The basic foundation of morality, according to utilitarianism, would be to urge people to help other people in the achievement of their own objectives, most of these objectives being immoral. In this sense, Harsanyi considers that morality is the servant of other human values, and not the highest value. The rejection of the categorical imperative then induces a radically different conception of the individual who is detached, or more exactly extricated, from his personal situation. It does not deal with a person endowed with reason, but with a rational individual calculating in a situation of risk.

3. The Impartial Discussant

The impartial discussant is another figure of the ideal observer. We shall use this term in reference to the ethics of discussion. Jurgen Habermas and Karl Otto Apel founded this new philosophical perspective. Habermas expressed himself several times on the meaning that should be given to the partners of the discussion, by proposing a formula close to that of the impartial spectator. In fact, he clearly uses the property of empathy, but he also greatly diverges from the conception of the impartial spectator, as it has been described previously. For this reason, the term of impartial discussant avoids any confusion.

The ethics of discussion relates both to the rational conditions of an *impartial* assessment of action and to the specific social context of modernity within whose framework it falls. In this sense, it takes into account both an ethical dimension of the individual who is able to extricate himself from his situation, and a social dimension of the individual who is embedded in social and historical modernity.

We shall not make a complete presentation of the ethics of discussion here. Our presentation will be limited to the elements which directly concern the construction of the impartial discussant‘s figure[10]. Given the importance of Kantian moral philosophy in the debate about the impartial spectator, the positioning of the ethics of discussion with regard to this philosophy will be the subject of the first part of the presentation. We shall then analyse the notion of the impartial discussant, before clarifying Habermas' position with regards to the principle of commitment.

3.1. The Ethics of Discussion: a Post-Kantian Philosophy

The ethics of discussion is a so-called post-Kantian form of contemporary ethics. Like Kant's moral philosophy, it tries to establish an universal procedure representing morality so that it may be transcribed into a maxim of action legitimating the use of practical reason. This procedure is consequently independent from the particular content to which it is likely to apply. Taken from this point of view, it falls within the tradition of Kantian moral philosophy, thus contrasts with the Aristotelian attempts to apprehend good life within particular contexts.

Nevertheless, it diverges from Kantian moral philosophy by reformulating the framework within which the search for universality, which is specific to the maxim of action, must be interpreted. Kantian moral philosophy is, above all, a philosophy of conscience. The Kantian categorical imperative is associated with a capacity for universalisation in such a way that we must always treat the others as an end in themselves. But this duty is an injunction which everybody's conscience, in a solitary way, addresses to itself. The respect of this duty then depends mainly on willpower.

Conscience addresses a duty of universality where an individual's will extricates itself from personal and self-interested motives. This will must get rid of egocentric tendencies. In a world where there are many solicitations not to respect this duty, an individual's will turns out to be fragile. The exercise is all the more difficult since the specificity of a fragile will is that it fools itself and conceals purely selfish interests under signs of universality (Cusset, 2001).

In these conditions, only a considerable amount of willpower, characterising a being of reason, may reach the target of giving the form of an universal law to the maxims of its actions. Although such a strength cannot be guaranteed, it is important to bear in mind that an individual's will is free and that it cannot be suspected of perversity or fragility.

The ethics of discussion, taking note of the weight lying heavily on solitary conscience, proposes to render the conditions of universalisation of the maxims of actions in the empirical world more effective. It abandons the philosophy of conscience, in which it perceives a surrealistic and heroic effort. On this occasion, it also levels a criticism at the philosophers, especially Rawls[11], who reproduce the "monologism" of the Kantian ethic. It thus rejects the position according to which I may inwardly, monologically, adopt all the roles in order to neutralise my own point of view and reach an ideal neutrality.

It shifts the centre of comprehension of the impartial formation of an individual's will through the construction of a procedure of intersubjective cooperation. The philosophy of conscience is replaced by a philosophy of intersubjective relations, where participation in a discussion free from any constraint constitutes an act which is representative of an individual's will. This shift of the centre of reflection is, for Habermas, a logical perspective of the deployment of post-Kantian philosophy. He underlines: "Autonomy is not a distributive concept and cannot be accomplished individually. In an empathetic way, we may assert that in this sense, a person can only be free if all the persons belonging to this community are also free. I want to underline here the following thing. With his notion of autonomy, Kant himself already introduced a concept which can only be fully deployed within an intersubjective context" (Habermas, 2003, p.22).

But above all, this intersubjectivist perspective is made necessary in a modern society where cultural pluralism implies, to a certain extent, that the world is perceived and interpreted from different perspectives which are specific to different groups. "We may therefore judge that a kind of interpretative pluralism intervenes in the determination of the vision of the world and the comprehension of oneself, the perception of the values as well as the interests which are specific to the persons whose individual story is embedded in traditions and particular forms of life which define the latter." (Habermas, 2003, p.17). In fact, to admit this pluralism presupposes another approach of the principle of universality of the maxims of actions. Habermas again supports this point of view by noting that "this multiplicity of interpretative perspectives is the reason for which any monological reflection leading to the recognition of maxims, which, from my point of view, would be acceptable as general laws, does not exhaust the meaning of the principle of universalisation." (Habermas, 2003, p.18).

Thus, the philosophy of conscience, associated with monological deliberation, or with the principle of introspective equilibrium, does not seem to hold. It is replaced by a dialogical deliberation which automatically involves several persons in their intersubjectivity. The will leaves the sphere of solitary conscience to enter into a practice of discussion. The Kantian principle of universality is translated into a principle of discussion.

The validation of moral norms now stems from a principle of discussion insofar as it means a form of practical intersubjectivity. "The norms that may aspire to validity are only the norms that are likely to meet with the adherence of all the parties concerned as participants in a practical discussion." (Habermas, 1991/1992, p.17).

But what discussion does it deal with? What is meant by participants in a discussion? All discussions are not ethical. Very often, the urgency of situations means a multitude of discussions that are as vain as they are ineffective, with participants whose arguments are close to conviction, but hardly acceptable for other participants. The goal of the ethics of discussion is precisely to clarify the framework within which a discussion becomes a procedure permitting to construct a point of view established in conditions of impartial universality and reflecting our practical choices.

3.2. The Impartial Discussant and Argumentation

Discussion is above all rendered necessary within contexts where disagreements occupy a central place and reflect the conflicts of our convictions. It is essential in conditions where the actions which we have undertaken produce conflicting interactions, forcing us to revise the situation and contemplate a new way of perceiving our practices.

The ethics of discussion is aimed at clarifying the framework within which the discussion becomes ethical. It deals with describing the procedure by which each participant in the discussion submits to the force of the latter, with a view of producing an universally accepted norm in accordance with our practical orientations. This discussion is not achieved under the pressure of an absolute search for consensus; discussion does not try to obtain consensus at all cost. It differs clearly from negotiation. It is the cooperative search for universality, a common interest, and as such, it contrasts with negotiation as a compromise between diverging interests. It produces a common interest eliminating the power struggles inherent to the negotiation.

It proceeds through a discursive exchange of words in which all the opinions are competing and are equally open to criticism. The validity of the norm stems from the non-restrictive force of the best argument. The ethics of discussion rests on the validation of argumentation.

To take up the economic terms specific to the impartial spectator, negotiation is carried out on subjective preferences which bring particular interests into play, while discussion refers to impartial ethical preferences characterising the quest for a common interest. Therefore, the ethics of discussion does not construct an intersubjectivist philosophy of actors negotiating on the basis of their subjective preferences. Rather, it constructs a philosophy where intersubjectivity presupposes everyone's ability to adopt an universal point of view, reflecting their aptitude for extricating themselves from their own situation and putting themselves in the place of others. The role of participant in a discussion presupposes the adoption of a hypothetical attitude, a cognitive capacity for empathy as a mode of enforcement of the Kantian categorical imperative. Habermas perfectly sums up this presupposition when he asserts: "It is only as participants in an inclusive dialogue aimed at a consensus, that we are led to exercise the cognitive virtue of empathy, in view of our reciprocal differences which arise in the perception of a common situation. We are supposed to learn the way every participant, on the basis of his own perspective, would proceed within the context of an universalisation of all interests concerned. We may thus understand practical discussion as a framework within which the problem of the enforcement of the categorical imperative would arise. The participants in a discussion may only hope to reach an agreement on what is in the equal interest of all as long as everyone gives in to this exercise which consists of trying to adopt the others' point of view..." (Habermas, 2003, p.18).

The ethics of discussion therefore constructs a new figure of the ideal observer, under the features of an impartial discussant endowed with the faculty for empathy. Therefore, the framework of the discussion is not a "normal communication" but a communication between persons adopting a hypothetical attitude. But unlike Kantian philosophy, this hypothetical attitude takes place within the framework of an intersubjectivity which is peculiar to the discussion. The aptitude for empathy which is recognised in every participant only constitutes a principle of generalisation, where everyone has this aptitude, but it is not sufficient to obtain the universal validity of norms. The ethics of discussion adds a procedure of universalisation to this principle, through the rule of argumentation. "It is not enough for an individual to wonder, after thinking twice, whether it would be possible for him to adhere to a norm. It is not even enough for all individuals to conduct this deliberation on their own for their vote to be then recorded. What is demanded is a real argumentation in which the persons concerned participate, in cooperation. Only an intersubjective process of comprehension may lead to an agreement of an introspective nature; it is only then that the participants may know whether they reached a certain conviction in common." (Habermas, 1983/1986, p.80).

Norms will only be valid if the side effects and the predictable consequences which they produce satisfy the interest of each participant. The intersubjective acceptability of the argumentation therefore stems from its rationality, the acceptance of the results and the consequences of this norm. This does not mean that the norm is set once and for all, on the basis of objective criteria. Only the intersubjectivity of the discussion permits to assess, in an impartial manner, up to what point the consequences of a norm may be accepted without restraint. The interchangeability of roles guarantees that intersubjectivity is compatible with an impartial point of view. But we must not see impartiality as a normative device. It takes root in the very structures of argumentation. The effort made by the participant in a discussion is not an extraordinary achievement, but is rather what the argumentative use of the language demands quite normally. This finally presupposes a universal pragmatic analysis of language.

Without going into the details of this analysis, the essential element consists in retaining that what a partner in the discussion says must be in agreement with the context of his enunciation. Although no positive criterion permits to judge the acceptability of an argument in the discussion, there nevertheless is a negative criterion of acceptability. An argument will be acceptable and will be the subject of agreement, at least temporarily, if it passes the negative criterion of acceptability of the *performative contradiction*[12]. The performative contradiction is the impossibility of reconciling the meaning of the proposal with the context of its enunciation, that is to say, the inability to render an argument effective within a given context.

The ethics of discussion constructs an impartial discussant who adopts a hypothetical attitude in regard to a normal mode of communication. His effort of extraction from his situation is not a metaphysical presupposition, but rather, it requires the use of language to aspire to the validity of the arguments on which the individuals' practical choices rely. Claims to validity in everybody's arguments, to be accepted, must be founded rationally and must be able to receive the assent of all; this ultimately presupposes each participant's ability to put himself in the place of others in order to establish this validity.

But, concerning the theme which is dealt with here, we are still to know what exactly urges an individual to keep his commitments and to respect the arguments that were validated during the discussion in his practical orientations. Is it not possible for his subjective preferences, and even his irrational convictions, to resurface once he is extricated from this discussion?

3.3. The Act of Discussion as Commitment

The ethics of discussion is based on intersubjectivity. Moral norms stemming from discussion are recognised as valid by the participants in this discussion. But to consider the genesis of norms on the basis of an argued discussion does not say anything about the ultimate recognition of these norms through a commitment to respecting them once they have been established. Finally, does not the fact that the subject considers these norms as legitimate and undertakes to apply them, imply that he ultimately recognises them as legitimate, in an internal relation between self and self, and not because they stem from a discussion? At the end of the day, is not the conscience of the subject essential for him to undertake the respect these norms? This would amount to legitimating the intersubjective practice of discussion through an ultimate resort to the solitary subject.

For Habermas, one must indeed recognise that self-awareness, the ability to adopt an introspective attitude with regard to one's own beliefs, is essential because it is a condition for participation in the public discussion. However, another at least equally important requirement appears through discussion. The participants in a discussion, as they enter into an argumentative practice, are ready to satisfy the expectations of cooperation held by the others. To that end, they adopt the attitude of the impartial spectator, but the discussion into which they enter only has a meaning because they also undertake to respect the terms of it. They respect the validity of the norms stemming from the discussion because the discussion itself makes them commit to do so. A participant who would not be ready to commit himself would simply not enter into the discussion. It is because we are willing to cooperate that we cooperate and that we respect the terms of this cooperation. "Once we enter into an argumentative practice, we let ourselves be caught up again, so to speak, in a social link which persists, even when we are dealing with individuals who entered into competition in search of the better argument." (Habermas, 2003, p.25).

This interpretation may be understood by the fact that the speech act is a committing act. The involvement in a discussion only takes on a meaning because the illocutory act implies at the same time the capacity of honouring what we say. Without this property, language would only be a piece of information or a manipulation, and not a communication or a discussion. Thus, when we enter into a discussion, we agree at the same time to respect the presuppositions of this discussion. The inter-subjectivist space of discussion is also, and above all, a space which already urges the individual to respect the conditions of the discussion and more particularly, respect the validity of the norms stemming from this discussion.

If communicational freedom is an essential condition, implying everybody's free involvement in the discussion, as long as everybody is committed, everybody also undertakes to respect the terms of the discussion. The discussion then takes on a form of authority.

This perspective implies three conditions: first, the freedom of involvement with regard to the discussion. Without the freedom of involvement, the discussion itself does not make any sense. The ethics of discussion therefore presupposes the freedom of discussion. Then, the participants' sincerity is required. Without sincerity, the very involvement in the discussion is truncated. Finally, it is important to mention the participants' symmetry, according to which everybody must be in a position to put themselves in the place of the others. If not, social positions and relations of authority would determine the validity of argumentations. These three conditions are concomitant. We cannot establish any classification between the three conditions, but all three must be respected. For example, demanding sincerity and symmetry would not make any sense if there were no freedom of involvement to enter into the discussion. But freedom is not a sufficient condition for sincerity. These conditions are strong and we may see in them an obvious limit to the ethics of discussion. The discussion concerns persons who are already willing to reach an agreement, who therefore do not have any divergent interests on the whole. Otherwise, how can struggles for power and manipulation be avoided? Where the ethics of discussion reproaches Kantian philosophy for its impracticability, demanding a heroic act of will or, failing that, postulating its freedom, it nevertheless finds itself in a similar situation. To suppose a discussion in which the illocutory act implies commitment and gives an universal force to the norms stemming from it, presupposes the freedom of discussion, sincerity as well as the participants' symmetry. How is it possible not to imagine that the egocentric interests limiting the will of any person may also be at work in a discussion-involving act, unless we consider that the discussion only takes place between persons who already have a common interest. But this indeed is a great limitation of all possible forms of discussion.

4. Conclusion

The ideal observer has taken several forms in economic analysis, even though its main form is that of the impartial spectator. The most recent form, which still has not been explicitly used in modern economic theory, is that of an impartial discussant. This concept might play a relatively important role in the coming years, given the interest which the ethics of discussion is arousing in fields of economic analysis, such as the environment or development. The participative approaches referring to the multiplicity of actors and their involvement in debates, with a view of defining the choices of economic policies are increasingly numerous indeed.

Nevertheless, whatever their forms, the main objective on which the construction of an ideal observer rests is the individual's possibility to extricate himself from his personal and subjective situation, in order to give these moral judgements an universal perspective. This mode of reasoning constructs a certain kind of duality between two aspects of the individual: a subjective, personal aspect and an universal, impersonal aspect. On this occasion, constructing duality without proposing a schizophrenic individual presupposes the question of the individual's commitment in regard to universal principles. From this point of view, an ethical question, that of the individual's commitment, is directly set in modern economic theory.

Notes

1. Here also, a distinction could be established between altruism and benevolence. On this subject, see F.R. Mahieu (1998).
2. In this section, we shall mostly follow the argumentation of John Rawls (2000).
3. In such a perspective, Smith would be much closer to Hume. It would then be interesting to see what actually separates both authors.
4. Vickrey also discussed this idea in two articles in 1945 and 1960.
5. For a presentation and detailed discussion, see Roemer (1996).

6. For the quotations, we use the 2003 edition of the book *A Theory of Justice* of 1971. Quotation p.24.
7. Ib. p.24
8. One of the major criticisms of Rawls' book was that of Nozick (1974). We shall not examine his criticism since it deals with a question which is different to the question treated here.
9. Although numerous parallels between Rawls and Kant may be drawn, important differences still remain. See Canivet's article for detailed descriptions.
10. For a more complete presentation, please refer the works of Habermas and Apel, but also Yves Cusset (2001).
11. See Habermas' work, *Morale et Communication* (*Moralbewusstsein und Kommunikatives Handeln*) .
12. The performative contradiction is a term initially proposed by Apel and also used by Habermas. However, it gave rise to a debate between the two authors to know up to what point this criterion may constitute a sufficient criterion. Apel, in opposition to Habermas, more particularly expresses the need to have resort to a transcendental analysis as an ultimate means of judging the universality of the enforcement of a norm.

References

Appel, K. O. 1989. *Penser avec Habermas contre Habermas*. French translation 1990. Paris: L'éclat.

Appel, K. O. 1994. *Ethique de la discussion*. Paris: éditions du Cerf.

Arnsperger, Ch. 2001. "Entre impartialité, horizons de sens et précarité existentielle, les fondements de l'éthique économique et sociale". In Arnsperger Ch., Larrère C., Ladrière J., *Trois essais sur l'éthique économique et sociale*, 19-67. Paris: INRA éditions.

Arrow, K.J. 1973. "Some Ordinalist Utilitarian Notes on Rawls'Theory of Justice". *Journal of Philosophy*, 70 (9), 245-263.

Binmore, K. 1998. *Game Theory and the Social Contract. Volume 2: Just Playing*. MIT Press.

Boudon, R. 2000. *Etudes sur les sociologues classiques*. Paris : PUF.

Canivet, M. 1984. "Justice et bonheur chez Rawls et chez Kant". In Ladrière J. and Van Parijs Ph. (eds), *Fondements d'une théorie de la justice*. Louvain-la-Neuve: Institut supérieur de philosophie.

Cusset, Y. 2001. *L'espoir de la discussion*. Paris: Michalon.

Eisenberg, N.; Miller, P. A.1987. "Empathy, Sympathy, and Altruism: Empirical and Conceptual Links". In Eisenberg N. and Strayer J. (eds),

Empathy and its Development, chapter 13, 292-316. Cambridge: Cambridge University Press.

Fontaine, P. 1997. "Identification and Economic Behavior. Sympathy and Empathy in Historical Perspective". *Economics and Philosophy*, 13, 261-280.

Forsé, M. ; Parodi, M. 2002. "Homo oeconomicus et spectateur impartial". *Revue de l'OFCE*, 82, 165-230.

Gaertner, S.L.; Dovidio, J.F. 1977. "The Subtlety of White Racism, Arousal, and Helping Behavior". *Journal of Personality and Social Psychology*, 35, 691-707.

Habermas, J. 1983. *Moralbewusstsein und Kommunikatives Handeln.* French translation 1986, *Morale et communication*. Paris: éditions du Cerf.

Habermas, J. 1991. *Erläuterungen zur Diskursethik.* Frankfurt: Suhrkamp Verlag. French translation 1992, *De l'éthique de la discussion.* Paris: éditions du Cerf.

Habermas, J. 2003. *L'éthique de la discussion et la question de la vérité.* Paris: Grasset.

Harsanyi, J.C. 1953. "Cardinal Utility in Welfare Economics and in the Theory of Risk-Taking". *Journal of Political Economy*, 61, 434-435.

Harsanyi, J.C. 1955. "Cardinal Welfare, Individualistic Ethics and Interpersonnal Comparison of Utility". *Journal of Political Economy*, 63.

Harsanyi, J.C. 1958. "Ethics in Terms of Hypothetical Imperatives". *Mind*, 47, 305-316.

Harsanyi, J.C. 1975. "Can the Maximin Principle Serve as a Basis for Morality? A Critique of John Rawls' Theory". *American Political Science Review,* 69, 2.

Harsanyi, J.C. 1977. *Rational Behavior and Bargaining Equilibrium in Games and Social Situations*. Cambridge: Cambridge University Press.

Harsanyi, J.C. 1986. "Individual Utilities and Utilitarian Ethics". In Diekmann A. and Mitter P. (Eds), *Paradoxal Effects of Social Behavior*. Heidelberg: Physica, 1-12.

Harsanyi, J.C. 1995. "A Theory of Prudential Values and a Rule Utilitarian Theory of Morality". *Social Choice and Welfare*, 12, 319-333.

Hart, H.L.A. 1973. "Rawls on Liberty and its Priority". *University of Chicago Law Review*, 40.

Hoffe, O. 1988. *L'Etat et la justice*. Paris: Vrin.

Hoffman, M. L. 1981. "Is Altruism Part of Human Nature". *Journal of Personality and Social Psychology*, 40 (1), 121-137.

Hume, D. 1738. *A Treatise of Human Nature*. Oxford: Clarendon Press 1966.

Kant, E. 1785. *Grundlegung zur Metaphysik der sitten*. French translation, Fondements de la métaphysique des mœurs. Paris: Delagrave, 1975.

Klévorick, A. 1974. "Discussion". *American Economic Review*, 64 (2), 158-161.

Mahieu, F-R. 1998. "Altruisme et ingérence. Modalités de l'altruisme dans l'analyse économique". In Mahieu F-R. and Raporport H. (Eds), Altruisme, analyses économiques, 113-137. Paris: Economica.

Mercer, P. 1972. *Sympathy and Ethics: A Study of the Relationship between Sympathy and Morality with Special Reference to Hume's Treatise.* Clarendon Press.

Mueller, D.C. 1980. *Public Choice*. Cambridge: Cambridge University Press.

Nagel T. 1973. "Rawls on Justice". *Philosophical Review*, 82, 220-234.

Nozick, R. 1974. *Anarchy, State and Utopia*. New York: Basic Books.

Piliavin, I.M.; Rodin, J.; Piliavin, J.A. 1969. "Good Samaritanism: An Underground Phenomenon". *Journal of Personality and Social Psychology*, 13, 289-299.

Rawls, J. 1971. *A Theory of Justice*. Cambridge Mass.: Belknap Press. edition 2003.

Rawls, J. 1974. "Some Reasons for the Maximin Criterion". *American Economic Review*, 64 (2), 141-145.

Rawls, J. 1975. "A Kantian Conception of Equality".Cambridge Review, 96 (2225), 94-99.

Rawls, J. 1980. "Kantian Constructivism in Moral Theory". *Journal of Philosophy*, 77, 515-572.

Rawls, J. 1982. "Social Unity and Primary Goods". In Sen A. and Williams B. (Eds), *Utilitarianism and Beyond.* Cambridge: Cambridge University Press, 159-185.

Rawls, J. 1990. *Justice as Fairness, A Restatement*. Miméo. Cambridge: Harvard University.

Rawls, J. 2000. *Lectures on the History of Moral Philosophy*. Cambridge Mass.: Harvard University Press, edition 2002.

Roemer, J.E. 1996. *Theories of Distributive Justice*. Cambridge Mass.: Harvard University Press.

Sen, A.K. 1989. *The Territory of Justice*. Discussion paper 1425. Cambridge Mass.: Harvard Institute of Economic Research.

Smith, A. 1759. The Theory of Moral Sentiments. Oxford: Oxford University Press, 1976.

Sugden, R. 2002. "Beyond Sympathy and Empathy: Adam Smith's Concept of Fellow-Feeling". *Economics and Philosophy*, 18, 63-87.

Vickrey, W. 1945. "Measuring marginal utility by reactions to risk". *Econometrica*, 13, 319-333.

Vickrey, W. 1960. "Utility, strategy, and social decision rules". *Quarterly Journal of Economics*, 74, 507-535.

Weymark, J. 1991."Areconsideration of the Harsanyi-Sen Debate on Utilitarianism". In Elster J. and Roemer J.E. (eds), *Interpersonal Comparisons of Well-being*. Cambridge: Cambridge University Press.

Kantian Economics: Retrospect and Prospect[1]

Jérôme Ballet
Patrick Jolivet

Although it is not unusual to broach the relation between ethics and economics through altruism (see the first part of this book), in this article, we propose to explore the concept of commitment, or the categorical imperative of Kantian type, as determining the behaviour of economic agents. Kant distinguishes hypothetical imperatives from categorical imperatives: "If the action is only right as a means *with a view of obtaining something else*, then the imperative is *hypothetical*; if it is represented as right in itself [...], then it is *categorical*" (Kant, 1785/1994, p. 88). Although the first imperatives comply with the economic approach, it is more original to try to introduce the second imperatives into such analysis.

While altruism consists in integrating the welfare of others into the objective function of an individual, the moral commitment prompted by the categorical imperative consists in acting in relation to a norm (ethics), whatever the behaviour and the welfare of others might be. The hypothesis of Kantian behaviour is therefore characterised by an attempt to found a non-selfish form of individual behaviour beyond altruistic behaviour, as it is usually formalised in economics. This hypothesis seems to be spreading and various developments now integrate it (Laffont, 1975; Sen, 1975; Collard, 1978; Cornes and Sandler, 1984; Bordignon, 1990; Roemer, 1996; *etc.*). According to Wolfelsperger (1999), this success might come from the mention, in Samuelson's founding article of public economics (1954), of the Kantian solution.

This article proposes a critical panorama of Kantian-inspired economics. By this appellation, we mean a set of works, which explicitly use a reference to Kant's moral philosophy, and more particularly, to the notion of the categorical imperative. This "Kantian economics" actually constitutes a relatively heterogeneous body; it leans on three different interpretations of the categorical imperative, founding an ordinary Kantianism linked to the principle of generalisation, a principle of unconditionality of action, and a concept of commitment[2]. Therefore, this article does not propose a reading of the various possibilities of integrating the hypothesis of morality into the economic theory[3], but rather, it is a presentation of a field, which is more restricted than that of the integration of Kantian ethics into the determinants of individual behaviour.

In a second section, we shall examine the various ways taken to formalise the Kantian hypothesis in economics from the principle of generalisation. They have enabled the construction of an "ordinary" Kantianism. This section is mainly focused on the first models which achieved this integration. A third section establishes the difference between the Kantian principle adapted to economics and the principle of reciprocity. It brings to light a principle of unconditionality of action. A fourth section focuses on the notion of commitment, which is interpreted within the Kantian framework, but takes on various forms, for example with the distinction between Kantianism and "super-

Kantianism". Finally, a fifth section concludes on the lessons, which should be drawn from the Kantian hypothesis in economics.

1. "Kantian Economics": Presentation

The so-called *Kantian economics* is an attempt to integrate the Kantian categorical imperative into economic theory. It deals with proposing a model of behaviour, which complies with the maxim of action formulated by Kant: "Act only according to the maxim which makes that you may want it to become a universal law at the same time"[4]. One of the first models trying this integration is that of Laffont (1975): he proposes to add a moral rule of behaviour to the process of individual optimisation. His hypothesis is that the agents may, in certain cases, deviate from the selfish behaviour generally attributed to the *homo oeconomicus*, and adopt "collective behaviours" voluntarily and individually (Pareto-improving at the macroeconomic level[5]).

1.1. The Position of Laffont

According to Laffont (1975), the Kantian ethics of behaviour would consist, for an agent, in acting by assuming that everybody else will act like him. Therefore, the so-called 'Kantian' solution refers here to the principle of universality of the Kantian categorical imperative; this hypothesis presupposes that the individual acts in search of personal objectives, but also in accordance with the moral rule as formulated by Kant in his maxim of action.

In order to represent this behaviour and its economic consequences, Laffont takes the example of a macro-externality of consumption: the welfare of an agent is affected negatively by an additive externality to which all the other agents contribute. Let us consider with him the case of a large beach to which numerous persons (who do not know each other) go every day;

bins are placed every hundred metres, and everybody's welfare depends on the total quantity of waste spread on the beach. The fact that an individual throws his own litter on the beach only marginally increases the total quantity of rubbish, therefore only affecting his welfare in an insignificant way; however, to go to the nearest bin requires a particular amount of effort[6].

In a situation where the individual welfare depends positively on the quality of the environment (public good), but negatively on the participation in its production, the best configuration for an individual in terms of welfare is one where everybody else participates in the production – except him, then one where everybody (including him) participates, then one where nobody participates, and finally, which constitutes the worst configuration, one where nobody participates – except him.

If this description is valid for all the individuals, we are faced with a situation of the prisoner's dilemma type, where nobody participates in the quality of the environment, while everybody's welfare would have been higher if everybody had participated. To go by Sen's writing (1975), any individual (*ego*, *E*) has the choice between doing nothing (E_0) or participating (E_1) in the production of the public good, knowing that the others (*alter*, *A*) are faced with the same alternative A_0 or A_1. The classic result of the above example is A_0E_0, while from the individual point of view, the situations are classified according to the following order of preference: $A_1E_0 > A_1E_1 > A_0E_0 > A_0E_1$.

Laffont wonders what is the decision-making process which makes that, individuals however, and still more in their majority, do not throw their rubbish directly on the beach (the reason must not be, according to him, an effect of demonstration, if it deals with anonymous individuals). In their majority, the agents adopt a rule of behaviour (not to throw one's litter anywhere), by assuming that the others will do the same. Laffont calls this a Kantian rule of behaviour. To go by what the author says, the economic question of the individuals' coordination may find part of its explanation in ethics, in "the social responsibilities of the citizens", going "beyond selfish maximisation" (1975, pp. 431-432).

Let us suppose that an agent consumes two goods *X* and *Y*, which provide him with utility, but that the total consumption of *Y* by all the economic agents negatively affects the agent's utility (which Laffront calls macro-externality of consumption). In the standard case, the consumer adopts a parametric form of behaviour in relation to the externality; there results from it a Pareto-inefficient situation of divergence between the agent's private marginal rate of substitution[7] and the social *mrs* (private *mrs* is above a social *mrs*, there is over-consumption by everybody of the good object of macro-externality, and everybody's utility is accordingly reduced). The modification of the representative agent's ethics consists in supposing that "when he maximises his utility function, he assumes that everybody behaves as he does" (1975, p. 433): the macro-externality on *Y* is integrated into the individual optimisation calculus in such a manner that the private and social mrs are equivalent, and Paretian efficiency restored. Laffont concludes that "this Kantian behaviour realises the optimum that would be attained with selfish behaviour only if appropriate taxes were imposed on the consumption of good Y" (1975, p. 433).

Let us sum up Laffont's position:

1. Kantian ethics (note that the author does not use the term of imperative, categorical and/or hypothetical in his article) consists in supposing a form of mimicry of the behaviours: "We postulate that a typical agent assumes (according to Kant's moral) that the other agents will act as he does, and he maximises his utility function under this new constraint. […] Our proposition is then equivalent to a special assumption of others' behaviour" (1975, pp. 430-431).

2. In the presence of a great number of agents, whose welfare is affected by an additive externality resulting from the individual consumption of a good, the adoption by everybody of a Kantian ethic permits the restoration of the equality of private and social mrs, and thus the Paretian efficiency. This presupposes that the agents choose their plan of consumption by knowing beforehand the optimum to be reached: it is necessary "to accept the (radical?) idea that *preferences and behaviour are endogenous to the system*, and to try by means of an information campaign to induce a Kantian type of behaviour, even if a negligible set of consumers does not comply" (1975, p. 434, *highlighted by us*).
3. From the point of view of the public policies, the existence of such behaviour modifies the traditional modes of internalising externalities. Taxation is not very pertinent in the above example, since the externality does not come so much from the consumption of the good as from the modes of rejection of the waste. The solutions of control and/or repression may then give way to other instruments for the State: "Such behaviour may be induced by making people aware of a macroeconomic constraint. The State may play a major role in the realisation of conditions favourable to the awakening of this consciousness" (1975, p. 430).

This example sets the question of the moral or ethical framework, within which individual choice is formed. According to our example, and in the absence of any moral rule of behaviour, the situation preferred by the rational *homo oeconomicus* is A_1E_0. The hypothesis of ethical behaviour is introduced in Laffont's article by assuming that the preferences are endogenous to the system and that the individual decides to act knowing that the optimal state will be achieved if everybody else acts like him. As the philosopher Peter Koslowski notes: "as soon as the individual assumes the universal in his preferences, his preference is transformed in such a way that he prefers the alternative A_1E_1 to the alternative A_1E_0 […]. The *prisoner's dilemma* disappears as soon as moral motivation is taken for a universal motivation" (1998, p. 44).

1.2. An "Ordinary" Kantianism

However, as Wolfelsperger (1999) points out, such a solution to the prisoner's dilemma actually implies solving two distinct questions. The first concerns the existence of a solution: supposing that everybody assumes the universal in their preferences, can we characterise the solution to the game as being Pareto-optimal? The second question is that of the feasibility of the solution: supposing that the solution exists, how can it be achieved? According to this author, the Kantian solution in economics fails in both cases: it is neither in a position to respond to the question of the existence of the solution, nor is it in a position to produce any satisfactory analysis from the point of view of the feasibility of this solution.

Let us sum up his arguments here. Concerning the question of the existence of a solution, the moral rule of Kantianism is insufficient: if it may produce the solution, it deals with exceptional circumstances. Indeed, "the categorical imperative is not aimed at guiding men towards the best fulfilment of their subjective ends by more particularly compensating for the imperfection in their institutions" (Wolfelsperger, 1999, p. 894). While the normal context of Kantianism consists in confronting the individual with the obligations which the institutions impose on him, the models proposed by the Kantian-inspired economics presuppose precisely that there are no institutions of coordination. This shift of problem makes the existence of the Kantian solution much more uncertain.

Concerning the question of feasibility, two arguments are put forward. Firstly, such an approach more or less contradicts

Kantian philosophy itself. As Wolfelsperger (1999, p. 883) underlines it perfectly, in this kind of reasoning, "what is supposed to urge the individuals to follow this law is that, actually, thanks to it, they will reach the Pareto-optimal state which they want. But, from a Kantian point of view, it is contradictory to make morality a means to attain an end. It is therefore necessary to dissociate the question of the nature of the rules from the question of the reasons for adhering to them." In *La métaphysique des mœurs* (*Metaphysik der Sitten*), Kant is very clear on this point: "The moral value of an action accomplished from a sense of duty does not come from the *aim* which is to be attained through it, but from the maxim on the basis of which it is decided" (1785/1994, p. 68).

The "Kantian behaviour" postulated by Laffont, which presupposes an *ex ante* knowledge of the optimum and a conditional principle of generalisation (such action is chosen further to the question *what would happen if everybody acted in the same way?*), comes within the framework of an utilitarian philosophy rejected by Kant himself when it deals with defining the categorical imperative. If the desire for happiness actually is a universal desire among men, "we may call prudence in the strictest sense of the word the skill in the choices of the appropriate means to attain our greatest personal happiness. Consequently, the imperative relating to the choice of the means with a view to personal happiness, that is to say the prescription of prudence, is still simply hypothetical; the action is not absolutely commanded, but it is only so as a means to attain another end" (Kant, 1785/1994, p. 90).

Furthermore, if the integration of morality depends on the sought result, then the behaviour is perfectly strategic. In this case, the prisoner's dilemma reappears insofar as it is always preferable to be amoral when the others are moral.

Finally, the Kantian solution as proposed by Laffont, offers a prospect of results, which is both unlikely and deviates singularly from Kantian philosophy. Supposing that this kind of model constitutes a solution to the prisoner's dilemma, it does not really deal with a Kantian solution. The philosophy retained and the conditionality of the principle lead to describe this framework as an "everyday Kantianism" (Elster, 1989, 1995), an ordinary Kantianism (Wolfelsperger, 1999), or a principle of rational commitment (Harsanyi, 1980)[8]. However, this proposal is not the only one that has been formulated: two other approaches referring explicitly to Kant have been put forward. They are also aimed at going beyond the framework of the prisoner's dilemma.

1.3. Two Alternative Approaches: the Emergence of the Norms and the Paradox of Isolation

A way of resolution could be contemplated to go by what Ulmann-Margalit says (1977). In a pragmatic perspective, the Kantian maxim of action is obvious since it permits to solve the problem the agents are faced with, and the establishment of this rule stems from an evolutionary principle or principle of natural selection of the development of the norms. The use by Bergstrom (1995) of a similar maxim, presupposed Kantian, falls perfectly within this logic. In a model where the nature of the human preferences stems from a biological law of evolution, that is to say that the individuals do not consciously choose their strategy but act according to a programme determined by their genetic structure, he introduces a rule which he describes as Kantian. He shows that a stable equilibrium of a monomorphic population (all of whose members have the same genotype) is obtained if this population acts in accordance with the Kantian maxim[9]. Within this framework, any mutant gene that would appear would reproduce less rapidly than the dominant gene; we are here within a dynamic perspective of the emergence of the Kantian principle. This type of approach, though it may supply a new perspective to the problem of coordination, clearly deviates from Kantian philosophy. Indeed, the latter does not come within a dynamic framework of the emergence of norms, but on the contrary, it presupposes their previous existence and wonders about the conformity and the internalisation of these norms by the individuals. Furthermore, the above perspective obviously considers morality as a means to attain an end and it thus very clearly deviates from the Kantian ethics.

In fact, a great number of models do not set the problem of the emergence of the norm, and consider it as present at a certain point in time. Therefore, it does not deal so much with setting the problem of the selection of the norm than that of its internalisation. The models integrating a Kantian behaviour generally consider that all individuals act in compliance with the Kantian maxim of action: their approach consists in comparing the situation of failure of coordination- which the prisoner's dilemma represents- with the 'solution' which ethical behaviour provides.

Another proposal is contemplated by transforming the prisoner's dilemma into what Sen (1967) described as the paradox of isolation. While in the prisoner's dilemma, no hypothesis is set as to the individual's morality, whereas in the paradox of isolation, the players are supposed to have a moral preference, or preference for cooperation. The paradox of isolation is based on an agent inclined to the respect of moral rules: if the individual is willing to respect moral rules, he will act morally only if he knows that the others will also follow this rule; in the contrary case, he will also break the rule. The information on the others' behaviour appears essential here: in the absence of this information, the individual may be considered to be in a situation of isolation. The paradox of isolation is then seen as a game of assurance, and differs from the prisoner's dilemma. According to the game of assurance, the revealed preferences place the cooperative solution above all others and the individuals behave "as if" they were trying to favour this solution first and foremost. In the prisoner's dilemma, the individual prefers everybody to respect the rule, except him. In the paradox of isolation, on the other hand, the individual prefers the situation where everybody, including him, respects the rule, but he is undecided as to his behaviour as he does not know that of the others. The individual has an ethical preference: what is at stake is the universalisation of ethical preference. Kantian ethics then appears as a means to get out of the paradox through the principle of universalisation or generalisation. It is then close to a game of assurance.

The commonly recognised and shared values have the effect of turning the problem into a situation of a game of assurance since, through the promotion of these values, the individual no longer acts in a state of uncertainty as to the moral character of the others' preferences (Sen, 1975). Given that the isolation comes from the fact that the individual does not know what the others will do, but prefers the respect of the moral rules, the fact of noting the others' action is enough to solve the problem. Everybody's behaviour therefore influences the others' decision.

However, this result presupposes an extremely strong hypothesis (in addition to that of perfect information), namely, the hypothesis of common recognition or the sharing of values. In the absence of this hypothesis, moral motivation is no longer sufficient to solve the prisoner's dilemma. Indeed, according to Koslowski (1988), this result is only a *petitio principii*, which consists in setting the respect by everybody of the moral rule, assuming in an *ad hoc* manner that the others simultaneously reason and act in an identical way. Now, in terms of decision, the individual cannot observe in advance the others' behaviour: the paradox of isolation lies precisely in this dilemma. As long as the situation remains uncertain, the principle of assurance cannot be guaranteed. In the paradox of isolation, as Koslowski underlines it, no assurance may therefore be given as to the others' moral behaviour, and no confidence in moral behaviour may either be founded. The Kantian principle, as a solution to the paradox of isolation, is then close to a simple principle of reciprocity. Yet, there is a difference of nature between these two principles.

2. Kantian Behaviour and Reciprocity

The works of Gouldner (1960) permitted to give the concept of reciprocity its full extent. He associates a dimension of strategic interaction with it. Kolm (1984a, b) particularly used the concept. For him, reciprocity is associated with a set of interdependent donations. The generalised donation, or general reciprocity, constitutes, according to Kolm (1984a), the application of the principle of the Kantian categorical imperative to economics: everybody gives assuming that everybody else gives. General reciprocity then supplies a coherent system of cooperation and coordination of the economic agents[10].

However, it seems to us that although the hypothesis of reciprocity is close to the Kantian analysis in regards to its results (in terms of coordination), it deviates from it in regards to its foundations. In particular, it overlooks Kant's concept of the autonomy of will, which Dupuy defines as the "ability to limit one's individuality by giving oneself a transcendental and fixed law or rule, and keep to it" (Dupuy, 1997, pp. 56-57).

We have already hilghlighted that the principle of universalisation of the maxim was not comparable, in Kant, to a principle of conditional commitment. In the categorical imperative, the maxim of action must not only be universalisable, but it must also correspond to the agent's intrinsic motivations, to the exclusion of any condition[11]. Therefore, the hypothesis of Kantian behaviour distinguishes itself from the behaviour based on reciprocity. Sugden (1984) particularly set a Kantian approach, which he calls the principle of unconditional commitment, against an approach in terms of reciprocity, which rests upon a conditional action based on the equivalence of advantages. Finally, reciprocity seems to be defined according to two essential criteria, which are conditionality and equivalence[12].

The Kantian principle requires a participation or an action independently of the others' participation or action. However, the principle of reciprocity, through an effect of identification, presupposes perfect interdependence. The principle of reciprocity is a principle according to which the individual will not behave as a stowaway providing that the others do not behave themselves as stowaways, or else: the individual will behave in a cooperative way or as if he wanted this cooperation, if the others also behave in a cooperative way. The opposition between these two principles could be summed up with the following sentences: "Act independently of the others' action" for the Kantian principle, and "Act according to the others' behaviour" for the principle of reciprocity.

Sacco and Zamagni (1996) proposed an overall vision of this difference within the framework of a two player game. Let us suppose two players *I* and *II* decide to give a certain amount of money to another poorer person, or act for a charitable organisation. This third party needs a monetary unit to survive, and the players have the choice between giving 0, ½ or 1. The players' preferences are represented by an order of preference ">" over the space of results; below, the first term in each parenthesis corresponds to the donation of agent *I*, the second to the donation of *II*. Individual *I*, who adopts a principle of reciprocity, is characterised by the following system of preferences:

$$\left(\frac{1}{2},\frac{1}{2}\right) \phi \ (0,0) \ \phi \left(\frac{1}{2},0\right) \phi \ (1,0)$$

$$\left(\frac{1}{2},\frac{1}{2}\right) \phi \ (0,1)$$

An individual who adopts a behaviour based on the principle of reciprocity is therefore an individual whose desire is that everybody contributes equally (here ½ in the case of two individuals). However, if *I* knows that individual *II* will not participate or will not act, then he does not wish to participate or act either. But *I* prefers to contribute if he knows that *II* contributes too. In other words, the behaviour of reciprocity presupposes that the weight of the contributions or actions is divided equally. If such is not the case, the individual then prefers to refrain from acting or participating rather than having to bear the action or participation alone.

Individual *I*, if he adopts a so-called Kantian behaviour, is characterised by the following system of preferences:

$$\left(\frac{1}{2},0\right) \phi \ (0,0)$$

$$\left(\frac{1}{2},0\right) \phi \ (1,0)$$

$$\left(\frac{1}{2},\frac{1}{2}\right) \phi \ (0,1)$$

Here, the Kantian individual respects two modes of behaviour: on the one hand, he is willing to act or participate independently of the others' participation (he therefore respects the principle of unconditionality of action); on the other hand, he postulates the universal in his preferences, *i.e.* he acts assuming that the result sought will be achieved *if everybody acts like him.* In other words, in case individual *II* is not willing to contribute, individual *I* will only participate up to his just share (in the present case half), in spite of the fact that his only action or participation is not sufficient to achieve the final result. This mode of behaviour reflects to the letter a Kantian maxim of action resting upon the argument of generalisation. Obviously, Kantian individual *I* prefers a situation where everybody contributes on an equal basis (½ each), rather than a situation where he would not participate and the others would assume the full burden.

According to Pereau and Tazdait (2002, p. 10), "economic literature refers to the Kantian principle if an actor supposes it reasonable to make his action tenable (in the eyes of his preferences) and compatible with the fact that the others might adopt the same attitude as him". This perception of the Kantian principle clearly underlines the attitude which one "could adopt" and not what one "adopts". The individual finds himself in a situation of uncertainty, and if he may hope that the others will act like him, he cannot base his decision on the observation of their behaviour: the moral rule then applies whatever the others' decision. Consequently, the equilibrium of the game will only correspond in a fortuitous way to Pareto's optimum: all the individuals should be Kantian and perfectly identical[13].

Here, the action implicitly rests upon the principle of autonomy, central in Kant's works, and better retranscribes the requirement of the categorical imperative, which implies that the moral rule must be followed for itself, regardless of its consequences, that is to say independently of others' behaviour. Sugden (1984) and Koslowski (1998) see in this scenario an implausible situation product of real moral heroism. Yet, it actually deals with a conception closer to Kantian philosophy. A stronger version may also be expressed through the idea of commitment.

3. Commitment, Which Conception?

The hypothesis of Kantian behaviour is based on the idea of moral commitment and the fact that the individual assumes his moral duty as it is retranscribed in the maxim of action. Despite the criticisms levelled against the use of the categorical imperative, for instance by Harsanyi (1958, 1995), who considers that all imperatives may be expressed in a hypothetical form and that consequently, morality is the "servant" of other human values and not the highest value, or even the criticism of Taylor (1982) for whom the distinction between the hypothetical and categorical imperative is extremely vague, Kantian ethics has given rise to various types of formalisation of the commitment.

3.1. Commitment as a Categorical Imperative

In the previous section, the individual's behaviour is associated with a sharing of values. His moral commitment is translated into an equal contribution to the donation made to the third party. However, this amounts to limiting the conception of the individual's commitment: a committed individual is not only concerned about fulfilling his own moral duty, but he also wants the objective for which he commits himself to be finally achieved. Thus, we cannot limit his objective function to his sole individual commitment, for example his commitment not to litter the beach. The individual also wishes to see beaches perfectly clean.

Sacco and Zamagni (1996) presented this difference by proposing a distinction between the "Kantian individual" and the "super-Kantian individual". As above, the representation of the system of preferences of a super-Kantian is the case of two individuals:

$$(1,0)\,\phi\left(\frac{1}{2},0\right)\phi\ (0,0)$$

$$\left(\frac{1}{2},\frac{1}{2}\right)\phi\ (0,1)$$

The main difference between Kantian and super-Kantian therefore, is that if the other individuals do not act or do not participate, the super-Kantian individual *I* is willing to bear the weight of participation alone, rather than limit himself to his participation on an equal basis. While a Kantian is first concerned about the morality of his own action, a super-Kantian is first concerned about the fulfilment of the final objective.

However, this hypothesis looks extremely strong, and even excessive in a great number of cases, since it seems impossible, in certain situations, to reach the final objective through the action of one person only. Collard (1978) thus takes the example of blood donors. A Kantian donor acts in the hope that others will do the same, and more exactly that a sufficient number of donors will act in a Kantian way with a view to distributing the donations equally to reach the desired stock. If such were not the case, the Kantian individual would perceive his donation as useless. But in this case, can we expect a super-Kantian to give the necessary stock of blood alone? The physiological limits obviously impose an unsurmountable constraint. This type of situations seems less frequent, however, than those which consist in the adoption of a Kantian principle based on everybody's just share. Still, if this conception actually confirms the autonomy of the subject's will, it conditions the behaviour to the end to be attained: therefore, such a vision of commitment does not really coincide with Kantian moral philosophy. An individual who acts with a view to reaching an objective does not conform to Kantian ethics, which claims that the action is committed because it is good in itself, and not because it permits to achieve a particular aim. If it deals with a form of commitment, the "super-Kantian" individual of Sacco and Zamagni is no longer Kantian.

3.2. The Concept of Commitment in Sen

Basing himself on a problem and an example rather close to those of Laffont (1975), Sen (1973) already discussed the difficulties, for microeconomic theory of rational choice, in taking into account a moral imperative as a rule of behaviour. Although Laffont considers that Kantian behaviour may be comparable to a preference of the individual, and therefore integrates it into his utility function, the option retained by Sen (1973, 1977)[14] consists in introducing an absolute constraint (admitting the categorical imperative as a commitment) between the couple preferences-set of possibilities on the one hand, and the actual choice on the other hand.

Let us go back over our example of section 2, when an agent (*E*) has the choice between participating (E_1) or not (E_0) in the production of a public good, such as the quality of the environment. Let us consider with Sen that the individual always prefers E_0 from the point of view of his personal welfare, but that he considers it *irresponsible* not to carry out E_1 – he therefore chooses E_1[15]. In such a situation, the individual's actual choice no longer reveals his preferences *and* his welfare simultaneously: if responsibility is part of the preferences and leads the individual to choose E_1, this does not reveal anything on the welfare of the individual, who hypothetically prefers E_0. If, conversely, the individual only acted on the sole criterion of his personal welfare, he would choose E_0 and would thus reveal his preferences; in this case, the theory of preferences is unable to describe an act of commitment as we describe it, and cannot logically explain why the agent will finally choose E_1[16].

The above-developed discussion is that of the impossibility, for the theory of the preferences, of taking a moral imperative as a rule of behaviour into account. According to Elster (1989), economic rationality rests upon a hypothetical imperative, which could be thus formulated: *if you want to satisfy your preferences, choose such action.* If, like in the previous example, there is a categorical imperative intervening between the preferences and the choices, then the latter no longer reveals preferences. Therefore, it is not so much the preferences as they are usually defined in economics which is important to discuss, or the hypothesis according to which the choices generally constitute a source of information on the preferences, but rather , it is important to discuss the hypothesis according to which the actual choices permit to know the preferences of an individual, since these economic preferences sum up all motivations guiding his behaviour.

Here, we are trying to represent the individual choice prompted by what Sen calls "morality" (Sen, 1974) or "commitment" (Sen, 1982), and which, to us, may give shape to the notion of categorical imperative. Unlike Laffont, Sen does not put ethical concerns and considerations of individual welfare on the same plane. He thus deviates from a strictly utilitarian philosophy, which seems, in any case on this point, more in keeping with Kant's thinking. According to Sen, it is the uniqueness of the set of preferences that should be called into question as a single ranking of all the actions realisable by an individual reflecting all his motivations[17].

Supposing that there is a plurality of motivations, each ordering the realisable actions within a specific set of preferences. Sen's proposal (1974, 1982) may be translated as follows: to the set of actions realisable for an individual correspond as many particular orderings as there are individual motivations of behaviour. We may suppose that this set of realisable actions will not be ordered identically if the guides of actions retained are the personal welfare, the respect of a philosophical or religious norm, the will to conform to the values of a community, *etc.* Furthermore, if we assume that the individual acts according to a certain ethic, he may then rank the orderings (or guides) of realisable actions according to his own ethics, that is to say express preferences over preferences. This technique of meta-ordering permits the introduction of the morality and the ethics, *etc.* of the individual as an element structuring the set of preferences and choice. This consists in expressing preferences *over preferences* (saying for example: 'I want the individual choices to come within the framework of such political priority').

This technique of preferences over preferences, or ranking of rankings, permits to integrate into the analysis various types of individual motivations, each of them making itself a ranking of the realisable actions. In the face of a consequentialist conception of rationality, which assesses the choices as an individual utility, without any other consideration on the rules of behaviour, Sen proposes to assess the rules before the consequences of the acts. Commitment, understood as the product of a meta-preference, is translated into a rationality over the rules, without it being possible to consider it as irrational from the point of view of the internal coherence of the choices. The action, which is finally retained by the agent, does not only depend on the rankings made by each of his motivations, but also on the ranking of the motivations themselves, which translates his individual ethics of behaviour.

According to Sen, the technique of the ranking of rankings permits to understand why the individuals who are in a prisoner's dilemma type situation do not adopt the selfish strategy, but conform to a Kantian principle of action:

> "A more fruitful approach may lie in permitting the possibility that the person is *more* sophisticated than the theory allows and that he has asked himself what type of preference he would like the other player to have, and on somewhat Kantian grounds has considered the case for himself having those preferences, or behaving *as if* he had them. This line of reasoning requires him to consider the modifications of the game that would be brought about by acting through commitment [...] and he has to assess alternative behaviour norms in that light" (Sen, 1982, p. 103).

The technique of meta-ranking appears like a means to represent commitment in the form of a Kantian principle.

3.3. Meta-Preference and Commitment

The representation of moral commitment through a process of individual optimisation is the subject of Arnsperger's article (1998). We shall only present the broad lines of it here. For a more detailed presentation and formalisation, refer previous chapter.

For this author, it deals with giving an operational form to the concept of meta-preferences proposed by Sen, by distinguishing the rule of behaviour representing the individual ethics from the choice of the ensuing action. The modelling which he proposes, however introduces an additional idea in relation to Sen: "The individual uses a lexicographical procedure within which several orderings are applied by descending order of priority" (1998, p. 193).

The introduction of meta-ordering implies that the individual does not try to satisfy, on the set of realisable actions, any particular ordering representing his welfare, but his meta-ordering of a set of morally realisable actions ranked by lexicographical order of ethical priority. It is therefore important to distinguish:

- The ranking of the guides of actions (the various sets of preferences translating the plurality of motivations) according to individual ethics;
- The maximising action itself.

Commitment ultimately amounts to a voluntary limitation of the choice space, since the individual no longer maximises on the set of realisable actions, but on the set of *morally* realisable actions. This set of morally realisable actions is understood as a meta-ranking of actions stemming from a ranking of the sets of actions according to individual ethics *and* the actions themselves within each set.

The action undertaken is therefore not characterised as "an action that yields a lower expected welfare than an alternative available action", which will break "the basic link between choice behaviour and welfare achievements in traditional models" (Sen, 1982, pp. 93-94). Arnsperger (1998, p. 200) underlines that it deals with a "far too restrictive conception of the moral commitment". The adoption by the individual of a priority guide of actions is then sufficient to define the responsible act, since the meta-ranking of morally realisable actions is not conditioned only by personal welfare. What constitutes responsibility (commitment) is the fact of being able to rank several sets of preferences, each reflecting a particular motivation, and then progressively restricting the set of morally realisable actions (according to a lexicographical order of ethical priority), with a view to determining a meta-ordering of the actions on which the satisfaction of preferences works. Therefore, *a priori*, there is nothing preventing the meta-ordering of morally realisable actions from ranking actions, which would have been chosen with individual welfare as the only guide: everything depends on the restriction imposed by the priority ideals on the set of realisable actions.

This conception of commitment permits to set, to a certain extent, specific non-consequentialist ideals, such as Kantian ethics, against other consequentalist ideals. In this respect, Kantian ethics appears relatively flexible, by not completely restricting the range of realisable action. However, this type of formalisation is not limited to this form of ethics, which *a contrario* only looks like a particular case.

4. Conclusion: What Lessons May be Drawn from Kantianism in Economics?

What lessons may be drawn from this brief review of "Kantian economics"? In his article, Laffont (1975) saw in

Kantian ethics a solution to the question of the individuals' coordination. If, historically heir to the moral philosophy, economics actually shares the ideal of coordination with ethics, we have attempted here to put into perspective the so-called Kantian approach in economics. It is important to recall in the first place that, in its 'ordinary' version, the *categorical* imperative is in reality *conditional* (the agent determines his action knowing that the optimal result will be obtained if everybody does the same), that is to say that it represents a means with a view to an end, which somewhat moves it away from the Kantian moral sense. By being preoccupied with the end to be achieved (a Pareto-optimal social state, a cooperative solution to the prisoner's dilemma), we forget that the ethics of the categorical imperative does not rest so much upon the principle of generalisation of action as upon the principle of generalisation of the maxim, "generalisation of the subjective practical principle belonging to the actor" (Koslowski, 1998, p. 89). In this respect, a conception of responsibility resting on the only argument of the generalisation of action could perfectly have fallen within the framework of, for example, Sartrian existentialism (Sartre, 1946, pp. 25-29).

Subsequently, we tried to show that the concept of commitment was more in a position to represent Kantian ethics. It is important to make the two following remarks here: first, despite the explicit reference to Kant, a conception of commitment in which the latter is conditioned by the objective to be reached, cannot translate Kantian ethics. Secondly, the version presented in the previous section compels us to get out of the utilitarian framework by resorting to lexicographical preferences. Commitment, as it is presented then, is *compatible* with Kantian ethics, but is not confined to it. It is easy to perceive that such a construction also applies to other forms of ethics. For instance, we may establish a ranking according to the virtues claimed by an individual: we would thus get a meta-ranking obtained from various values ranked by order of preference such as justice, honesty, prudence, *etc*. Since all these values are not necessarily compatible on all occasions, priorities also apply.

Finally, commitment, even if it corresponds to the Kantian principle, does not in any way guarantee the resolution of the prisoner's dilemma. It would be necessary for all the individuals to act in the same way, that is to say to make exactly the same ranking and decide exactly on the same action within the framework of this ranking. In other words, it would be necessary for all individuals to be perfectly identical. These developments are actually not proposed with a view to responding to this dilemma, and they do not give any solution to the problem of coordination. The question of the individuals' coordination remains on hold. Nevertheless, a solution might be found in the articulation of the reasonable with the rational, the universalisation of the maxim of action resting on the shoulders of the impartial spectator (Mongin and d'Aspremont, 1998, p. 446; Rawls, 2000).

Kantianism in economics is mainly based on the principle of generalisation. Every rational individual deliberates by taking into account the maxim of action. But this rational deliberation is only a part of the Kantian ethics. The individuals are certainly rational but also reasonable, and commitment in the Kantian sense presupposes the priority of the reasonable over the rational. As Rawls underlines it perfectly in his lessons on Kant:

> "In my opinion, it is therefore important to consider that Kant's objective is to present the principles according to which a fully *reasonable* and *rational* ideal agent would act, even if he were led to go against all his objective desires if it were necessary to respect the requirements of the moral rule" (2000/2002, p. 153, *highlighted by us*).

Let us take an example given by Kant himself and taken up by Rawls (2000/2002, p. 198) to better understand the importance of the term reasonable. Kant distinguishes between the categorical imperative and the golden rule expressed by "Do unto others as you would have them do unto you". This golden rule is compatible with the situation of a criminal who would tell the judge: "If you were in my place, you would not like to be sentenced, consequently, *etc.*". The principle of generalisation applied in this sense and in a rational way is obviously not compatible with morality. In fact, the criminal, as a reasonable and not only rational being, should consider the judge's action not from the point of view of his own situation, but from the point of view of an ideally neutral person who would refer to the procedure of the categorical imperative.

To give substance to commitment – in the sense of Kantian ethics – then implies considering individuals as rational and reasonable beings, and giving priority to the reasonable over the rational. In such a perspective, cooperation would no longer rest on the individuals' rationality, even if it is rational to do so, but on the reasonable, including if it is more advantageous from a rational point of view not to cooperate.

By way of conclusion and opening, a last remark seems necessary to us. A certain number of authors in moral philosophy underlined the limits of Kantian ethics when it deals with putting the theory of responsibility within a dynamic perspective (Jonas, 1979; Simon, 1993; Koslowski, 1998). According to the latter, the ethics of the categorical imperative is not much concerned about the consequences of the maxim of action on the empirical world. Now, according to Jonas (1979), the foundations of the ethical theory are disrupted by the switch to what he calls the technological civilisation, which introduces a phenomenon of cumulative irreversibility through the transformation of nature, which it implies: the conditions of the future human actions will no longer be the same as those of the present subjects[18].

The switch to the technological civilisation then compels us to extrapolate the consequences of our actions on another person who does not share our present. The new categorical imperative becomes: "Act in such a way that the effects of your action are compatible with the permanence of a genuinely human life on earth" or "Act in such a way that the effects of your action are not destructive for the future possibility of such a life" (Jonas, 1979, pp. 30-31). The categorical imperative is thus reformulated on account of the temporal dimension of human action, but this temporal dimension itself is different from the past: from a static constitutional state, which was perpetuated from period to period (which does not mean that it was unchanging, but that the environment's conditions of reproduction were not affected), the technological civilisation implies a state of potential transformation. Hence the necessity of basing the maxim of action on a precautionary principle since the ethics of responsibility can no longer be extricated from temporal considerations (Jonas, 1979, 1998; Birnbacher, 1994; Dupuy, 2002).

Notes

1. A different version of this paper was first published in *Social Science Information*, 42 (2), 185-208. London: Sage Publications. We wish to thank D. Diatkine, J.C. Péreau, Ph. Mongin, T. Tazdaït and A. Wolfelsperger for their comments on a previous version of this article.
2. We are indebted to A. Wolfelsperger for making us clearly aware of this distinction.
3. See for example Wolfelsperger (2001).
4. Let us note that we only deal here with one of the formulations of the categorical imperative proposed by Kant in *La métaphysique des mœurs* (*Metaphysik der Sitten*).
5. The fact that the agents adopt "collective behaviours" voluntarily and individually means, according to Laffont (1975, p. 430) (*i*) that the behaviour is "in contradiction to the maximisation of direct personal interest" (voluntary aspect) (*ii*) "without any direct communication between the agents" (individual aspect).
6. The case of voluntary contributions (private) to the supply of public goods constitutes a privileged field of study of the so-called Kantian behaviour; Bontemps and Rotillon (1998) observe along these lines, that if the quality of the environment is often regarded as a public good, its particular characteristic is that it is produced in a decentralised way by a great number of agents.
7. Let us recall that the marginal rate of substitution (mrs) between two goods is

the rate at which the individual is willing to exchange these two goods, while remaining at constant utility.

8. On the putting into perspective of instrumental rationality in relation to Kantian philosophy, please refer the presentation and notes of A. Renaut in *La métaphysique des mœurs* (*Metaphysik der Sitten*), and especially p. 30, p. 188 (note 15), p. 190 (note 25), pp. 192-193 (note 34).

9. He expresses the Kantian maxim with the following formula: "Act toward your sibling as would be in your own best interest if your sibling's actions would mimic your own" (Bergstrom, 1995, p. 61).

10. Elster (1995) also goes along these lines by putting ordinary Kantianism within the category of the norms of cooperation.

11. See for example Mongin and d'Aspremont, 1998, p. 378 and p. 446.

12. Kolm's works are more balanced as to the application of these two criteria to define the principle of reciprocity. If conditionality is truly present, it comes within a broader framework than an inter-individual conditionality. Indeed, it is not a particular donation which influences another particular donation, but the fact that there is a set of donations permitting a set of counter-donations. As there is no precise relation between each donation, equivalence no longer makes much sense.

13. Bordignon (1990) underlined this result in a model close to that of Laffont. When the individuals are different, the Kantian maxim no longer helps obtain a Pareto-optimal result.

14. We shall subsequently refer to the reprint of Sen (1977) in Sen (1982).

15. Which is quite comparable to the example of Laffont: the individual on the beach *prefers* not to have to go to the nearest bin to drop his litter in it, knowing that his personal contribution to the cleanliness of the beach is marginal; however, he considers it *irresponsible* to act in this way, and he therefore goes to the nearest bin.

16. See Sen (1973); also see Mongin and d'Aspremont (1998, pp. 388-394) for a detailed discussion on this topic.

17. "A person thus described may be 'rational' in the limited sense of revealing no inconsistencies in his choice behaviour [...]. Economic theory has been much preoccupied with this rational fool decked in the glory of his *one* all-purpose preference ordering" (Sen, 1982, p. 99).

18. Jonas takes the example of nuclear energy and the potential catastrophes, which it entails. We could quote other global threats to the environment, such as the greenhouse effect of anthropic origin.

References

Arnsperger, C. 1998. “Engagement moral et optimisation individuelle”. In F.R. Mahieu and H. Rapoport (eds.), *Altruisme, Analyses économiques*, 191-214. Paris: Economica.

Bergstrom, Th. C. 1995. “On the Evolution of Altruistic Ethical Rules for Siblings”. *American Economic Review*, 85 (1), 58-81.

Bontemps, Ph.; Rotillon, G. 1998. *Economie de l’environnement*. Paris: La Découverte.

Bordignon, M. 1990. “Was Kant Right? Voluntary Provision of Public Goods Under the Principle of Unconditional Commitment”. *Economic Notes*, 3, 342-372.

Collard, D. 1978. *Altruism and Economy. A Study in Non-Selfish Economics*. Oxford: Martin Robertson.

Cornes, R.C. ; Sandler, T. 1984. “The Theory of Public Goods: Non-Nash Behaviour”. *Journal of Public Economics*, 23, 367-379.

Dupuy, J-P. 1997. “Temps et rationalité; les paradoxes du raisonnement rétrograde”. In J-P. Dupuy. and P. Livet (eds.), *Les limites de la rationalité. Tome 1, Rationalité, éthique, cognition*, 30-58. Paris: La découverte.

Elster, J. 1989. *The Cement of Society*. Cambridge: Cambridge University Press.

Elster, J. 1995. “Rationalité et normes sociales: un modèle pluridisciplinaire”. In L-A. Gérard-Varet and J-C. Passeron (eds.), *Le modèle et l’enquête. Les usages du principe de rationalité dans les sciences sociales*, 139-148. Paris: Editions de l’EHESS.

Gouldner, A.W. 1960. “The Norm of Reciprocity: A Preliminary Statement”. *American Sociological Review*, 25, 161-178.

Harsanyi, J.C. 1958. “Ethics in Terms of Hypothetical Imperatives”. *Mind*, 47, 305-316.

Harsanyi, J.C. 1980. “Rule Utilitarianism, Rights, Obligations and the Theory of Rational Behavior”. *Theory and Decision*, 12, 115-133.

Harsanyi, J.C. 1982. “Morality and the Theory of Rational Behaviour”. In A. Sen and B. Williams (eds.), *Utilitarianism and Beyond*, 39-62. Cambridge: Cambridge University Press.

Harsanyi, J.C. 1995. “A Theory of Prudential Values and a Rule Utilitarian Theory of Morality”. *Social Choice and Welfare*, 12, 319-333.

Kant, E. 1785, 1797. *Métaphysique des mœurs I. Fondation de la métaphysique des mœurs (1785), Introduction à la métaphysique des mœurs (1797)*. Paris: Flammarion, 1994.

Kolm, S-C. 1984a. *La bonne économie. La réciprocité générale*. Paris: PUF.

Kolm, S-C. 1984b. "Théorie de la réciprocité et du choix des systèmes économiques". *Revue économique*, 35(5), 871-907.

Koslowski, P. 1998. *Principes d'économie éthique*. Paris: Editions du Cerf.

Laffont, J-J. 1975. "Macroeconomic Constraints, Economic Efficiency and Ethics: an Introduction to Kantian Economics". *Economica*, 42, 430-437.

Mongin, Ph.; d'Aspremont, C. 1998. "Utility Theory and Ethics". In S. Barbera; P. Hammond; C. Seidl (ed.), *Handbook of Utility Theory*, vol. 1. Dordrecht & New York: Kluwer Academic Press.

Péreau, J.C.; Tazdaït, T. 2002. *Une analyse économique de la coopération*. Paris: Miméo.

Rawls, J. 2000. *Lectures on the History of Moral Philosophy*. Harvard: Harvard University Press. French translation 2002, *Leçons sur l'histoire de la philosophie morale*. Paris: La découverte.

Roemer, J.E. 1996. *Theories of Justice*. Cambridge Mass.: Harvard University Press.

Sacco, P.L.; Zamagni, S. 1996. "An Evolutionary Dynamic Approach to Altruism". In F. Farina, F.; Hahn, S.; Vannucci (eds.), *Ethics and Economics*, 265-300. Oxford: Clarendon Press.

Samuelson, P.A. 1954. "The Pure Theory of Public Expenditure". *Review of Economics and Statistics*, 36, 387-389.

Sartre, J-P. 1946. *L'existentialisme est un humanisme*. Paris: Nagel, 1970.

Sen, A. 1967. "Isolation, Assurance, and the Social Rate of Discount". *Quarterly Journal of Economics*, 81(1), 112-124.

Sen, A. 1973. "Behaviour and the Concept of Preference". *Economica*, 40, 241-259.

Sen, A. 1974. "Choice, Orderings and Morality". Reprinted, In Sen (1982), *Choice, Welfare and Measurement*, Oxford: Basil Blackwell, 74-83.

Sen, A. 1975. *Ökonomische Ungleichheit*. Francfort: Campus.

Sen, A. 1977. "Rational Fools: a Critique of the Behavioural Foundations of Economic Theory". Reprinted, In Sen (1982), *Choice, Welfare and Measurement*. Oxford: Basil Blackwell, 84-106.

Sen, A. 1982. *Choice, Welfare and Measurement*. Oxford: Basil Blackwell.

Sugden, R. 1984. "Reciprocity: the Supply of Public Goods Through Voluntary Contributions". *The Economic Journal*, 94, 772-787.

Taylor, Ch. 1982. "The Diversity of Goods". In A. Sen and B. Williams (eds.), *Utilitarianism and Beyond*, 129-144. Cambridge: Cambridge University Press.

Ulmann-Margalit, E. 1977. *The Emergence of Norms*. Oxford: Oxford University Press.

Wolfelsperger, A. 1999. "Sur l'existence d'une solution kantienne du problème des biens collectifs". *Revue économique*, 50 (4), 879-902.

Wolfelsperger, A. 2001. "La modélisation économique de la rationalité axiologique. Des sentiments moraux aux mécanismes sociaux de la moralité". In R. Boudon; P. Demeulenaere; R. Vialle, *L'explication des normes sociales*, 63-91. Paris: PUF.

PART THREE

Responsibility

For a Positive Analysis of Responsibility and Duty

Jérôme Ballet
François-Régis Mahieu

Since 1971, John Rawls's theory of Justice has given rise to many debates regarding the criteria of Justice by equity. These debates revealed the importance, in Anglo-Saxon philosophy, of individual rights; to such an extent that people's duties[1] were relegated to a subordinate role. In the context of *civil rights*, there is an abuse of right and a calculating conception of responsibility, so that we are all liable for the use of our freedom. In his interpretation of Rawls, John Roemer (1994) calculates the responsibility of the person. It can be deduced from the "type" considered, by crossing the handicap (positive or negative) and the merit (positive or negative), therefore from the mixing of circumstances and autonomous choices. To a certain extent, society's responsibility (or the government's) originates in the calculus it does on the responsibility of individuals.

In this case, several problems arise. First of all, the person is not a responsible subject; he/she is a set of characteristics thereby allowing a calculation of responsibility. The second problem lies in the priority given to rights over obligations. By a reversal of perspectives, one can oppose the ethics of Just (unquestioning obedience to the LAW) to the ethics of justice by equity (based on the GOOD). Finally, the third problem lies in the analysis of the difficulties to the implement principles of justice enacted by these theories. The implementation of such principles clashes with the behaviour and reaction of people as immediately (and not by calculus) responsible subjects. It is necessary to consider responsibility as a direct component of individual decisions of economic agents. But before highlighting these issues, we will detail the relation these theories have with rights.

The chapter is structured in the following way. In a first part, we will show in what sense contemporary theories of social justice are based on the priority of rights. In a second part, we will emphasise that, in such an interpretation, obligations are only a remainder used for a second-rate calculus. In a third part, we will develop the idea that these approaches overlook reflection on the moral subject, and we will draw several consequences from it, particularly by opposing the ethics of Just to the ethics of justice by equity.

1. Priority of Rights in Theories of Justice

As an introduction, let us recall the distinction Dworkin (1977) suggested, when defining three categories of theories. He suggested distinguishing between political theories based on the *aim*, those based on *rights* and those based on *obligations*.

1/ According to a theory based on the aim, a kind of *status quo* is an aim if a political action improves, delays or threatens this *status quo*. From such a point of view, what counts is what is aimed by actions and not the actions themselves. In other words, this theory suggests referring to an aim, and analyses the impact of actions in the achievement of this aim. The aim can be specific such as full-employment, but also general such as the improvement of well-being or the realisation of a good life based on a specific concept. Utilitarianism perfectly matches a kind of theory based on the aim.

2/ According to a theory based on rights, an individual has a right to a specific political act. This right is a permission for the individual to carry out this act, even if the act in question is harmful for the achievement of an aim that the theory is trying to attain. In this case, priority is no longer given to the aim to be achieved, but to certain acts that individuals have a right to carry out. For example, they have the right to speak their mind, to meet, to vote etc. These rights, as permissions to act or have, define the theory's outline.

3/ A political theory is said to be based on duty if the act is constrained, regardless of any sought-after aim. According to Dworkin, such a theory might stipulate, for instance, that individuals must worship God, even if this duty is required and serves no aim whatsoever. In this situation, individuals obey the Law or principles, not because these principles aim at protecting rights or even because they help attaining an aim, but simply because these principles are self-sufficient. For example, a sentence such as "you shall not lie" implies absence of lying, even if it would be favourable in order to achieve a certain goal, and not because other people have a right not to be lied to. Therefore, there is an unquestioning obedience to the principle or to the Law.

Of course, such a typology is only used to present a wider set of possibilities. Indeed, some theories can very well combine an aim and a right. In this case, the force of the granted right depends on its specific relation to the sought-after aim. In the same way, a theory combining duty and aim would imply that the constrained act is a necessary requirement for the achievement of an aim. The constraint on this act would then depend on its relevance or on its value in the achievement of the aim.

According to this distinction, we can consider contemporary theories of justice which appeared in the wake of Rawls's *Theory of Justice* (1971) as theories mainly based on rights. The theory suggested by Rawls is an original attempt to break with utilitarianism. It clearly rejects this approach by drawing on the concept of rights. Let us recall that this theory suggests two principles of justice. The first one deals with freedom, we all have an equal right to it, provided it is compatible with the system of freedoms for all. Basic freedoms can range from political freedom, to freedom of speech, of assembly, of thought and of conscience. In this liberal framework, the rights of the person (integrity) and of property are protected, but this protection does not always match the freedom to have certain forms of property and the freedom of contract in its "laisser faire" sense. The second principle tackles the issues of social and economic inequalities which must be: a) to the greater benefit of the worst-off people within the limits of a just saving principle, b) related to functions and positions open to everybody, in accordance to the principle of fair equality of opportunities. In other words, inequalities are arbitrary until they fairly contribute to the advantage of everybody, and provided the positions and functions they are related to, or from which they can be attained, are open to everybody. The maximin rule is related to this second principle, i.e. "maximum minimorum" rule, applied in a lexicographic way, i.e. the leximin.

There are two priority rules which are linked to these two principles. The priority order is such that each principle must be completely fulfilled before the implementation of the following one. According to the first priority rule, basic freedoms cannot be restricted. A reduction of freedom is only conceivable if it strengthens the system of freedoms shared by everybody. The second rule establishes the priority of justice over efficiency (assimilated to Pareto-optimality).

From this interpretation, we are tempted to conclude that the theory is based on a right to an inalienable freedom. But that would be taking the theory's result for its base. The right of freedom is the result of an individual's rational reflection under the veil of ignorance. Part of Dworkin's theory consists in showing that Rawls' theory is based on the idea that "individuals have a right to equal concern and respect in the design and administration of the political institutions that govern them"[2]. According to him, "the right to equal respect is not, on his account, a product of the contract, but a condition of admission to the original position"[3].

Nevertheless, it is advisable to wonder what is meant here by rights. Are they individual rights or a general abstract rights? Rawls puts individuals in an original position, under a veil of ignorance, a kind of borderline case of individuals' ignorance about their own interests. It does not mean they are not capable of giving a judgement on their interests, but simply that, not knowing their personal interests, they have to pass a judgement taking into account all the combinations of interests that could be theirs. The notion of right is inevitably abstract, that is to say rights cannot be related to personal interests. Therefore, following Dworkin, we can assert that Rawls' abstract fundamental right is the right to equal attention and to equal respect. But if this base is accepted, rational reflection under the veil of ignorance produces a principle of equal freedom conceived as a set of rights or permissions to carry out these acts. The theory of justice by equity suggested by Rawls is thus doubly based on rights; first in its base, then in its results. Individuals are above all considered as right holders, whose rational reflection under the veil of ignorance establishes validity. Of course, such an approach rejects the notion of duty as a founding element of reflection.

2. Right or Duty, what Priority?

Rawls' theory of justice gives priority to rights over duty. Indeed, this does not mean that the notion of duty is neglected in his reflection. For example, in section 19 chapter 2 of his book, he uses the concept of natural duties. He dedicated chapter 6 to this question. He refers to positive and negative natural duties, but these natural duties are not at the origin of the practise of justice. They only endorse, through practise, once the veil of ignorance has been removed, what individuals have decided under this veil. In chapter 6 (p.293), Rawls says that " from the standpoint of the theory of justice, the most important natural duty is that to support and to further just institutions. This duty has two parts: first, we are to comply with and to do our share in just institutions when they exist and apply to us; and second, we are to assist in the establishment of just arrangements when they do not exist, at least when this can be done with little cost to ourselves"[4]. Further on, "we can define the natural duty of justice as that to support and to further the arrangements that satisfy these principles; in this way we arrive at a principle that coheres with the criteria for institutions"[5].

The natural duties, mentioned by Rawls, are the result of rights accepted beforehand. Therefore, Rawls depicts duties that individuals set themselves in the original position; but it is not the same to say that the theory is based on duties. Indeed, he clearly distinguishes between these natural rights and obligations. " Now in contrast with obligations, it is characteristic of natural duties that they apply to us without regard to our voluntary acts. Moreover, they have no necessary connection with institutions or social practices; ... "[6]. The fact that individuals set themselves duties is actually because they have rights. As such, these rights must be respected and a share of responsibility lies with the individuals in the implementation of the institutions that govern them.

However, this conception has deeply marked post-rawlsian developments on justice. Indeed, theories of justice based on responsibility are remarkable examples of it[7]. The responsibility of individuals is considered as a calculus done on their merits and their handicaps, in order to determine what share of responsibility can be attributed to them and what share of responsibility, in their situation, belongs to society. Actually, the idea is to see to what extent individuals have rights and to define the outline and the limits of these rights. These responsibilities are in no way duties. They only stand for shares of efforts or non-efforts, of good luck or bad luck, and consequently allow determining the allocation of an allowance and the amount of it. The calculus of responsibility only aims at setting the limits of the calculus of rights and is derived from it. Responsibilities are derived from rights.

The priority of rights over duties or responsibilities, and the derivation's direction, are not neutral. Dworkin explains this problem very well in the case of lying. "There is a difference between the idea that you have a duty not to lie to me because I have a right not to be lied to, and the idea that I have a right that you not lie to me because you have a duty not to tell lies. In the first case I justify a duty by calling attention to a right; if I intend any further justification it is the right that I must justify, and I cannot do so by calling attention to duty. In the second case it is the other way around"[8]. The direction in which this derivation is done has strong implications. If in both cases, moral rules are referred to, theories based on duty consider that these rules are attributed to the individual by society, by him/herself or even by a superior entity; they concern the essence of the subject. On the contrary, theories based on rights consider these rules as instrumental above all, guaranteeing the coordination with others' rights or behaviours.

Rawls's strong Kantian inspiration may lead to think he gives a considerable role to duty. He insists in particular on the fact that the original position must be interpreted in a Kantian framework. "The original position may be viewed, then, as a procedural interpretation of Kant's conception of autonomy and the categorical imperative within the framework of an empirical theory"[9]. He reinforces this point of view in a 1980 article entitled *Kantian Constructivism in Moral Theory*. In this article, he gives his conception of the moral person. He strengthens the idea that the original position is much more than a mere self-interested negotiation under a veil of ignorance; the original position resembles Kantian autonomy. The partners' autonomy in the original position does not only concern a rational autonomy, but also a full autonomy which refers, beyond the rational, to the reasonable. The reasonable presupposes and subordinates the rational. The reasonable takes precedence over the rational. The rational corresponds to the Kantian hypothetical imperative, to the promotion of individual interests with an eye on determined aims. The reasonable, on the contrary, implies accepting constraints set in the original position, and consequently is associated to the categorical imperative.

Moreover, Rawls defines "formal constraints" of right, perfectly and clearly explained in the conditions of the contract related to the original position. Among these constraints, we may note the universality of the implementation of law, and its acceptability by all. Individuals are not only rational, they are also reasonable and consequently they abide by the principles set in the original position, not because these principles are given to them as an external law, but because individuals have set themselves these principles by committing to the original position, and they hold their commitment in pursuance of the reasonable. Therefore, duty could be present in the case of the Kantian influence of Rawls's theory.

However, as a reaction to the criticisms he received, Rawls clarified his position, especially regarding the inadequacy of the freedom principle defined in his original position (Hart 1973), but also regarding the availability of information and the calculus of probability (Harsanyi 1975, Hoffe 1988), or the risks of disobedience once the veil of ignorance has been removed (Arrow 1973, Klévorick 1974, Sen 1989). These three criticisms actually have the same aim, which is the status of the individual and his/her behaviour in the theory of justice. Is there a radical change in the answers made by Rawls, shifting from a "Rawls I", first manner with a theory of justice giving priority to the right, to a "Rawls II", second manner giving priority to duty? Probably not. If Rawls gives a major role to the duty, it is above all to strengthen the 1971 structure. People entering the rational process built from the original position are obviously moral people, who respect the contract they define in this position, but their moral status has as sole role to guarantee rights derived from this contract. As for the contract, it has a meaning only because individuals are considered to be on an equal footing, based on the right to equal respect and to equal attention. Let us remind that according to Dworkin's interpretation, the right to equal respect is not a product of the contract, but an admission condition, and this right has a meaning only because it concerns moral people. Let us quote Rawls himself: "We see, then, that the capacity for moral personality is a sufficient condition for being entitled to equal justice. Nothing beyond the essential minimum is required. Whether moral personality is also a necessary condition I shall leave aside. I assume that the capacity for a sense of justice is possessed by the overwhelming majority of mankind, and therefore this question does not raise a serious practical problem. That moral personality suffices to make one a subject of claims is the essentiel thing"[10]. In other words, being a moral person has a dual role. First of all, it is enough to obtain rights, but it is also a guarantee that everybody will respect the rights thus defined.

The insisting way in which Rawls reiterates his conception of justice, drawing on Kantian philosophy, enables him to give its place to duties as a counterpart of rights. Duties follow from rights and not the opposite. However, such a conception, although it extends the scope to the individual's responsibility, also confines it to a precise limit, that is to say what is defined by rights. Therefore, the approaches of justice based on a calculus, dividing the responsibility between an individual share and a social one are perfectly within the Rawlsian tradition.

But this perception of things, which gives priority to rights, is not neutral. The order of rights and obligations is important, since it implies a radically different conception of the individual. The priority of rights specially sets aside all anthropological reflections on the moral subject.

3. The Abuse of Right or the Setting Aside of the Reflection on the Moral Subject

Many contemporary theories of justice, amongst them the theory of Rawls, are alternatives to utilitarianism. They are based on the priority of rights, thus rejecting the priority of aims. Still, we may consider they have something in common with utilitarianism, whose idea is to free philosophy from the religious context and more generally from LAW. Associated to hedonism and to the cult of pleasure, it deliberately rejects the idea of duty; but theories based on rights do the same. Duties are not derived from rights. It follows that they share a common conception of the individual.

As emphasized by Dworkin, the main idea of a theory based on rights is that individuals have interests they have a right to protect if they wish to do so. Rawls's ultimate reference is the Good, even if it is subordinate to Fairness: *the Good is the fulfilment of rational desire* corresponding to the project of each individual.

Therefore, it does not diverge from the utilitarian conception of the individual[11]. Such an economic theory implies that the person follows moral rules in return for rights, and that obedience to these rules actually represents an advantage in social organisation. On the other hand, an approach that gives priority to obligations does not necessarily imply that an advantage must be produced in terms of social organisation. It does not consider that fair institutions are those corresponding to the interests of each individual. The approach only implies that the person adopts a virtuous behaviour for him/herself.

Both approaches thus see the individual from a different perspective. In a theory based on obligations, the moral quality of acts lies in conformity to a principle or to LAW. An act is considered to be good or bad not because of the effect it has, but because it abides by a rule or it does not. In an approach based on rights, the main point is not the compliance of the act with a particular principle, but the independence of these acts. The aim of rights is to reinforce a set of individual and independent acts, aiming at a social organisation, in other words, aimed at the coordination and restriction of these acts. Therefore, while assuming the existence of a moral person, theories based on the right set the reflection on the person aside.

Furthermore, in certain circumstances, these theories radically deny the existence of the person. Of course, they suggest considering the citizen as free. He/she has inalienable rights. Responsibility is derived from this freedom, and this responsibility can be calculated according to the citizen's use of his/her freedom and according to the social environment in which the citizen moves. But this calculus implies a central database by the people in charge of equal opportunities, in order to avoid the manipulation of characteristics and to objectively determine the share of individual responsibility as well as the share of responsibility of the social environment. This interpretation leads us from Rawls to Orwell and reminds us through Roemer, of the central data storage. In this case, the citizen becomes a calculating individual, potential victim of the Taliban of liberty.

Still, how can we overlook a reflection on the moral subject, in a world where over half of the individuals more or less rigorously adopt religious practises and consequently comply above all with duties? A theory based on duties allows us to no longer consider an ethics of justice by equity, as theories based on rights understand this notion, but an ethics of Just, understood as an ethics of the respect of duties. Such ethics can be found in reflections on redistribution, and therefore the idea of social justice, but the latter does not follow from rights, is the result of precepts that bind each of us beforehand to the respect of others' rights.

The ethics of Just is not an ethics of justice as equity based on GOOD. Tensions between both ethics are inevitable, between compliance with the law and the social contract. By setting aside all reflection on the moral subject, there is then necessarily a conflict with the ethics of justice.

But setting aside the reflection on the moral subject does not have this opposition as its only result. It can also, and above all, produce a certain inefficiency of the theory of justice in its will to implement. Under constraint, people adapt. Max Weber used to point out that protestant ethics is the adaptation of moral principles with selfish aims. In other situations, the implementation of principles resulting from theories based on rights will produce other adaptations. These adaptations will themselves produce perverse effects in relation to principles of justice. These adaptations can not be anticipated because of the absence of reflection on the moral subject and in the end, these principles become ineffective.

As a conclusion, in addition to a normative ethical theory of justice, a reflection on positive ethics, understood as an ethics of moral agents who internalise norms and act under their constraints, is required.

Notes

1. On several occasions, Rawls separates natural duties (good, justice) from obligations which are the result of voluntary acts related to institutional positions. According to him, natural duty is general and obligation more specific in its form and in its nature. Nonetheless, he uses one for the other. For Rawls (and also for A. Sen) the most important point is responsibility in relation to the institution and not immediate responsibility otherwise defined in relation to the other.
2. Dworkin, p.180, edition 2001 of his 1977 book
3. Id. p.181, edition 2001.
4. Chapter 6, p.293-294 of the 2003 edition.
5. Id. p.295, edition 2003.
6. Id. p.98, edition 2003.
7. See for example Roemer (1985, 1993a, 1993b), Fleurbay (1995), Bossert (1995) and others…
8. Dworkin, id. p.171, edition 2001.
9. Rawls, id., p.226, edition 2003.
10. Rawls, id., p.442-443, edition 2003.
11. Arrow's criticism of Rawls can thus be understood, when Arrow says that the Rawlsian theory lies within the framework of collective choice and therefore is compatible with utilitarianism.

References

Arrow, K.J. 1973. "Some Ordinalist-Utilitarian Notes on Rawls' Theory of Justice". *Journal of Philosophy*, 70, 245-263.

Bossert, W. 1995. "Redistribution Mechanisms Based on Individual Characteristics". *Mathematical Social Sciences*, 29, 1-17.

Dworkin, R. 1977. *Taking Rights Seriously*. London: Duckworth. Edition 2001, Cambridge Mass.: Harvard University Press.

Fleurbaey, M. 1995. "Equality and Responsibility". *European Economic Review*, 39, 683-689.

Harsanyi, J.C. 1975. "Can the Maximin Principle Serve as a Basis for Morality". *American Political Science Review*, 69 (2), 594-606.

Hart, H.L.A. 1973. "Rawls on Liberty and its Priority". *University of Chicago Law Review*, 40, 534-555.

Hoffe, O. 1988. *L'Etat et la justice*. Paris: Vrin.

Klévorick, A.K. 1974. "Discussion". *American Economic Review*, 64 (2), Papers and proceedings, 158-161.

Rawls, J. 1971. *Theory of Justice*. Cambridge: Harvard University Press.

Rawls, J. 1980. "Kantian Constructivism in Moral Theory". *Journal of Philosophy*, 77 (9), 515-572.

Roemer, J.E. 1985. "Equality of Talent". *Economics and Philosophy*, 1, 151-187.

Roemer, J.E. 1993a. "A Pragmatic Theory of Responsibility for the Egalitarian Planner". *Philosophy and Public Affairs*, 22, 146-166.

Roemer, J.E. 1993b. "Distributing Health: The Allocation of Resources by an International Agency". In Nussbaum, M. and Sen A. (eds.). *The Quality of Life*. Oxford: Clarendon Press.

Roemer, J.E. 1994. *Egalitarian Perspectives: Essays in Philosophical Economics*. New York: Cambridge University Press.

Sen, A.K. 1989. "The Territory of Justice". *Discussion paper n°1425*. Cambridge Mass: Harvard Institute of Economic Research.

The Economic Person and Responsibility

Jérôme Ballet
Damien Bazin

Economic theory traditionally proposes the concept of an individual devoid of all morality. At its best, morality becomes the object of a rational calculation. However, a person is not as untarnished as economic theory presupposes him to be. Each person is submerged into a social world and more or less integrates the norms of the society in which he lives. If he is unable to internalise them, he would at least partially fear the sanctions that could be imposed upon him if these norms are not respected by him.

In the vast majority of cases, persons act in a responsible manner, be it through willingness or constraint. They make their choices by taking social norms and morals into consideration. Economic calculation should hence take this aspect into account. It cannot totally dismiss the fact that the individual is above all a social and responsible being.

However, traditional economic calculation most often does not recognize responsible calculation. Furthermore, it interprets economic agents as individuals and not as persons. Such a manner of dealing with the subject-individual is probably due to the strong influence of utilitarianism that still remains an important reference in economic theory. In the utilitarian tradition however, the individual is not taken seriously into consideration. One is barely able to highlight the autonomy of preferences. More generally speaking, individuals are quasi-objects. They are not persons, but a mere set of characteristics that help define them. Under such circumstances, one individual could be substituted to another. Just as the consumer optimises his choice between two brands of washing powder, the Utilitarian optimises his choice between two individuals with different characteristics (part 1).

Taking responsibility into consideration is hence not an easy task. In Kantian tradition however, the individual is capable of responsible action and responsibility could be imposed upon him. By taking economic calculation into account, responsibility could be dealt with according to two different angles. It could first be considered through the internalisation of moral norms by the individual. This implies that the agent's preferences shall take these norms into account when making his decision. He could thus prefer a less paid, but moral, action instead of a better paid action that goes against his values. On the other hand, responsibility could also be perceived through the conception of norms as an external phenomenon whose respect is imposed through sanctions that accompany these norms. This implies that the individual faces a social constraint in his decision-making (part 2).

These two modalities of integrating responsibility are of course complementary. When a person is simultaneously faced with several responsibilities, he is obliged to classify them. Following such reasoning, economic calculation is rendered more complex since it now consists not only of possible substitutions but also of specific priorities. Here, we notice the emergence of various strategies that help the classification of responsible calculation. These models of economic calculation do not bring the agent's rationality into question, rather, this rationality merely becomes subordinate to responsibility (part 3).

1. The Notion of the Person

The concept of the person dates back to the 6th century. The person is an individual substance of a rational nature: "*Persona est rationalis naturae individua substantia*"[1].

Such a definition does not seem to pose any problem to economic theory. The latter describes the economic man as a rational individual. However, upon close inspection, this definition makes a clear distinction between the person and the *homo œconomicus*. Economic man is mainly a result of the utilitarian tradition. Nevertheless, according to this tradition, and as highlighted by Sen and Williams (1982, p.4) "Essentially, utilitarianism sees persons as locations of their respective utilities -as the sites at which such activities as desiring and having pleasure and pain take place". A couple of lines further, they note that: "persons do not count as individuals in this any more than individual petrol tanks do in the analysis of the national consumption of petroleum". Other critics of utilitarianism highlight the same problem. Rawls (1982, p.181), for instance, states that: "Co-ordinal utilitarianism (and general utilitarianism) starts by regarding persons in terms of their capacities for satisfaction".

The problem seems to be strongly embedded in the utilitarian tradition with which economics is particularly associated. But what exactly is the problem? Is it the fact that economic theory, in all its utilitarian tradition, places greater importance to pleasure and sees the individual as someone who maximises his pleasure and minimises pain? This of course is partially true. But the problem goes far beyond this. Hedonism and utilitarianism do not totally ignore the existence of a personality. Utilitarianism, for instance, takes utility or preferences into consideration and seeks to obtain the greatest possible amount of them. These utilities or preferences reflect persons. It is hence the representation of the person, as described in utilitarianism that is fundamentally unique and restrictive.

The problem of the person when faced with utilitarianism shall be dealt with through the use of three distinct but complementary features, namely: 1/ The representation of the person according to utility. According to this approach, all persons will not have the same importance. 2/ The negation of the person. The individual is perceived as a quasi-object and not as a subject. 3/ The third feature is a direct result of the second: since persons are quasi-objects, they are substitutable.

1.1. Person, Utility and Preferences

Economic theory, following the utilitarian tradition, and following the latter's influence on the modern perception of economic theory, introduces us to an individual whose system of preferences is represented by the utility function. This utility function is associated to hedonism. Indeed, hedonism presents itself as a psychological base that is at the origin of all rational behaviour and judgements adopted by individuals. Nonetheless, such a perception of things is not only rather restrictive, but most importantly, it does not take the person as a whole into full consideration. Such a perception merely represents the person through a single facet- the quest for pleasure.

However, all individuals are not at the same stage in their quest for pleasure. According to the famous saying of John Stuart Mill, it is better to be an unsatisfied man than a satisfied pig. This manner of reasoning implies that the pleasures of a pig cannot be considered as similar to the pleasures of educated persons. Nevertheless, the pleasures of a pig are not any less intense than the pleasures of an educated person. If so, the maximisation of pleasure should take the intensity of pleasure of *everyone* into account, including the most unpleasant.

Modern utilitarianism has of course attempted to overcome such complexities. Authors such as John Harsanyi (1977), for example, propose a reasoning based, not on utility as the representation of pleasure, but on preferences. Here, utility becomes the mere mathematical representation of a system of preferences. Given that preferences are of a purely subjective nature, it enables us to measure the importance placed by an individual upon each of his preferences. Through such a shift of reasoning, utilitarianism now becomes an utilitarianism of preferences. According to Harsanyi, this form of utilitarianism favours the preservation of the individual's autonomy. Autonomy, as employed in this context, should be understood as the autonomy of preferences and not in the Kantian sense of the term. Thomas Scanlon (1977) defines this autonomy as the ability of a person to independently make a decision. This ability could refer to reason, as seen in the writings of Kant, but the utilitarianism of preferences does not limit autonomy to this simple interpretation. The ability of independent decision-making could also result from sensitive motives such as feelings.

This shift from pleasure-utility to preferences does not however solve the problem. If we state that the utilitarianism of Mill implied that each one's pleasures are not on the same level- those of a pig being less important than those of a man- the utilitarianism of preferences fares no better, even if it admits that the preferences of saints carry the same weight as the preferences of sadistic persons. Yet, Harsanyi explicitly rejected the sadistic preferences of utilitarian calculation. From the very onset, through his articles that date back to 1953 and 1955[2], he makes a distinction between ethical and subjective preferences. Ethical preferences reflect the individual's preferences solely according to social and impersonal considerations. Subjective preferences express real preferences, whether they be dependent on the individual's mere personal interest or on other criteria such as sadism. However, we should not merely reject sadistic preferences here, but also, all other forms of preference towards the other. Harsanyi further proposes to eliminate all benevolent motivations or behaviour from the social choice function. Such systematic elimination is essential if one is to respect the utilitarian principle as reflected in the Bentham maxim that Mill (1861) decides to inscribe below the principle of utility as an explanatory note: "Everyone must count for someone, but no one for more than one". Yet, all preferences that are not oriented towards myself but to the Other produce an interdependency of preferences. This implies that some would not have the same weight as others in the utilitarian calculation.

As such, although ethical preferences, as defined by Harsanyi, develop a certain morality of the individual, the rapprochement of the notion of the person, as seen in the writings of Kant, does not permit such an interpretation. The objective of ethical preferences is above all to delete the interdependence of preferences that could put utilitarianism ill at ease. Moreover, Harsanyi (1995, p.319) clearly highlights his rejection of Kantian morality: "I shall argue against Kant that morality is primarily a servant of many other values rather than being in itself the highest value of human life". The rejection of morality is considered at the same level of that of sadism. What Harsanyi actually does is to propose the concept of a neutral and distant individual. Within this context, we no longer deal with a person, but a simple individual amongst a series of other individuals, whose only distinctive characteristic is his or her preferential function. This indeed is a very poor representation of the person.

1.2. The Individual: A Quasi-Object

The preceding argument stated that utilitarianism runs into many difficulties when it has to take all persons equally into account. We could go even further and state that the representation of the individual within the utilitarian tradition brings forth the problem regarding the recognition of the individual. Two examples shall be employed to illustrate our argument.

The first example deals with certain formulations of the utilitarian theory of justice. Various attempts at constructing a theory of justice upon a utilitarian foundation clearly reflect this difficulty. Kolm (1966, 1972), for example, proposes the notion of fundamental preference as the basis of calculation. He believes that all individuals have the same preferences, the same tastes and the same needs. Two persons have seemingly different preferences because they find themselves in two objectively different situations. As such, it is possible to include into the object of preferences everything susceptible of causing differences in preferences of various members of the society. If these parameters are integrated into the object of preferences, a preference thus obtained would then be identical to all members of the society. This preference if known as a *fundamental preference*. It is a priority that describes the preferences and the needs of the individual who is representative of society.

Several points could be made regarding such a procedure. Firstly, the concept of fundamental preference eliminates the irreducibility of individual preferences; this implies that we can no longer make reference to the autonomy of preferences when defining an individual. Next, the differences between persons that we see here are differences of objective characteristics such as age, sex and education. This in turn implies that persons are not considered for themselves but for the set of characteristics to which they could be reduced. The person is not a person but a single individual amongst a collection of others. His sole uniqueness is to possess certain characteristics such as age, sex and education etc. According to John Rawls (1982), this fundamental preference or all other "shared highest order preference" defines the person as a "bare person", as suggested by John Bennett[3].

This expression suggests that such a concept resembles a certain vision of the individual where it is only the concept of satisfaction that is taken into account. The person is reduced to an insignificant element. Furthermore, authors such as Arrow (1977) acknowledge that in its cardinal form, utilitarianism seems to overlook all aspects of personal individuality. As Arrow states (1977, pp.222-223) "reducing the individual to a specified list of qualities (...) is denying his individuality in a deep sense. In a way that I cannot articulate well and am none too sure about defending, the autonomy of individuals, an element of incommensurability among people, seems denied by the possibility of interpersonal comparisons. No doubt, it is some such feeling as this that has made me so reluctant to shift from pure ordinalism, despite my desire to seek a basis for a theory of justice". Indeed, if one follows Arrow's reasoning, cardinal utilitarianism leads us to reduce the individual to a list of qualities or characteristics. But the problem is not unique to cardinalism. It is general to utilitarianism since the fundamental preferences as defined by Kolm are present in ordinal utilitarianism too. According to Kolm, if the objects of preference are described by points of an Euclidean space and if the order of fundamental preferences could be represented by an ordinal function of utility, equity will then be noticed where the points representing the situations of various individuals consist the same hypersurfaces of indifference.

It is not merely cardinalism that is under threat here, but all forms of utilitarianism. The second example perfectly illustrates this problem.

Here, we shall make use of a fable presented by Bernard Williams (1973). Jim, a Texan explorer in search of the ruins of a pre-Columbian civilisation, finds himself one day in the village square of a small south American town. Moving towards a gathering of people standing around a group of men in uniform, he makes his way forward and is surprised to see twenty Indians with their hands bound, backs towards the wall and facing the armed soldiers. Pedro, the head of these armed soldiers, surprised and ill at ease at being disturbed by Jim, a citizen of an ally, explains to Jim that the citizens were chosen at random and were going to be shot so that this would serve as an example to the rest of the citizens. In this manner, he proceeded to explain, the citizens will remain calm and not protest against the government. But as Jim is a guest of honour, the captain proposes him to kill one of the Indians himself and that the rest would be set free. If, on the other hand, Jim refuses to do so, the twenty Indians shall be killed as planned. Upon close reflection and much thought, and with the crowd jeering and cheering, he takes the gun, chooses the oldest Indian and shoots. After ensuring that the remaining Indians were freed, Jim goes on his way.

Looking at it from an utilitarian point of view, Jim's decision is right. By killing one single man, he saves the lives of nineteen others. In this manner, Jim minimizes the total damage. But such reasoning only makes sense because the person is not considered alone. The individual is none other than a quasi-object amongst many others. Let us now imagine the following situation: a container ship is caught up in a stormy sea. The excess weight of the containers makes its journey even more dangerous. If we do not get rid of one of the containers, we run the risk of losing all the cargo on board. The captain is now faced with the choice of throwing a container overboard or losing all of them. Of course, the logical solution would be to get rid of the single container. This same type of reasoning is used in the story of Jim. The Indians were treated just as the containers. A single person, taken by himself or herself, has no value. The person is almost a container, a quasi-object. Such a perception of a quasi-object is rendered possible because persons do not really exist. They are a mere collection of characteristics. In the example of Jim, he chooses the oldest Indian. This seems to render his choice legitimate. If, on the other hand, Jim had chosen the youngest, would this not have shocked our moral intuition? What justifies his choice is then finally the fact that all persons do not have the same value. The old Indian is less worth than the young. Such reasoning is however possible only when the person is defined according to certain characteristics that he or she possesses and not according to the very fact that he or she is a person.

The utilitarian concept of the person cannot be accepted since at the end of the day, it refuses to recognize the person as such and since it legitimises the principle of the innocent sacrifice[4]. It could then be legitimate to kill a person if this would lead to a greater amount of satisfaction for the rest of the community. Let us imagine, as does Rawls (1967), that the employees of a particular institution have the right to file a case against an innocent person, each time they believe that this is in the interest of the society. Such an act would maximise the community's total utility through the sacrifice of innocent individuals but would at the same time negate the value of the person. Utilitarianism thus does not take the concept of the person seriously into account.

1.3. Quasi-Object and Substitution

The preceding argument highlights that the person is nothing more than a quasi-object within the utilitarian tradition. If we go further down this path, we could say that one individual could be replaced by another. He could be replaced, just as oil reserves or containers could be. What is most important is the total value that is finally achieved. Persons, taken alone, have no value. They merely represent a part of the total value. An individual is perfectly substitutable to another.

Peter Singer believes that such a perception of human value is at the heart of our reasoning and that the utilitarian argument thus has a lot of relevance when dealing with practical questions. Take for instance his example where a woman who carries out an amniocentesis finds out that her child is handicapped and decides to have an abortion, in the hope of having a healthy child later on, which in turn will maximise her happiness.

But could such an action really be classified as substitution? Does the woman who chooses to have an abortion consider that the foetus that she destroys could be replaced by another, this time of better quality? Does she really make the conscious choice between a malformed foetus that she already has and a healthy foetus that she may have later? In other words, does she maximise her utility? Bernard Baertschi (1995) objected to such reasoning by stating that: "abortion (in this case) occurs to destroy a defective foetus and not to produce a better foetus later on. And if the parents later decide to have a second child, this is a wholly different question, even though the way to console the loss of a child is to have another. As such, it is not because a human occupies a special place that he could replace another" (pp.60- 61).

The question as to whether one should destroy a fœtus is distinct from the question as to whether one should produce another. One cannot replace the other. In this case, we are dealing not with the choice between two foetuses but with two distinct decisions: destroy a foetus or produce another[5]?

Utilitarianism, in considering individuals as quasi-objects, recognises substitution between such individuals. As such, given that our objective is to maximise our utility, interest or our system of preferences, an Utilitarian will consider an object substitutable to another. This *in fine* negates the value of the person. Still, a person cannot be reduced to a particular value according to his characteristics. The person is not a mere copy existing in society as is a book in a library. A person is not a prototype and cannot be reduced to an ensemble of characteristics. It is a person's integrity and moral values that characterise him or her as a person. The person is not a quasi-object. Stated otherwise, a person is not the sum of the characteristics that represent him.

At its best, utilitarianism, in its form of "utilitarianism of preferences" defines the autonomy of persons through the autonomy of preferences. This implicitly admits a certain individuality of each person. At its worst, utilitarianism generally considers that a person has no autonomy. He or she is a quasi-object characterised by a certain number of characteristics. A person could be of a particular age, be male or female, just as a vase could be blue or red, big or small, etc.

However, within a Kantian perspective, autonomy is recognised as having greater meaning than the mere autonomy of preferences. Autonomy is a part of the perception of the person as a moral person who is free and equal. According to Kant: "A person is that subject whose actions reveal responsibility. The moral person is nothing more than the freedom of an individual who is reasonable under moral laws". Thus, a person is above all a responsible being, who deserves to be respected in turn. Responsibility is at the heart of the notion of the person.

2. Responsibility

Since utilitarianism does not give full recognition to the notion of person and since it reduces the person, at its best, to the concept of autonomy of preferences, utilitarianism is unable to deal seriously with the concept of a responsible person. This does not however imply that no concept pertaining to responsibility can be integrated into utilitarian theory. Rather, such integration will be limited. This is seen in the doctrine of negative responsibility as described by Bernard Williams (1973): if I am aware that doing X will produce O_1 and that not doing X will produce O_2, and given that O_2 is worse than O_1, I shall be responsible of O_2 if I purposely abstain from carrying out X.

Going back to our previous example, if Jim refused to kill an Indian, he would have been responsible for the death of twenty. According to Williams, such reasoning does not make sense. If Jim had indeed refused to kill an Indian, the death of the twenty Indians would not have been the result of his refusal to kill since he himself did not shoot any of them, nor did he give the order to shoot. The twenty Indians could, after all, have been freed. He who is responsible for the twenty deaths is thus the captain and not Jim[6]. This doctrine has been used to justify the strong responsibility of persons. It has nevertheless been contested within the very tradition of utilitarianism. Let us take another example proposed by Harsanyi (1982, p.60): "Thus, if I feel like reading a book for entertainment, I must always ask myself whether my time could not be more usefully devoted to looking after the poor, or to converting some as yet unconverted colleagues to utilitarianism, or to taking part in some other socially beneficial project, etc.". Such a proposition will imply that we use every minute of our lives to do good. This will lead to moral fanatism. Smart (1973) contested this doctrine. According to him, not doing a good deed today would increase our ability of doing one tomorrow. Even though this answer helps us get away from moral fanatism, it does not however solve the main problem. And if tomorrow I think of the same thing as today, I put back my actions for the day after tomorrow and the day after.... Harsanyi's argument (1982, p.20) is more clear since he categorically rejects this doctrine: "There is obviously something wrong with this moral choice criterion. It is not hard to see where the problem lies. Any reasonable utilitarian theory must recognise that people assign a non-negligible positive utility to free personal choice, to freedom from unduly burdensome moral standards, trying to regulate even the smallest details of their behaviour". The freedom of choice generates positive utility that cannot be eliminated for moral reasons independent from the voluntary choices of the individual. This reply from Harsanyi clearly poses the limits within which utilitarianism could take the responsibility of the moral person into consideration. This responsibility is of course reduced to an insignificant element.

A finer analysis of responsibility could nevertheless be introduced into positive economic thought. For practical reasons, we shall distinguish two categories of responsible behaviour, namely: forms of behaviour resulting from "being" and certain other forms resulting from "doing". Although these two categories seem contradictory, this does not however mean that there is no relationship between the two. This relationship could be illustrated by the following example: I can give money to a person in need because I am generous or, on the contrary, I can give money to a person in need because I want to seem generous.

In the first case, it is because "I am" that "I do", while in the second case "I do" because I want to give the impression that "I am". Being and doing are linked, but in one case "doing" results from "being" and in the other, "being" is implied by "doing". As such, I am responsible and this leads me to act in a certain responsible manner or, on the other hand, I behave in a responsible manner in order to seem responsible.

The meaning of relationships is thus important since I carry out a particular action because I deem it good and essential and because it corresponds to my preferences. In the other case, I carry out an action because I seek to achieve a result that depends on the behaviour of the others.

Let us take another example. There are speed limits when driving on the road. We see two oppositions in this case. In the first and probably the most frequent, I do not exceed the speed limit because I know that there are police surveillance cameras and that I run the risk of a fine if I do not respect the speed limit. In such a context, if I know the proper positioning of the surveillance cameras and am assured that I shall not be fined, then there is nothing to stop me from exceeding the authorised speed limit. In the second case, less frequent this time, I respect the speed limit because I am convinced that speed limits are good. This implies that I respect these limits whether I have information on police surveillance or not. Even when I know that there are no surveillance cameras, I will respect the speed limit since I believe that such respect is good.

The difference between such behavioural attitudes results from the concept linked to "being" and "doing". Certain norms are internalised by individuals whereas other norms are respected with the mere aim of producing a particular effect or avoiding a penalty. Here, we do not aim at creating a classification of norms that are internalised or not. Each person internalises certain norms and respects certain others because of fear or sheer desire to avoid penalisation or because of his desire to generate a certain effect in response to the behaviour of others. Such a distinction enables us to deal with norms as follows: they can either be treated as an internalised element that favours "being" or, as stated by Elster (1989, p.131) "people have an internal gyroscope that keeps them adhering steadily to norms, independently of the current reactions of others"; or as an element of a calculation that implies that we "do" something and that if they are to be efficient, norms would have to be associated with sanctions. If not, their respect should produce a beneficial result, through the others, for the person who acts.

We shouldn't forget that within the context of internalised norms, the individuals "are" something. It is this that determines their action. In the case of norms that are a mere external constraint, the individuals do that which enables them to be: to be considered as generous, not to be penalised etc. In the latter case, it is above all the behaviour of the others and rules imposed by society or life in general that govern an individual's behaviour pattern.

This enables us to deal with personal responsibility in economics in two distinct ways. On the one hand, responsibility can directly be integrated into the structure of preferences. This would correspond to internalised norms. On the other hand, responsibility could be treated as a constraint imposed from outside. This corresponds to external norms that imply the risk of sanction.

Economic theory can thus integrate responsible calculation at two distinct stages: preferences and constraint[7]. These two stages could be considered as two distinct approaches, as seen in the example of speed limits. Indeed, it is possible to account for the responsible behaviour of the individual, either through his way of being, because he has internalised the proper norms, or it could be accounted for through the sanctions that could be faced if he does not follow the given norms. It should however not be forgotten that a combination of both these factors is highly possible. Let us take the following example:

Let us imagine that one of your friends rings at your door one night. He has come to seek your financial assistance. You feel obliged to help him, but you have already planned to buy a present or some flowers for your partner with the money you have because the following day is your partner's birthday. You have a certain moral obligation in this case. In order to solve this dilemma, you will have to determine which is the most important moral obligation, regardless of the sanctions that you will have to face. If, for example, you chose to give the money to your friend, you run the risk of having to face a discontented partner because he or she was not your priority. On the other hand, you can estimate the sanctions you will have to face in both cases and then make your decision.

In such an example, responsibility due to moral duty and responsibility resulting from sanction are combined together. You could moreover consider that, if you did not give your partner a present, he or she will not be angry as you had made the right decision in helping your friend. But is this a sufficient reason that will make you help your friend? Could you not, after all, conclude that celebrating your partner's birthday is more important than helping your friend, even though you know that your partner will not be angry with you for not choosing to celebrate?

Both levels of responsibility could thus be combined in various ways and are embedded in the dilemmas faced by individuals when having to make a decision.

Whatever said, the positive analysis of responsibility in economics considerably enriches economic calculation. The following section presents us with illustrations of the interest of this calculation and modalities.

3. Modalities of Responsible Economic Calculation

Persons cannot be considered as quasi-objects that are substitutable amongst themselves or that are substitutable with goods. If not, why would one spend great sums of money to save a baby who fell into a coma at birth? Or why would one spend such money to save a group of miners trapped in a mine when these same sums of money could be used to develop prenatal medical research or improve the safety conditions of miners? Indeed, this would surely stop many future catastrophes (Hausman and McPherson 1993). Choices regarding persons limit substitution because priority and urgency interfere with the optimal allocation of resources. Here, we are no longer dealing with the definition of a priority in calculation regarding persons, in relation to calculation regarding goods. Rather, we establish priorities in our choices regarding persons in time and space.

The other imposes himself upon me, and I hence have even more obligations towards the Other. But given that the Other implies certain priorities, my priorities become conflictual the moment that the Other is "multiple". In other words, when there is a third party who also represents the "Other" to me. I am then obliged to calculate my priorities. Given the limited resources that an individual possesses, he must establish a particular choice regarding his relations with others. Several modalities of calculation could be highlighted at this point. From a more pragmatic point of view, the order of one's priorities could be determined through the introduction of the consequences of the acts, of time and money, into the equation.

Reasoning through the analysis and comparison of consequences is the first means of solving the conflict between priorities.

3.1. The Consequences of Acts as a Modality for Responsible Calculation

Reasoning through consequences is the first element in solving conflicts between priorities. Sen (1993), for instance, proposes a reasoning on norms through consequences. A genocide within a particular country, for example, shall present the problem of external intervention or, in other words, we are faced with the conflict between sovereignty and solidarity. Intervention implies that solidarity primes over sovereignty. A particular law is violated in the name of another. Justification through the consequences of non-intervention could hence serve as an argument for the violation of the law of sovereignty.

Reasoning through consequences highlights several paradoxes. Above all, it enables the creation of a positive theory of norms. The individual makes a choice according to the consequences of his action (probable sanctions). Substitution is not eliminated but it can take on a more limited form.

However, as noted by Sen (1982, 1987), the desire to do certain things, rather than the pleasure taken from the consequences of having done them, has important consequences on the order of preferences and choice.

Moreover, choice through consequences could be a relatively insufficient model when dealing with particular situations. It does not in any way represent a perfect and unique guide for action. This approach takes only a mere fraction of the importance of norms into consideration when dealing with economic calculation. Let us for example imagine an extreme situation, similar to that faced by Jim before the Indians, (Hausman and McPherson 1993) where committing a particularly immoral act such as torturing a child could prevent other individuals from torturing two children. The approach through consequences presupposes torturing the child in question. But it is evident that measuring the consequences of these acts is totally forbidden by morality, which, on the contrary, implies that "I should not torture children".

However extreme this example may seem, it is nonetheless significant. It could for instance be transformed into the question:

can I employ children in my factory in order to have an edge over my competitors? After all, this is common practice in other countries. By this very question, we could come to the deduction that employing a child in my factory for a low wage could prevent two children being employed by another competing firm in another country. In this instance, moral norms prevent me from using children for production. In other words, admittance of a certain degree of consequentialism within responsible economic calculation does in no way imply the abandoning of the notion of person. The consequentialism as proposed by us is delimited by the fact that the economic subject is above all, a responsible person. As such, this form of consequentialism is differentiated from the utilitarian perception of consequentialism.

3.2. Time as a Modality for Responsible Economic Calculation

The second element in solving conflicts between priorities is the element of time. If I promised my future bride that I will marry her next Saturday, I cannot substitute marriage to going out fishing with a friend, even though I had already promised to go fishing with him if the weather was good. Reasoning regarding persons limits substitutions. Similarly, we could imagine that the same individual has to choose between going out fishing and helping another friend move house. In this case, substitution is relatively easy. While I cannot get married in the morning and then go out fishing in the afternoon, I can however help move house in the morning and then go out fishing. Reasoning regarding persons and the obligations that are linked to it automatically imply the element of time. All obligations exert a certain constraint on the allocation of time and resources. Nevertheless, the element of time enables the individual to respond to certain obligations by differentiating between them. If my friend has to move house on that particular day, I could always put back my fishing for another day. As such, we see that the element of time brings with it the possibility of postponement.

On the other hand, certain obligations cannot be postponed. If I have to help a friend shift, and if I also have to be at work that same day, the conflict could be solved by accepting a temporary vexation of the friend I was supposed to help. I could also make use of my networking skills and ask another of my friends to help with the shifting. In this case, the conflict of norms is handed over to the second friend who, himself, has to make a choice between particular obligations. Another possible solution would be to financially participate in the shifting. One could thus help rent a vehicle or pay the movers. As such, I am able to execute certain obligations by substituting goods in time.

3.3. Currency as a Modality for Responsible Economic Calculation

Currency or money, represents the third element that helps resolve conflicts between priorities. Responsibility does not prohibit substitution, especially a rational choice that uses money as a medium in order to solve a conflict resulting from integration or exclusion. The quantification of man by money enables us to solve the radical difference between men: According to Levinas (1982, 1983, 1989), for example, "the problem of human violence could be solved only through vengeance or forgiveness". The Other leaves no choice to the subject. But the response to the Other could be of monetary form. Divorce and the monetary arrangements that go with it are an important example of this form of conflict resolution.

Mobilising money and one's network of relations is a solution that largely enables the person concerned to preserve substitution and continuity. However, this solution represents the calculation of the Other as a means or an altruism of means, and not as an end or an altruism of an end. It generally implies that the element of altruism of an end is either given up or postponed. In the example of a friend moving house, if I send a friend j instead of going, I use my friend as a means to fulfil the ends of my friend i who is moving house. At the same time, I generate an obligation towards my friend j who could, in turn, ask me to help him. In other words, obligation towards i now shifts to obligation towards j.

On the other hand, if I had promised "in my youth" that I will marry a particular young lady when I had a more stable financial situation and that ten years later I meet her again, would I still have the obligation to marry her? Is it the same person I have before me? If I decide not to marry her, this would certainly not involve any monetary compensation.

Of course, currency enables us to solve a certain amount of conflicts regarding responsibility. But it cannot solve them all. I could for example spend little time with my children, but could on the other hand earn more money for their well-being. I substitute money to time. But would I be perceived, in the eyes of others and in my own children's eyes as a responsible person? Nothing can be more certain. Being responsible and seeming responsible to others could well go hand in hand, but this does not mean that there are no incompatibilities at all.

Through the above modalities of reasoning, we have attempted to highlight that taking responsibility into consideration does not negate economic calculation, it merely generates a certain hierarchy. Economic calculation is thus created not merely by the definition of the priorities of the person with regards to goods, but also through the construction of priorities between the persons themselves. The order of these priorities presupposes the agents' rationality. But here, rationality is subordinate to responsibility. Rational economic calculation develops within a framework where the economic agent is responsible. The utilitarian framework of thought thus seems little adapted since it minimizes the moral subject by defining it as a set of characteristics rather than a full-fledged person.

Notes

1. See Ladrière, P. 2001. "La notion de personne, héritière d'une longue tradition". in Novaes S., *Biomédecine et devenir de la personne*. Paris: Seuil, for more on this definition and its history.
2. Harsanyi, J.C. 1953. "Cardinal Utility in Welfare Economics and in the Theory of Risk-taking". *Journal of Political Economy*, 61; Harsanyi, J.C. 1955. "Cardinal Welfare, Individualistic Ethics and Interpersonal Comparisons of Utility". *Journal of Political Economy*, 63.
3. Cf. footnote 25 in J. Rawls 1982.
4. Refer Baertschi (1995) for further details.
5. Here, we shall not enter the much debated topic of the value of a fœtus. Could the foetus really be considered as a person? If so, when? Our example is a mere attempt to illustrate the problem raised by utilitarianism, without however positioning ourselves on the question of the foetus.
6. See Williams (1973) and Baertschi (1995) for a more detailed discussion of this doctrine.
7. These two levels globally correspond to two modalities of calculation in economic theory that have until now, been contradictory. Cf. for example Sen (1974, 1977) for the level of the calculation of preferences and Becker (1974) for the level of calculation of constraints.

References

Arrow, K.J. 1977. "Extended Sympathy and the Possibility of Social Choice". *American Economic Review*, Papers and Proceedings, 219-225.

Baertschi, B. 1995. *La valeur de la vie humaine et l'intégrité de la personne*. Paris: Presses Universitaires de France.

Becker, G.S. 1974. "A Theory of Social Interactions". *Journal of Political Economy*, 82 (6), 1063-1093.

Elster, J. 1989. *The Cement of Society*. Cambridge: Cambridge University Press.

Harsanyi, J.C. 1953. "Cardinal Utility in Welfare Economics and in the Theory of Risk-Taking". *Journal of Political Economy*, 61, 434-435.

Harsanyi, J.C. 1955. "Cardinal Welfare, Individualistic Ethics and Interpersonal Comparison of Utility". *Journal of Political Economy*, 63.

Harsanyi, J.C. 1958. “Ethics in Terms of Hypothetical Imperatives”. *Mind*, 47, 305-316.

Harsanyi, J.C. 1975. “Can the Maximin Principle Serve as a Basis for Morality? A Critique of John Rawl’s Theory”. *American Political Science Review,* 69 (2).

Harsanyi, J.C. 1977. “Rule Utilitarianism and Decision Theory”. *Erkenntnis*, 11, 25-53.

Harsanyi, J.C. 1982. “Morality and the Theory of Rational Behaviour”. in Sen A. and Williams B. (eds.), *Utilitarianism and Beyond.* Cambridge: Cambridge University Press, 39-62.

Harsanyi, J.C. 1986. “Individual Utilities and Utilitarian Ethics”. in Diekmann A. and Mitter P. (eds.), *Paradoxal Effects of Social Behaviour.* Heidelberg: Physica, 1-12.

Harsanyi, J.C. 1995. “A Theory of Prudential Values and a Rule Utilitarian Theory of Morality”. *Social Choice and Welfare*, 12, 319-333.

Hausman, D.M. and Mc Pherson, M.S. 1993. “Taking Ethics Seriously: Economics and Contemporary Moral Philosophy”. *Journal of Economics Literature*, 3 (2), 671-731.

Kolm, S.C. 1966. *La production optimale de justice sociale.* Conférence de l’AISE. *in* Economie publique. Paris: CNRS.

Kolm, S.C. 1972. *Justice et Equité.* Paris: Editions du Centre National de la Recherche Scientifique.

Ladrière, P. 2001. “La notion de personne, héritière d’une longue tradition”. In Novaes S., *Biomédecine et devenir de la personne.* Paris: Seuil.

Levinas, E. 1982. *Ethique et infini.* Paris: Fayard.

Levinas, E. 1983. *Le temps et l’autre.* Paris: PUF.

Levinas, E. 1989. *Répondre d’Autrui.* Neuchâtel: A la Baconnière.

Mill, J.S. 1861. *Utilitarianism.* In The Collected Works of John Stuart Mill. J.M. Robson (ed). Toronto and London: University of Toronto Press, 1963-1991.

Rawls, J. 1967. “Two Concepts of Rules”. In Foot Ph., *Theories of Ethics.* Oxford: Oxford University Press.

Rawls, J. 1982. “Social Unity and Primary Goods”. In Sen A. and Williams B. (eds.), *Utilitarianism and Beyond.* Cambridge: Cambridge University Press, 159-185.

Scanlon, T. 1977. “A Theory of Freedom of Expression”. In Dworkin R.*, The Philosophy of Law.* Oxford: Oxford University Press.

Sen, A.K. 1974. “Choice, Ordering and Morality”. In Körner S. (ed.), *Practical Reason*, Oxford: Blackwell.

Sen, A.K. 1977. “Rational Fools: A Critique of the Behavioural Foundations of Economic Theory”. *Philosophy and Public Affairs*, 6, 317-344.

Sen, A.K. 1982. *Choice, Welfare, and Measurement.* Oxford: Blackwell.

Sen, A.K. 1987. *Hunger and Entitlements*. Helsinki: World Institute for Development Economics Research.

Sen, A.K. 1993. *Ethique et Economie*. Paris: PUF.

Sen, A.K. and Williams, B. 1982. "Introduction: Utilitarianism and Beyond". In Sen A.K. and Williams B., *Utilitarianism and Beyond*. Cambridge: Cambridge University Press.

Smart, J.J. 1973. "An Outline of a System of Utilitarian Ethics". In Smart J.J. and Williams B., *Utilitarianism, for and Against*. Cambridge: Cambridge University Press.

Williams, B. 1973. "A Critique of Utilitarianism". In Smart J.J. and Williams B., *Utilitarianism, for and Against*. Cambridge: Cambridge University Press.

Some Reflections on Responsibility and Happiness in Economics

Jérôme Ballet
Vinca Bigo
Jean-Luc Dubois
François-Régis Mahieu

In this chapter, we use the concept of "Person", as defined by Emmanuel Mounier and Emmanuel Levinas, for economic purposes. The person has the same characteristics as a philosophical subject, i.e. she is an autonomous consciousness, with the capacity to decide and choose a way of life, the capacity of reflection upon decision (the person is reasonable), the capacity of reciprocity which induces responsibility, and the capacity of making efficient choices through rationality.

In fact, the person, defined in such a way, is a much more complex and complete entity than the individual, as considered by the utilitarianism theory[1]. Nevertheless, the relationships of this person with others persons can still be analysed in an utilitarian way, either by considering the social interactions or through the search for a rational solution in the case of focused dilemma.

One of the key characteristics of a person is his capacity to be responsible towards others. A responsibility which results from his involvement in a nexus of social relationships, out of which it is impossible for him to escape. All types of relationship generate a series of rights, on one side, and associated obligations, on the other side, which express the person's level of responsibility towards the others. This can be formally represented by a specific tool: the right and obligation map (ROM).

In his regular search for happiness, the person's consciousness of responsibility may enter an internal conflict. Searching for his individual pleasure on one side may not be compatible with satisfying his social obligation. A balanced solution between responsibility and happiness has to be found. Therefore he can consciously adjust his level of responsibility, by prioritising the various obligations, but this adjustment has to appear reasonable. He must keep in mind that any of her actions have to look reasonable for the others. Such an attempt to conciliate responsibility and happiness leads naturally to a refusal of the simple criteria of satisfaction that the utilitarian philosophy considers. It implies to refer to another type of ethics, the ethics of joy and happiness.

1. The Right and Obligations Map (ROM): A Formal Representation of Responsibility

A person is normally embedded in various social networks, or in institutions, which give him rights but also impose obligations based on reciprocity. A. Sen (1981) already discussed this issue when he discovered that famines occur in situations where enough food is available to feed the whole population but remains stocked. He developed his analysis of entitlements to explain the surge of the famine. However, this explanation did not fit in well when analysing the 1972 Sahelian famine; despite a situation of starvation, the rate of mortality was much under the level it was supposed to be (Caldwell J. and Caldwell P. 1987). In fact, the distribution of rights and obligations among family relatives, between urban and rural areas, allowed adequate transfers, which helped overcome the situation. But, these rights, and their related entitlements, could only be used once the obligations were fulfilled (Mahieu 2001).

This relation between rights and obligations can be formalised by introducing a specific entitlement tool: the Rights and Obligations Map (ROM). Each person has his own ROM, which defines the set of obligations he is subjected to and the potential rights he disposes of, according to his age and sex, the role played within the family and the social status at a given date.

Two types of relationships are represented by the ROM. First, the family links, or vertical relationships, which are based on the lineage system (patriarchy, matriarchy, etc.). They are usually the most intensive and oppressive ones. Second, the horizontal relationships which express the mutual aid that exists between age groups, community groups, social networks, and which can be used to complement the lineage authority. Both relationships generate rights and obligations based on political, economic, religious and other foundations.

On such a map, the Y-axis of the diagram represents the intergenerational balance of rights and obligations by showing the opposition between younger and older people. On the X-axis, the range beyond zero represents the intensity of rights, in positive terms, and the amount of obligations, in negative terms (see graph. 1).

The diagram can be used to analyse various situations. For instance, if obligations are totally balanced by rights, in the long run, the distribution of points will be symmetrical. A non-symmetrical distribution appears when the amount of obligations exceeds that number of rights, especially between generations.

This is the case for the points in the "South-West" quarter of the diagram, which represent the situation of the youngest having many obligations towards older people, either through tradition (as in the developing countries) or by law (the pension system in the developed countries). Therefore, the younger generations can be considered as a "sacrificed generation", once compared to others. However, this may change over time, during their life cycle, and the "once sacrificed generation" may then become, a few years later, a "lost generation" (for it may become spoiled by affluence and power).

Graph.1 :The Rights and Obligations Map (ROM)

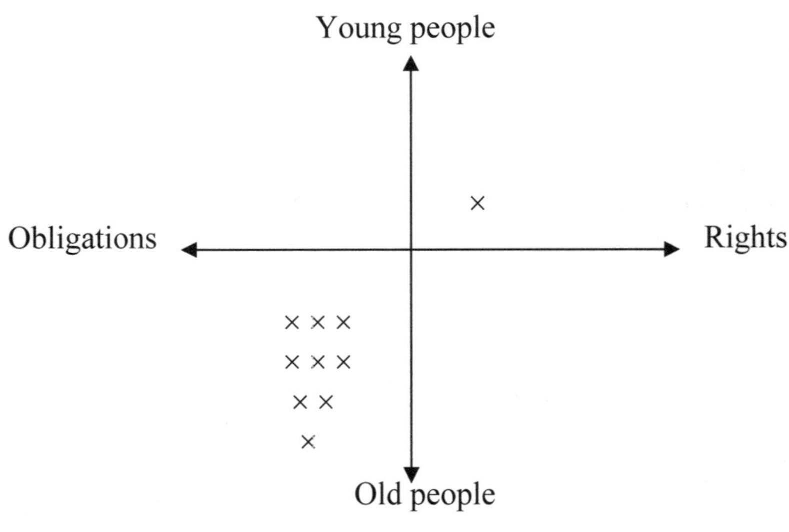

Everybody has to fulfil obligations towards the community in order to benefit from rights. Obligations are usually expressed by constraints on time and resources. Resources cover the transfers of money or goods to the original village and the aid to the members of the community living in urban areas. Time obligations include visits to parents, attending funerals, participation in collective work, etc. For a given level of obligations, time and money may become substitutes. For instance, sending money for funerals or the required goods to parents can compensate being unable to attend and to give time to support the family. All these events are captured through the use of targeted surveys which measure the community pressure on personal income and time allocation.

Substitution between time allocation and transfer of goods can be formalised, in economic terms, by indifference curves of obligations, such as those presented in graph. 2. Each curve expresses, for a given person, the level of obligations based on his double allocation of time and expenses on goods. More generally, the final balance between amounts of time, money, goods, and caring relationships, is a function of the way in which a person is imbedded in community relationships. It depends on the community's preference for this person.

While facing obligations on one hand, the person has also potential rights, on the other, which means that he can use these rights later on, when need be. The effective ability to exercise these rights depends, amongst other things, on how the person respects his obligations towards the community. Some rights can be considered as fundamental for they are related to a social position in the community, to the protection from evil forces and to survival in case of disasters. Rights are circumstantial and concern access to assets, goods and services, e.g. access to the land managed by the community, to children's fosterage, to help for fieldwork, and cash money or gifts in the case of funerals. Having such a set of rights is an insurance against actual or potential difficulties. In West Africa, for instance, subscribing to mutual benefit pools such as the "tontines" enables one to receive collective help in the event of financial trouble.

The main issue, for a given person, stands in the balance between the number of rights and obligations. At the inter-personal level, reciprocal obligations can be analysed, in theory, with the classical Edgeworth box. In practice, rights and obligations may be difficult to compare due to their different substance and content. Obligations often materialise by flows of goods in real terms, while rights remain frequently a potential which can only be mobilised within community. It becomes difficult to set up a balance at the personal level, for it will depend on the relationship between the person and his community .

Moreover, rights and obligations vary according to the socio-economic status of its members. For instance, the "first born" of a family and the "older brother" are more strongly subjected to obligations than other members. On the other hand, they also have more rights. But, since these remain potential, they may in the short-term be overburdened by obligations and be unable to compensate the corresponding expenses with their current resources. By contrast, those who are lower down in the family hierarchy may be never obliged to return, in one way or another, the small benefits they get from their position.

Other distortions or difficulties may appear within this obligation-right pattern, through urban-rural relationships and intergenerational exchanges. For instance, the flows of given goods are usually directed from the village to family members in the urban areas. The village community compensates for this by giving potential rights to land, fosterage for children, and stocks of supplies once the harvest completed. But this may not be sufficient to equitably compensate the efforts made by the urban members for this particular community.

Meanwhile, such relationships generate social capabilities, i.e. abilities to generate social income (e.g. transfers), investment in social matters and social capital through reciprocity. These constitute "altruistic resources", which depend on the person's social status and are distributed according to social norms, i.e. the set of rights and obligations.

In conclusion, it appears clearly that intra and inter-generational balances between rights and obligations remain a condition for social sustainability at the personal and community levels. This is the case in all societies, whatever their level of development. For instance, the social security and pension system in France are an illustration of such arrangements in the North.

2. Responsibility and Happiness: A Conflicting Duet

Each person is plunged into a intragenerational and inter-generational pattern of rights and obligations, which reflects his responsibility towards other people. The introduction of this responsibility, besides his freedom to choose the life he expects to live, may be a source of conflict and therefore of disturbances in his own set of preferences. To a certain extent, his belonging to a series of social networks may restrain his personal search for happiness. Therefore, there is a risk of conflict between the personal quest for a better life (with the objective of reaching happiness in the end) and the level of responsibility towards others.

This is particularly true in societies where the power of the community is so strong and oppressive, that it is difficult to escape from the social obligation of solidarity without the risk of serious sanctions such as exclusion, sorcery matters, or life prosecution. In this case, the traditional obligation of solidarity may become a burden, a kind of plot on generations being "persecuted". In this context, counter-adaptation such as disregarding personal responsibilities is extremely difficult. It may generate other egoistic attitudes based on the dissimulation of information (e.g. hiding the level of the income) and the manipulation of events (e.g. omitting to declare the right personal status), etc.

In practice, the capacity of a person to behave in a purely egoistic way is quite limited since he lives in a social environment that imposes limits and defines his set of associated rights and obligations. No one can deny this situation and effectively avoid it. This is as true in developed countries as it is in developing countries. However, since the legal social security system (e.g. system of family support, health insurance, retirement pension, old age assistance, etc.) is more extended in developed countries, the importance of the traditional pattern of rights and obligations is normally less. Either way, the best solution is to adapt to the constraints of the social environment through thinking and appropriately reflecting upon actions. Responsibility thus informs adaptive preferences and this may even help, through the use of the "affiliation capabilities", to revise the set of obligations without rupture in the social capacity to co-operate.

To summarise, by adapting his preferences, the person will look for a balance between his egoistic and altruistic attitudes. In a context of scarce resources, he will have to adapt according to the corpus of social norms, which defines his responsibility, using assets such as time allocation or intergenerational transfers. In this way, the moral and economic constrains should fit together.

Another question remains: to what extent is a person's quest for happiness compatible with others' quests of happiness?

First, this takes us back to the capacity of relating to others, to participate in others' happiness. M. Nussbaum (2000) considers the capacity for reciprocity as part of the "affiliation capabilities" that she describes in her central list of capabilities, i.e. "to be able to imagine the situation of another and to have compassion for that situation". R. Misrahi goes further, in his ethics of joy and happiness, by demonstrating that higher levels of happiness are a deeply thought construct which cannot be reached without a strong reciprocal link to others.

Secondly, admitting reciprocity raises the issue of responsibility when confronted to the question: to what extent will my chosen actions, realisation of capabilities, achieved functionings, positively or negatively affect others? More precisely, what rules could guide the trade off between my personal freedom and responsibility towards others? Taking responsibility into account leads to two alternatives. A priority is given either to personal freedom or to responsibility.

In the European continental philosophical tradition of phenomenology, priority is always given to responsibility, which is considered as an ex-ante phenomenon related to the social context. It induces a self-constrained responsibility, based on the Kantian golden rule "behave as you would like others to behave". It is not, as in the Rawlsian tradition, an ex-post concept. It leaves the person a certain degree of freedom through his capacity to adapt, or to counter-adapt, his set of preferences (Elster 1983).

An extreme case of an infinite responsibility is given by E. Levinas (1983) (for intragenerational responsibility) and H. Jonas (1979) (for intergenerational responsibility). In both cases, the person has limited freedom. For E. Levinas, priority is always given to the other and makes it necessary to sacrifice personal freedom to ensure the happiness of others. For H. Jonas, the "precautionary principle" sets the priority . It ensures that future generations won't suffer from decisions taken by the present generation. For both authors, the priority of the others' happiness makes responsibility supersede freedom.

A different, and intermediary answer, is given by P. Ricœur (1995), who admits neither the rule of infinite responsibility, nor the short-term egoistic view of utilitarianism. He defines, as a primary capability, the capacity of a person to impute responsibility on his current actions. This is a capacity of "imputatio", which expresses the ability to freely assume finite actions and recognize the corresponding impacts on others.

Mostly, obligations need to be fulfilled before rights can be exercised. This shows the relevance of the "imputatio" theory of responsibility and through it "multiple realisability" in various contexts. Happiness still remains the synthesis of joy's events. But it has to be constructed within the framework of a self-constrained freedom, where preferences on finite actions are adapted to fit in with the dominant context.

3. On the Ethics of Joy and Happiness

According to R. Misrahi (2003), actions originate from human desire. Desire is a drive and an intrinsic part of human nature, which gives value to all things. Within this desire, there is freedom for choices including the choice to generate joy.

The desire can lead to the sole search of spontaneous individual hedonistic pleasure, but this will be too narrow a view, since we are all embedded in social networks. Our spontaneous desire will inevitably encounter the desires of the others. Differences in desires, whether perceived or real, generate resentment, conflicts and violence. This is a common experience of humanity.

But the human being, i.e. R. Misrahi's Subject, is able to perceive the others consciously. He has the capacity to "project himself on the other as a mirror", i.e. to imagine the situation of another, the risk of conflict when the respective desires do not match, and even to have compassion. As such, it is possible to avoid violence and conflicts, to define rational exchanges through the setting up of agreements and contracts according to which one will give something and receive the equivalent in exchange. This is the juridical expression of reciprocity based on a reciprocal recognition of the other. From this, a new form of ethics can be generated: not based on the usual ethos of pleasure - of spontaneous pleasure since this is often inconsistent with reality - but on an ethos of deeply thought out joy.

However, switching into such an ethic of joy implies going through several stages of conversion in order to abandon a spontaneous, inconsistent, egoistic and tormented life, and reach a more reasoned and peaceful stage. The first step involves a "knowledge conversion". It is based on the understanding that the Subject itself gives sense to all things in life and that it is not just the reverse. The Subject is at the origin of all the meanings and values. Therefore, he can change the world if he wants to, since he is the one giving sense to all its components. The second step is an "existential conversion". It means that the vocation of the Subject, through the realisation of its full desire, is not ontologically limited to anxiety and torment, but to fulfilment and joy. This happens by understanding the situation, developing a relationship with others, and, more generally, appreciating the world itself. The third conversion is the "reciprocal conversion", i.e. a conversion to reciprocity with others. It involves becoming conscious that the others are also Subjects, i.e. "alter egos" with their own sets of desires.

According to this view, joy is generated by the desire of an autonomous and conscious Subject who has the freedom to make *reflected upon* choices, to *focus* on finite actions in a reciprocal relationship that recognises mutual vulnerabilities, needs and desires. Such a three dimensional attitude gives meaning to all actions, and particularly to those having an economic end. For instance, earnings offer the capacity to achieve freedom and ensure responsibility, the house becomes a loving-living place, food integrates the long-standing culture of the people, and so on.

Within this framework, three types of joy may be experienced by the Subject: (i) by being conscious of creating his life with its autonomy of choice, (ii) by establishing reciprocal and loving relationships with others, and (iii) by enjoying the world in a wider sense.

Happiness is then attained through a combination of deeply thought out choices, at each stage deciding what action should be undertaken and bringing joy through the corresponding achieved functions. Personal and deep thought lead to a synthesis of related events of joy. This situation constitutes what can be called the "Preferable", i.e. a set of choices and achieved functions, each bringing specific joy. For instance, the joy of understanding things through lectures, of getting the right expected diploma, of making others happy, etc. The sum and interrelated nature of these events of joy lead to happiness and to the enjoyment of the world. Happiness then represents an absolute for the Subject. It is at the top of his preferences. But, it remains a lifestyle generated by the Subject's choices, i.e. his preferred way of being, based on the fulfilment of existence, which leads to enjoyment.

In conclusion, the ethics of joy and happiness define and explain the link which exists between personal actions and a potential "capability for happiness", intrinsic to human nature. But, to reach such an end, the classical individual has to be superseded by the concept of the Subject. Freedom of choice and preferences have to result from reasonable actions, i.e. reflected upon actions, and the focus must be on achieved functions and on reciprocity in relation to others.

4. Conclusion: Enhancing Capabilities Towards Happiness

The reasonable choices of a Subject, in order to achieve certain functions, bring us back to the key notion of capability, i.e. the "capacity of doing and being" (Sen 1987). On one hand, "the capacity of doing" can generate joy through chosen actions. On the other, "the capacity of being" can bring fulfilment by realising what was initially expected. The combination of the two generates a series of achieved functions, which are sources of joy and which lead to a certain level of happiness.

This expresses what can be called the "capability to achieve happiness", i.e. a capability which is the result of "combined capabilities" (doing and being) and which respects the two key principles of "each person as the end" and of "multiple realisability" in the various social contexts encountered (Nussbaum 2000). It calls on the idea that improving the people's capabilities during their life cycle will give them the means of achieving functions and realising the life they aspire to. Therefore, enhancing people's capabilities as an objective for development is the best way to improve this "capability to achieve happiness", as they make it possible to bring about one's existence.

Such a process may take time, since it needs a series of freedoms in order to make the reasonable choices, to undertake the appropriate actions, to develop the requested capacities and to achieve functions. But, happiness remains above all a complex process, i.e. the result of a permanent build-up towards higher levels of contentment, and the whole life cycle can be used for such an objective. However, it also requires appropriate public policies to provide useful information to the Subject, to guarantee his freedom of action, to generate social opportunities in education, health, employment, culture, and, more generally, to focus on the improvement of capabilities (Sen 1999).

In this context, the "Preferable" appears as something greater than a set of achieved functions in various domains, even if these might generate joy. It is rather the expression of realised capabilities at their upper level. Naturally, such an end goes further than what is proposed to human beings by the utilitarian standpoint, which mainly remains at the level of the individual, the standard of living, and pleasure.

Notes

1. See the chapter 8 of this book. See also J-L. Dubois, and F-R. Mahieu, 2003. "Personalism, Capability and Sustainability: From Mounier to Levinas, Ethics for a Socially Sustainable Development". 3rd Conference on

Capabilities *From Sustainable Development to Sustainable Freedom*, 7-9 September 2003, University of Pavia.

References

Caldwell, J. and Caldwell, P. 1987. "Famine and Africa". Seminar on *Mortality and Society in Sub-Saharan Africa*, IFORD: Yaounde.

Critchley, S. and Bernasconi, R. 2002. *The Cambridge Companion to Levinas*. Cambridge: Cambridge University Press.

Dubois, J-L. and Mahieu, F.-R. 2003. "Personalism, Capability and Sustainability: From Mounier to Levinas, Ethics for a Socially Sustainable Development". 3rd Conference on Capabilities. *From Sustainable Development to Sustainable Freedom*, 7-9 September 2003. Pavia.

Elster, J. 1983. *Sour Grapes*. Cambridge: Cambridge University Press.

Jonas, H. 1979. *Le principe responsabilité*. Paris: Cerf.

Levinas, E. 1983. *Le temps et l'autre*. Paris: PUF.

Mahieu, F.-R. 2001. *Ethique économique*. Paris: L'Harmattan.

Misrahi, R. 2000. "Construire son bonheur". In *Philosophies de notre temps*, 287-289. Paris: Editions Sciences Humaines.

Misrahi, R. 2003. *Le sujet et son désir*. Paris: Editions Pleins Feux.

Nussbaum, M. 2000. *Women and Human Development. The Capabilities Approach*. Cambridge: Cambridge University Press.

Ricœur, P. 1995. *Le Juste*. Paris: Esprit.

Ricœur, P. 2003. "Capabilities and Rights". Workshop on *Transforming Unjust Structure: Justice and Capabilities*, 26-27 June 2003. Cambridge: VHI, University of Cambridge.

Sen, A. 1981. *Poverty and Famines, an Essay on Entitlement and Deprivation*. Oxford: Clarendon Press.

Sen, A. 1987. *The Standard of Living*. Cambridge: Cambridge University Press.

Sen, A. 1999. *Development as Freedom*. Oxford: Oxford University Press.

Notes about the Authors

Jérôme Ballet is Senior Lecturer in economics at University of Versailles (France) and Senior Research Fellow at the C3ED (Economics and Ethics Center for Environment and Development). He is editor of the review *Ethics and Economics* (http://Ethique-economique.org). He has published several articles and books on ethics and economics.

Damien Bazin is a Research Fellow at the C3ED (Economics and Ethics Center for Environment and Development). His *Research Specialisation* is Economic philosophy. A great part of his work is devoted to Hans Jonas' philosophy. He is associate editor of the review *Ethics and Economics*.

Augendra Bhukuth is a Research Fellow at the C3ED (Economics and Ethics Center for Environment and Development). His main research topic is child labour.

Vinca Bigo is a Research Fellow at the University of Cambridge. Her research areas cover: Feminist economics, philosophy, in particular ethics, that of responsibility and more generally, the way any theorising needs to be underpinned by ontology.

Aurélie Carimentrand is a Research Fellow at the C3ED (Economics and Ethics Center for Environment and Development). Her main research Topic is Fair trade and organic value chains .

Alejandro Caparrós is Senior Research Fellow, at the Institute of Economics and Geography (IEG). Spanish Council for Scientific Research (CSIC), Madrid, Spain. He is also Assistant Professor at Marne la Vallée University (France), and Post-doctoral Research Fellow at CIRED (International Research Centre on Environment and Development, CNRS-EHESS). He won Second Prize in the Premio de Economía Regional de la Comunidad de Madrid (*Madrid Regional Economics Prize*) for his PhD Thesis 'Valoración económica del uso múltiple de un espacio natural: análisis aplicado en los pinares de la sierra de Guadarrama' (Economic valuation of multiple use of a natural space: analysis applied to the Pine forests in the Guadarrama Mountains). He has published several articles on environmental economics.

Jean-Luc Dubois is Director of Research within the French Institute of Research for Development (IRD). He manages a research unit focussing on "Socially Sustainable Development" at the University of Versailles. His main interests are on households' living conditions, poverty reduction, social and human development.

Patrick Jolivet is Research Fellow, Erasme, Ecole Centrale de Paris. His main Research interests concern Environmental Economics, Economic Philosophy, and Rationality. He has published several articles on these subjects.

François-Régis Mahieu is Professor of economics, University of Versailles. He has published several books and articles on Development and Ethics. Main references are: *Logique déductive et théorie économique*. Paris: L'Harmattan 1989; *La crise économique en Afrique*. Paris: L'Harmattan 1990; *Altruisme, analyses économiques*. Paris: Economica 1998; *Ethique économique, fondements anthropologiques*. Paris: L'Harmattan 2001; *Ethique Economique*. Paris: Ellipses 2003.

Jean-Christophe Pereau is Professor of Economics at Marne-la-Vallée University (France) and Research Director at

OEP, Marne-la-Vallée University. He has Published several articles on the Game theory.

Tarik Tazdaït si Senior Research fellow at the Centre International de Recherche sur l'Environnement et le Développement (CIRED, CNRS-EHESS). He has Published several articles on the Game theory and Environmental Economics.